THE
PINK PLAQUE
GUIDE
TO
LONDON

THE
PINK PLAQUE
GUIDE
TO
LONDON

Michael Elliman
Frederick Roll

Preface by
Jackie Forster

First published June 1986 by GMP Publishers Ltd,
  P O Box 247, London N15 6RW
World copyright © 1986 Michael Elliman and Frederick Roll
Preface world copyright © 1986 Jackie Forster
Photographs of buildings and statues world copyright © 1986 Ed Heath

British Library Cataloguing in Publication Data

Elliman, Michael
  The pink plaque guide to London.
  1. Homosexuals – homes and haunts – England – London
  2. London (England) – Description – 1981 – Guide-books
  I. Title II. Roll, Frederick
  914.21 DA 689.H6

      ISBN 0–85449–026–4

Front cover: 10 Downing St, SW1 (William Pitt, the Younger)
Photoset by M C Typeset, 34 New Road, Chatham, Kent
Printed and bound by A Wheaton & Co Ltd, Exeter

Acknowledgements

Sources of photographs in this book include:

The National Portrait Gallery, London; the Tate Gallery; the BBC Hulton Picture Library; the Mansell Collection; the Victoria and Albert Museum; the Fawcett Library, City of London Polytechnic; the Royal Opera House Archives; and the Provincial Archives of British Columbia, Canada.

We would like to extend our special gratitude to the following:

The Master, Fellows and Scholars of Pembroke College, Oxford, for permision to reproduce the portrait of Thomas Lovell Beddoes by Nathan C Branwhite (1824); Routledge & Kegan Paul Ltd, for permission to reproduce the photograph of Harold Monro published in Jay Grant's *Harold Monro and the Poetry Bookshop* (Routledge, 1967); The Cavafy Archive, Athens, for permission to reproduce the photograph of Constantine Cavafy; Lewis Morley, for permission to reproduce his photograph of Joe Orton; Renate Belina, for kind permission to reproduce her portrait of Ronald Firbank; The National Museum of Labour History, London, for permission to reproduce the photograph of Eva Gore-Booth; The Fine Arts Society Ltd, for the Emil Otto Hoppé photograph of Gluck; Anna Wilson, Lilian Mohin and Onlywomen Press, for the photograph of Frances Power Cobbe; Barbara Grier and the Naiad Press, for the photograph of Renée Vivien published in *A Woman Appeared to Me* by Renée Vivien, tr. Jeannette H Foster (Naiad Press, 1976); Jay Landesman, for the photograph of George Ives; John Murray Ltd, for the photograph of Mary Renault; François Lafitte, for the photograph of Edith Lees Ellis; The Council of Westfield College, University of London, for permission to quote from the unpublished autobiography and diaries of Constance Maynard; David Doughan of the Fawcett Library, City of London Polytechnic, for his enthusiastic assistance; and to Ed Heath for the photographs of buildings and statues taken especially for this book.

Though every care has been taken, if through inadvertence or failure to trace the present owners, we have included any copyright material without acknowledgement or permission, we offer our apologies to all concerned.

Preface

No doubt, like me, you will flip the pages of *The Pink Plaque Guide to London* to the well-known names, read about them and then lay the book aside to dip into again later on. Don't.

Through the most fascinating biographical sketches, Michael Elliman and Frederick Roll introduce us to lesbians and gay men long dead, unknown and until now unsung. These are the ones who linger with me the longest; about whom I ponder – even fantasise. For many months to come I shall be doing weekend walks in different parts of London tracking down the homes and places associated with the hundred or so people presented here.

Reading about these folk is a bit like standing in a reception line for a cavalcade of strong personalities and lifestyles. The authors must have spent a most strenuous three years chasing leads, amassing the information, verifying facts, checking and cross-checking – let alone the selection of names to be included. Inevitably I wonder about the ones left out and why?

This *Guide* works on many levels: it provokes discussion about other names; it is a historical/herstorical record ranging from 1459 to 1983; it reveals to us *our* London – our lesbian and gay London of five centuries; it tells us about the remarkable contributions made to society on many levels and in diverse areas, by people who had each and every one to cope with the stigma of perversion if not criminal charges. The *Guide* is much else besides – it is coolly written, which gives it greater impact. It is full of illuminating anecdotes: for example, Edward Carpenter's report that when his biblically ignorant lover, George Merrill, heard that Gethsemane was the place where Jesus had spent his last night, Merrill inquired "Who with?" Jane Harrison, who described herself as "a cheerful agnostic", said that "Life does not cease when you are old: it only suffers a rich change. You go on falling in love – only you fall so gently."

What *is* in a name? It can hardly be pure accident that homosexual women and men have such a divine ear for high-camp names: Bryher, Constantine Cavafy, Menlove Edwards, Desiderius Erasmus, Radclyffe Hall, Sophia Jex-Blake, Winnaretta Singer, James Whale – to mention but a few. Another intriguing factor unearthed by this monumental research is how restless most of the people were. They ceaselessly move home, travel, visit with friends, much as we do today. Is this a general feature of homosexual lifestyles?

By an accident that I'm sure is typical, I myself lived at 13 Connaught Square, Marble Arch, without ever knowing that Frances Power Cobbe, who declared her chief interest as "everything concerning women", had lived next door at no. 15 sixty years before. It would have helped to know that at the time, while struggling to come out. It is equally gratifying to note how many within these pages had affairs, pursued their own destiny, survived and went on to great things in my present locality of Maida Vale.

In my reading of the *Guide* it is the women more than the men who foreshadow the liberation movements of today. Some make singularly prophetic noises, such as Cicely Hamilton, who maintained that the improvement of the position of women had been particularly effected through the efforts of women who chose to be single – she meant, of course, not married to men. The single woman, she wrote, was "a witness to the unpalatable fact that sexual intercourse is not for every woman an absolute necessity", and the "spinster", far from being the pitiable "unchosen", was generally a woman who had chosen to be seen as independent of men, economically, psychologically and sexually.

I know that considerations of length have forced Michael and Frederick to restrict the *Guide* to a hundred entries, but I hope they continue and expand their work to include all those still omitted as a record of how much richer society is for our lesbian and gay existence.

Jackie Forster
Maida Vale, March 1986

Canonbury Tower, Canonbury Road, N1 (Francis Bacon)

J R Ackerley

(4 November 1896 – 4 June 1967)

Joe Randolph Ackerley was born in Herne Hill, the son of Alfred Roger Ackerley, a director of Elder and Fyffes, the banana importers, and Netta Aylward, an actress. He was educated at Rossall School in Lancashire, where he began writing poetry.

During the First World War Ackerley fought in the trenches on the Western Front, and rose to the rank of captain. He was taken prisoner in 1917 and spent eight months in Germany before being interned for a year in Switzerland.

In 1919 he went up to Magdalene College, Cambridge. He read law for a while but then switched to English literature. For several years after he left university he tried to make a career as a writer, all the time encouraged and financially helped by his father.

Through E M Forster, whom he first met in 1922, and whose friendship he described as "the longest, closest, and most influential" of his life, Ackerley secured a job in India, as companion and secretary to the Maharajah of Chhatarpur, and tutor to his son. This period of his life is brilliantly described in his first prose work, *Hindoo Holiday*. The prim Forster, however, thought that by alluding to the Maharajah's homosexuality, and detailing his sexual behaviour, Ackerley had gone too far.

When Ackerley's play *The Prisoners of War*, which derived from his experiences as an internee, was first produced in 1925, the strong undercurrent of homosexuality from which its emotional tension is drawn was apparently unrecognised by the critics. It was a huge popular success and was revived in 1955. Siegfried Sassoon called it "the most powerful . . . the most impressive" play that he had ever seen.

From 1928 to 1935 Ackerley worked as an assistant producer in the Talks Department of the BBC. But it was as literary editor of *The Listener* that he found his niche. During his twenty-four years as editor (1935–59) he was exceptionally fair, and his eclecticism and courage were remarkable. He helped several young unknown writers, such as Francis King and James Kirkup, to establish their careers,

while such luminaries as Forster and Christopher Isherwood readily contributed reviews anonymously, out of friendship and esteem for him.

Ackerley was a tall, slim, good-looking man with gold-blond hair and chiselled features. At school he had looked for a special intimate companion; at Cambridge, and subsequently in his sexual adventures involving guardsmen, waiters and policemen, he searched for the Ideal Friend. While his play was being produced he had several affairs with actors, some of them notable: "I don't like to boast," he wrote in his autobiography *My Father and Myself*, "but Ivor Novello took me twice into his bed." His longest relationship was with a sailor who was based at Portsmouth, which lasted for four years.

In his late forties he found that his Alsatian bitch Queenie gave him what his search for the Ideal Friend had never yielded. "She offered me what I had never found in my sexual life, constant single-hearted, incorruptible, uncritical devotion," he wrote. "From the moment she established herself in my heart and my home, my obsession with sex fell wholly away from me." In his autobiographical novel *We Think The World Of You* he tells of his relationship with a young man in the East End and of how he gains the affection of the man's dog. *My Dog Tulip* is an account of his life with Queenie.

Finding and telling the exact truth, in his life and in his work, was an obsession with Ackerley. With a candour which startled many, he laid bare in *My Father and Myself* all his own and his family's secrets. After his father died in 1929 Ackerley learned, from a letter marked "Only in the case of my death", that he had been simultaneously supporting, in addition to the family of Joe, his elder brother Peter (who was killed in the First World War), his sister Nancy and their mother, a second family, of his mistress and their three daughters, in his "secret orchard" in Barnes. As well as giving a frank account of his own sexual adventures, Ackerley describes his attempts to discover the extent of the role his father's early patron, the homosexual Count de Gallatin, had played in his life. It pained Ackerley that he and his father should have felt unable to be open with each other about their secret "other lives".

After Queenie, who died in 1961, and his sister Nancy, who lived with him for many years, what Ackerley cared about most in life were his many friends, who included Forster, Sebastian Sprott (John Maynard Keynes's lover), William Plomer, and Francis King, whom he appointed as his literary executor.

Ackerley died in his sleep at his home in Putney and was cremated at Putney Vale Cemetery. On the last page of his last diary he had written a line from the *Antigone* of Sophocles, "We have only a little time to please the living, but all eternity to love the dead".

Addresses

4 Warmington Road, SE24 – Ackerley's birthplace. (*Note:* In *My Father and Myself* he gives the address incorrectly as 4 Warminster Road.)

Apsley House, 106 Queens Road, Richmond – the Ackerley family's home c1906–10.

Grafton House, 89 Mount Ararat Road, Richmond – their home 1911–c1922.

Blenheim House (now Hillbrow), 76 Richmond Hill, Richmond – the family's home from c1922. Ackerley lived here until 1925.

11 Half Moon Street, W1 – he rented a room here occasionally during his undergraduate days, as he had heard that it was a "discreet establishment" near Piccadilly.

76 Charlotte Street, W1 – site of his home in 1925.

6 Hammersmith Terrace, W6 – he lived here in 1925.

Maida Vale, W9 – he had a flat in this road in 1933.

17 Star & Garter Mansions, 6 Lower Richmond Road, SW15 – his home for many years. (Died here.)

Works include

The Prisoners of War (1925); Escapers All (1932) – poetry; Hindoo Holiday (1932); My Dog Tulip (1956); We Think The World Of You (1960) – won the W H Smith £1,000 Annual Literary Award; My Father and Myself (1968); E M Forster: A Portrait (1970); Micheldever, and Other Poems (1972); The Letters of J R Ackerley (1975) – edited by Neville Braybrooke; My Sister and Myself: The Diaries of J R Ackerley (1982) – edited and introduced by Francis King.

Portraits

Photographs by Howard Coster (c1939) – National Portrait Gallery.

Fictional portrait

Captain Jim Conrad, the central figure in Ackerley's play *The Prisoners of War*, is a self-portrait, as is Frank in his novel *We Think The World of You*.

More Adey

(1858–1942)

If William More Adey is remembered at all today it is as the friend of Robert Ross and Oscar Wilde, the loyal and devoted shadow, always around to help and support the more robust and illustrious members of the group. Indeed his devotion to Ross, with whom he shared a house, amounted more to a dependence and after his friend's death he seems to have lost all sense of direction and his life ended tragically.

Adey, who was known to his detractors as the 'Bearded Lady', was a respected art critic and joint editor of the *Burlington Magazine* (1911–19). In 1891 under the pseudonym of 'William Wilson' he published the first English translation of Ibsen's *Brand* and he collaborated with Eric Stenbock in translating Balzac's short stories. He was co-director, with Ross, of the Carfax Art Gallery.

After Wilde's trial and imprisonment many gays, fearing a purge, fled abroad. Adey, however, decided to stay and regularly visited Wilde in Reading Gaol. When Wilde's wife heard of a visit in November 1895 she wrote to her husband: "I hear with horror that Mr More Adey has been to see you. Is this your promise to lead a new life? What am I to think of you if you still have intercourse with your old infamous companions? I require you to assure me that you will never see him again, or any people of that kind." Needless to say, the visits did continue and it was Adey who met Wilde on his release from prison on 19th May 1897. However, his bad business sense earned him the wrath of Wilde, who accused him of losing the money he had entrusted to Adey during his confinement, and the friendship cooled further after Adey criticised Lord Alfred Douglas for his part in Wilde's downfall.

In appearance More Adey was a strange, unkempt little man, with cropped hair and a long matted beard, and dark lustreless eyes, given to black moods of depression alternating with high spirits and playfulness. Most evenings he would appear at Ross's rooms in Half Moon Street, staying behind when other guests had departed, to chat into the early hours with his friend and confidante. There was an intensity and awkwardness of manner which kept most of his contemporaries at a distance, and his way of repeating Ross's opinions word for word, as if they were his own, gave the impression that he was but a cipher and a hanger-on. Although he accomplished much in his own right he was not a creative artist and deferred to those who were.

After Ross's death in 1918 Adey retired to an old manor house in Gloucestershire which he had inherited as a young man. For a time he was happy as the lord of the manor, walking about in a long black cloak with a tame rook perched on his shoulder. Then one day he became convinced that there was treasure buried somewhere in the house and he employed a number of workmen to demolish the place. Of course, no treasure was ever found and Adey was left with his life and his property in ruins. Nowhere to go, no Robbie Ross to turn to! He was finally taken away to live out the last few years of his life as a certified case of derangement in a hospital for the insane.

15 Vicarage Gardens, W8

Addresses

★*24 Hornton Street, W8* – Adey lived here with Robert Ross c1905.

★*15 Vicarage Gardens, W8* – lived here with Robert Ross c1906–08.

★*86 Kensington Church Street (formerly 10 Sheffield Gardens), W8* – the home of Reginald Turner. Adey moved here in 1908. (See also *Robert Ross*.)

Works include

Life of Charles Robert Maturin (1892) – with Robert Ross.

C R Ashbee

(17 May 1863 – 23 May 1942)

Best known as the founder of the Guild of Handicrafts and as a designer of metalwork, Charles Robert Ashbee was also a prolific writer and the architect of some sixty buildings, mostly houses, the best of which were built in Cheyne Walk, Chelsea, and in Chipping Campden, Gloucestershire.

He was born at Isleworth into a wealthy business family. His father, Henry Spencer Ashbee, was a collector of pornography who published, under the pseudonym 'Pisanus Fraxi', a three-volume catalogue of erotic works, *Notes on Curious and Uncommon Books,* the first of its kind to be published in English.

Ashbee was educated at Wellington and at King's College, Cambridge, where he became a friend of Goldsworthy Lowes Dickinson who described him as "a long youth, enthusiastic, opinionated". While he was at Cambridge he met Edward Carpenter who became one of the most important influences on his life.

After university Ashbee moved to Whitechapel and trained as an architect. Enjoined by Carpenter to get to know the working classes, he began giving lessons on Ruskin and design at Toynbee Hall, the pioneer East End settlement. This led to his inauguration in 1888 of the Guild of Handicrafts, a cooperative group of thirty craftsmen working in various branches of the decorative arts. Ashbee based the Guild on the mediaeval and Italian Renaissance craft guilds, and on Carpenter's theories of homogenic love as "the basis or at least one of the motors of social reconstruction".

In 1891 the Guild expanded and moved into its own workshops in Essex House in Mile End Road. Meanwhile, Ashbee continued his work as an architect, cycling to and from his office in Chelsea. Through the Guild Ashbee strove to build "a community of free men" where everyone had a say in policy-making and where the creation of the object was recognised as being part of the growth of the craftsman. There were lectures by visiting artists and festive suppers followed by folk songs and catches. They performed masques and had a cricket team whose players wore scarlet scarves and blazers embroidered with white pinks, the flowers which grew in the garden of Essex House.

In 1898 Ashbee married nineteen year old Janet Forbes. He wrote to her before the marriage explaining that hitherto he had based his life upon his love for men: "Some women would take this perhaps rightly as a sign of coldness to their sex, and they would shrink from a man who revealed himself thus and fear a division of affections," but while "there may be many comrade friends, there can only be one comrade wife."

Janet became an excellent comrade and took an active part in the Guild, but her longing for children and her husband's lack of sexual interest in her left her feeling unfulfilled. She fell in love with a family friend, Gerald Bishop, and had a platonic relationship with him which she wrote about in her unpublished novel *Rachel.*

In 1902 Ashbee decided to move the Guild out of London, as "good honest craftsmanship is better done the nearer people get in touch with the elemental things of life." He chose Chipping Campden, a mediaeval wool town very much in decline, with many empty houses and an old silk mill which could be converted into workshops. One hundred and fifty people made the journey "from Whitechapel to Camelot".

By now Ashbee had become well known as an architect and a designer. He travelled extensively abroad as a spokesman for the arts and crafts in England. He founded the London Survey Committee and edited, in 1900, the first volume of *Survey of London,* and he was one of the first members of the National Trust.

Ashbee loved rural life. He campaigned for the improvement of conditions in the village and opened the Campden School of Arts and Crafts as a way of reviving local craftsmanship.

In 1908 the guildsmen held a celebration dinner to mark the twenty-first birthday of the Guild. They knew, however, that the future was uncertain. Competition from factory production and from amateur craftworkers was threatening their livelihood.

The Ashbees remained in Chipping Campden until 1919, and eventually they had four daughters. Sometime before the First World War Ashbee had an affair with a young soldier called Chris. Although little is known about their relationship he probably wrote about it in *Confessio Amantis,* his private notebook which Janet burnt after his death. She was afraid of the possible effect his revelations might have.

When the war came Ashbee supported Goldsworthy Lowes Dickinson's call for a League of Nations and toured America campaigning for disarmament. He went to Egypt to teach English at the University of Cairo and to Jerusalem, where he worked as a town planner. After his return to England he lived at Janet's family home, Godden Green, near Sevenoaks. He devoted himself to the mammoth task of editing his journals, the record of a long life, recalling the years spent in Chipping Campden and the Guild of Handicrafts, which remained for Ashbee the symbol of his highest aspirations.

Memorabilia

A large collection of material relating to the Guild, including minute books, prospectuses, reports and photographs – Victoria and Albert Museum. His drawings for the houses in Cheyne Walk – the Royal Institute of British Architects; Victoria and Albert Museum; and Chelsea Public Library.

Addresses

★*Bedford Way (formerly Upper Bedford Place), WC1 – site* of Ashbee's childhood home.
★ *Toynbee Hall, 28 Commercial Street, E1* – he lived here in 1886.
★*Essex House, 401 Mile End Road, E3 – site*. He lived here in 1891–98.
★*37 Cheyne Walk, SW3 – site*. He designed and built the house which stood here for his mother, and he lived here for a time (c1894). He also had his office here. (House demolished in 1969.)
★*74 Cheyne Walk, SW3 – site*. He and his wife lived here 1898–1902 in a house which he designed and built. (House destroyed by a parachute mine in 1941.)

Works include

Houses: Only two of the houses Ashbee designed and built in Cheyne Walk still remain. They are Nos. 38 and 39 (1898–99).
Publications: *From Whitechapel to Camelot* (1892); *The Essex House Song Book* (1905); *Echoes from the City of the Sun: Poems* (1905); *Where the Great City Stands* (1917).
Journals: The complete set (44 volumes) of his journals is in King's College Library. A shorter version, edited by Ashbee in 1938 (7 volumes), is in the library of the Victoria and Albert Museum and in the London Library.

Portraits

Drawing by William Strang (1903) – Art Workers Guild. Bust by Allan G Wyon (1929) – Art Workers Guild.

W H Auden

(21 February 1907 –
29 September 1973)

The poet Wystan Hugh Auden was born in York, the youngest son of a doctor. At his preparatory school, St Edmund's, Hindhead, he met Christopher Isherwood; at Gresham's School, Holt, at the instigation of a fellow pupil, Robert Medley, he first entertained the possibility of becoming a poet. By the end of his schooldays he had come to terms with his homosexuality, helped considerably by reading Edward Carpenter.

He went up to Christ Church, Oxford, as an Exhibitioner in Natural Science, but switched after a term to English. At Oxford, in 1925, he renewed his acquaintance with Isherwood, and they became lifelong friends and allies. Another close friend and fellow undergraduate was Stephen Spender, who printed Auden's first volume of poems in 1928.

Down from Oxford, and eager to escape from what he called the "great batshadow of home", Auden went to Berlin. There he became interested in the teachings of the American psychologist Homer Lane. One of Lane's theories – that uninhibited love could be a liberating force – was particularly appealing to him and provided justification for his casual relationships with the young men he met in the city's numerous gay bars. He learnt German and hoped to make Berlin, in the heady years of the Weimar Republic, his literary territory, but it was Isherwood, who came to visit him and was introduced by him to the bars and boys of Berlin, who was later to achieve this in his stories of the city.

For some years after his return to England, in 1929, Auden earned his living by giving private tuition and by teaching in prep schools. His poetry during his undergraduate years had been in the style of T S Eliot, and it was to Eliot, at the publishers Faber & Faber, that he submitted his "country house charade" *Paid on Both Sides* in 1929. Eliot published it, the following year, in *The Criterion*. His *Poems*, published in 1930, began to influence a new school of poets, and *The Orators* (1932) – the titular poem of this volume is often cited as being one of the few modern poems which can stand in comparison with Eliot's "The Waste Land" – confirmed his enormous reputation.

His early poems are perhaps his most personal and most moving, particularly the love poems; later his poetry became much more intellectual, the inspiration being cerebral and critical more than emotional.

In Germany Auden had, inevitably, become aware of politics. His poetry during the Thirties began to reflect, with a growing intensity, the subjects of class differences, unemployment, the rise of Fascism and the approach of war, which, as his obituary in *The Times* stated, "made him for a whole young generation the poetic and satiric exponent of the anti-Fascism of the Left, almost an English Brecht."

He joined the GPO Film Unit in 1935. For the film *Coal Face* Benjamin Britten provided musical settings for Auden's verse commentary. This was the first of their several collaborations and it led to a long-lasting friendship between them. Auden's association with the Group Theatre during this period gave rise to another notable collaboration, the writing of two plays with Isherwood – *The Dog Beneath the Skin* and *The Ascent of F6*. (His first work for the Group, into which he had been recruited by Robert Medley whose friend, Rupert Doone, was the Group's choreographer and director, was a one-act play, *The Dance of Death*.)

In 1935 Auden married Erika Mann (daughter of the novelist Thomas Mann) in order to give her British citizenship, as she had been declared an enemy of the Third Reich by the Nazis and had fled from Germany.

He went to Spain in 1937 in support of the Republican cause in the Civil War, where he drove an ambulance and served as a stretcher bearer. In 1938 he and Isherwood visited China, in search of "a war of our own" to write about. At the beginning of 1939 they left England for America, and they were much criticised for their decision to remain there after the outbreak of the Second World War. (Both later became American citizens.)

At a poetry reading, in which he took part, in New York in April 1939, Auden met Chester Kallman (1921–75), a student and poet who had been in the audience. He later celebrated his good fortune at having fallen in love with Kallman, in his poem "Perhaps I always knew what they were saying". They were lovers for only two or so years, for Kallman was essentially promiscuous by nature, but once Auden had become reconciled to the fact that their relationship was not to be the monogamous "marriage" that was his ideal, they settled into a close and rewarding friendship which lasted until Auden's death. Kallman collaborated with Auden on several projects, most notably on the libretto for Stravinsky's *The Rake's Progress*. It was under Kallman's influence that Auden became a devotee of opera.

During the early 1940s Auden took up teaching again, and he taught and lectured at a number of American schools and colleges. During this period also he returned to the Anglo-Catholic faith of his mother.

He was appointed Professor of Poetry at Oxford in 1956; some of his lectures given there over the following five years were published in *The Dyer's Hand* (1962). Winning the valuable Feltrinelli Prize in 1957 enabled him to buy the first home he had ever owned, a house in Kirchstetten, near Vienna. His reputation was in decline in the 1960s, but in 1971 he was given an honorary D. Lit. of Oxford; in the following year London University also made him an honorary D. Lit.

Auden's return, in 1972, to his old college at Oxford, where he was given a "grace-and-favour" cottage, was not a happy one: he disliked the changes which the town and the university had undergone since his undergraduate days; his ribald table-talk offended some of the dons; and the students and younger dons barely tolerated him, regarding him as a kind of living relic of a literary past.

He died suddenly, of heart failure, in his hotel room, while on a visit to Vienna with Kallman. He is buried in the Kirchstetten cemetery.

Addresses

★*43 Chester Row (formerly Chester Terrace), SW1* – Auden stayed here in 1930 at the home of the Benensons, whose son Peter he was tutoring.

★*46 Fitzroy Street, W1* – stayed here with Robert Medley and Rupert Doone in 1932.

★*25 Randolph Cresent, W9* – lodged here briefly in 1933 at Stephen Spender's home.

★*38 Upper Park Road, NW3* – site of William Coldstream's home where Auden stayed c1934.

★*2 West Cottages (formerly West Cottage Road), NW6* – stayed here with Benjamin Britten in 1936.

★*559 Finchley Road, NW3* – stayed here with Britten (December 1936 – January 1937).

★*Thurloe Square, SW7* – stayed at his brother John's home in the 1930s.

★*15 Loudon Road, NW8* – stayed at Stephen Spender's home in November 1963 and again in 1972.

Works include

Poetry: *Poems* (1930) – printed privately by Stephen Spender in 1928; *The Orators* (1932); *Look, Stranger!* (1936) – for which he was awarded the King's Gold Medal for Poetry in 1937; *Spain* (1937); *Another Time* (1940); *The Double Man* (1941) – republished in UK as *New Year Letter* (1941); *The Age of Anxiety* (1947) – won Pulitzer Prize of 1948; *The Shield of Achilles* (1955); *Homage to Clio* (1960); *Collected Poems* (1976) – edited by Edward Mendelson.

Plays: *The Dog Beneath the Skin, or Where is Francis?* (1935) – with Christopher Isherwood; *The Ascent of F6* (1936) – with Isherwood; *On the Frontier* (1938) – with Isherwood.

Travel: *Letters from Iceland* (1937) – with Louis MacNeice; *Journey to a War* (1937) – with Christopher Isherwood.

Critical essays, review articles, etc.: *The Dyer's Hand* (1962); *Forewords and Afterwords* (1973) edited by Edward Mendelson.

Libretti: For Stravinsky's opera *The Rake's Progress* (1st perf. 1951) – with Kallman. For Hans Werner Henze's opera *Elegy for Young Lovers* (1st perf. 1961).

Songs: (see – Benjamin Britten)

Film commentaries: *Coal Face* (1935); *Night Mail* (1936); *The Way to the Sea* (1937) – music for these by Britten.

Portraits

Pen and ink drawing by Don Bachardy (1967) – National Portrait Gallery. Several photographs of Auden; Auden and Isherwood; Auden, Isherwood and Spender, by Howard Coster (1930s) – N.P.G.

Fictional portraits

Hugh Weston in *Lions and Shadows* (1938) by Christopher Isherwood is Auden. Nigel Strangeways in Nicholas Blake's (pseud. C Day Lewis) detective novels is part inspired by Auden. MacSpaunday in Roy Campbell's *Talking Bronco* (1946) is a composite of Auden, Spender and MacNeice. Evelyn Waugh based Parsnip in his novels *Put Out More Flags* (1942) and *Love Among the Ruins* (1953) on Auden.

Memorial

Memorial stone (unveiled by Sir John Betjeman in October 1974) – Poets' Corner, Westminster Abbey.

Sir Francis Bacon

(22 January 1561 – 9 April 1626)

There is a legend that Francis Bacon was the illegitimate son of Elizabeth I and Robert Dudley, Earl of Leicester. Some believe that he is the true author of Shakespeare's works. There is no doubt, however, that the deductive system for empirical research which he devised justly earned him the title of the "Father of Modern Science", nor that, as an essayist, he was one of the greatest prose stylists of English literature. At the height of his career, as Lord High Chancellor, Bacon was one of the most powerful men in England, being second in public office only to the throne itself.

In 1582 he began practising law, a profession at which he excelled. He was appointed Queen Elizabeth I's Counsellor in 1591, was knighted in 1603, became Solicitor General in 1607, Attorney General in 1613 and Lord High Chancellor in 1618. The titles Baron Verulam and Viscount St Albans were conferred on him in 1618 and 1621 respectively.

Although Bacon was undoubtedly a brilliant, charming man and a most able politician, his swift rise to power was aided, in no small part, by his personal friendship with King James I.

The King's homosexual loves were so well known that his subjects quite openly referred to him as "Queen James". Of necessity, Bacon was rather more discreet. The execution in 1631 of his brother-in-law, Mervyn Touchet, and two of Touchet's servants on account of their homosexuality would seem to bear out Bacon's belief that "A habit of secrecy is both politic and moral."

Nevertheless, it was fairly widely known that Bacon was homosexual. Sir Simon D'Ewes, in his *Autobiography,* says of Bacon: "Nor did he ever, that I could hear, forbear his old custom of making his servants his bedfellows so to avoid the scandal that was raised of him." He describes a particular Welsh serving-man of Bacon's as being "a very effeminate-faced youth" and "his catamite and bedfellow". In *Brief Lives* John Aubrey states: "He was a pederast" (meaning, then, simply 'homosexual') with "ganymedes and favourites". Lady Ann Bacon, writing to her other son, Anthony (who was also homosexual), rails against "that bloody Percy" whom Francis kept "yea as a coach companion and a bed companion". (It is probable that this was the Henry Percy to whom Bacon left some money in his will.)

Bacon's preference for "masculine love", a term for homosexual love which he was the first to use (in *New Atlantis,* 1617), is evident in his essays on love and friendship, and his essay "On Beauty" deals exclusively with the beauty of the male.

He married Alice Barnham in 1606, when she was fourteen years old and he was forty-five, probably because his career and social position made this necessary. He held that "Nuptial love *maketh* mankind, friendly love *perfecteth* it," and that "He who hath wife and children hath given hostages to fortune; for they are impediments to great enterprises, either of virtue or mischief. Certainly the best works, and of greatest merit for the public, have proceeded from the unmarried and childless men, which both in affection and means have married and endowed the public."

Bacon's fall from power occurred in 1621. He was put on trial by his enemies in the House of Lords who resented his friendship with the King (who tried that same year to abolish Parliament), and was found guilty of having accepted bribes while serving as a judge. It counted for little that Bacon had delivered judgement against the men from whom he had received these gifts, and that it was fairly common practice for public officials to expect and receive "extra payments", since the trial was politically, rather than morally, inspired. A fine of £40,000 was imposed on him, he was barred from sitting in Parliament and forbidden to come within the verge of Court.

Almost equal to the grief Bacon felt at the ruin of his career was that caused by the forced sale of York House to the Duke of Buckingham, the favourite of James I. Bacon had written: "York House is the house where my father died and where I first breathed and there will I yield my last breath." The greater part of his sentence had been remitted earlier, but it was only upon his agreement to sell the house that he was allowed to return to London.

Retiring from public life, Bacon devoted himself to writing and to scientific research.

One of his best known experiments is that which led to his death in the winter of 1626. Whilst out riding in a coach with a friend near Highgate, Bacon decided to test the effect of freezing with snow on the preservation of meat. He bought a chicken which he stuffed with snow. The experiment was conducted out of doors in a blizzard and Bacon became ill with a severe chill. He was taken to the nearby home of the Earl of Arundel. The bed he was put into was in a damp, seldom-used room and, not surprisingly, his chill developed into pneumonia, of which he died a month later.

He is believed to be buried in St Michael's Church, Gorhambury, but the relevant page of the burial register is missing. References to his funeral cannot be found, nor could his coffin during recent excavations at the church.

Addresses

★*York House – site*. Stood at corner of Villiers Street and Strand, WC2. Bacon's birthplace.

★*1 Gray's Inn Square, WC1 – site*. Bacon had chambers here for nearly fifty years. He is believed to have directed the laying out of the gardens here in 1586 when he became a bencher, and to have planted the catalpa tree growing in the garden, the seed being one brought back from Virginia by Sir Walter Raleigh.

★*Twickenham Park* – Bacon lived here 1595–1605.

★*Coleman Street, EC2* – he was confined in a house here in 1598 after his arrest for debt.

★*Canonbury Tower, Canonbury Place, N1* – Bacon held the lease on the property from 1616 to about 1621. There is a tradition that the mulberry tree in the garden was planted by him. Inscription Room: It was believed by some until recently, when cleaning was undertaken, that the name which had been obliterated from the inscription outlining the line of royal succession was that of Francis Bacon.

★*Bedford House, Strand, WC2 – site*. Bacon lived here 1621–23 after selling York House.

★*Arundel House (St Michael's Church, Highgate, and Old Hall, 17 South Grove, N6, now stand on the site)* – home of the Earl of Arundel, where Bacon died.

Works include

Essays (expanded version, 1625); *New Atlantis* (1617); *Novum Organum* (1620); *The Advancement of Learning* (1623); Poetry; Plays.

Portraits

Canvas, attributed to William Larkin (c1617) – University of London Library. Francis Bacon as Lord High Chancellor, by J Vanderbank (1731) – National Portrait Gallery. Canvas by unknown artist (after 1731) – N.P.G.

*Portrait on p. 8;
photo of Canonbury Tower on p. 9.*

Statues and memorials

Statue at City of London School, Victoria Embankment, EC4, – stone figure between windows on 2nd floor, facing Blackfriars Bridge – by J Daymond & Son (1882). Bronze statue at South Square, Gray's Inn, WC1, erected to mark his tercentenary as Treasurer of Gray's Inn (he wears the robes of Lord High Chancellor) – by F W Pomeroy (1912). Statue on wall of Islington Central Library, Fieldway Cresent, N5 (Holloway Road side of library building). (Statue at St Michael's Church, Gorhambury, St Albans – it represents him in a characteristic attitude; the inscription is "Sic sedebat" / "Thus he used to sit". There is an electrotype of this effigy in the National Portrait Gallery.) Statue on facade of Museum of Mankind, Burlington Gardens, W1. Monument in Marylebone Parish Church, Marylebone High St, W1. Figure in stained glass windows in the library of Sion College, Victoria Embankment, EC4.

Memorabilia

Documents by and concerning Francis Bacon – Dulwich College. Francis Bacon's autograph – British Musuem. Letters from Francis Bacon – British Museum and Public Records Office. Bacon's Lane, N6 is named after him.

Dame Lilian Barker

(21 February 1874 – 20 May 1955)

Born over her father's tobacconist's shop in Kentish Town, Lilian Charlotte Barker was the fifth of seven children. When "Lily" was ten years old her mother became ill with a crippling disease which confined her to a wheelchair. She loved and cared for her mother and bitterly resented the additional strain which her father's heavy drinking placed on the family.

Her first job, after leaving the National School, Kentish Town, at fourteen, was as an apprentice in a florist's shop. However, she had to leave after a few months because of a weak chest. Her next job took her back, as a pupil-teacher, to her old school, where she remained until she was twenty, when she was accepted for two years residential training at Whitelands Teachers Training College in Chelsea.

The next five years were spent teaching juniors, followed by a seven year break in her career when she stayed at home to nurse her mother who was now virtually paralysed. She became a Sunday School teacher at Holy Trinity Church during this time and it was there that she met Florence Francis, another Sunday School teacher and a few years younger than herself, who became her lifelong companion.

After her mother's death Lily returned to teaching. She became (in 1913) principal of a new experimental evening institute in Bell Street, NW1, which was sponsored by the LCC. The institute soon outgrew these premises and a year later was moved to a larger building in Cosway Street, NW1.

Having successfully established the evening institute, she then set up a day school at the Lock Hospital, a clinic for girls and women with venereal diseases. Evening entertainments at the school were provided by Lily's friends, whom she had roped in to give concerts, talks and filmshows.

Early in 1914 she went to live with Florence and her family. At the outbreak of the war she organised classes for women in semaphore and signalling and in cooking. This led to her being asked by Lady Londonderry to set up the cookery section of the newly formed Women's Legion.

She was appointed Superintendent of the Woolwich Arsenal in 1916 with responsibility for effecting its transition to a female workforce. She recruited, engaged and allocated all female labour: when she arrived fewer than one hundred women worked there; a year later the number had risen to thirty thousand. She was later to recall: "I liked the idea of all those girls and women coming to do work which only men had done before."

Her concern for the welfare and morale of the women of the arsenal led her to start the Lady Superintendent's Benevolent Fund. With money raised from garden fêtes and concerts she was able to establish for them maternity and convalescent homes and day nurseries. The evening classes in fencing, gymnastics, embroidery, art and drama which she organised were always well attended, as were the mixed clubs which she ran. (She nevertheless observed: "No amount of 'welfare work' will remedy low wages or bad working conditions.")

In 1917 Lily was awarded the CBE. She was appointed, after the war, Principal Officer of the Ministry of Labour's training scheme for disabled, widowed and unemployed women, and then served as Executive Officer for the Central Committee for Women's Training and Employment.

When she became Governor of the first girls' Borstal Institution at Aylesbury, Buckinghamshire, in 1923 she immediately set about improving conditions for the inmates, building up their self-esteem and teaching them practical skills. Dances were held, seaside trips organised and a programme of hobby activities initiated. She planted a flower garden inside the main gates to brighten the place up for both the girls and their visitors. The sympathy and understanding which she showed the girls gained her their respect and confidence, and she made a point of joining them every evening for a chat and a cigarette. "Have a pear drop," she would say, digging into her pocket and producing a bag of sweets, "or have a couple, one for each side."

Short and stockily built, her iron grey hair closely cropped, Lily usually wore severely tailored tweed suits and pork pie hats. In her later years she liked to wear capes.

Her remarkable achievements at Aylesbury led to her appointment in 1935 as the first woman Prison Commissioner for England and Wales.

On Lily's retirement in 1943 she and Florence went to live in a cottage in Wendover,

Devon. She was soon coopted onto several local committees; the rest of the time she and Florence spent gardening or going for long country drives.

Florence ("Fuff") had learned to drive a car when they lived in Aylesbury so that she could be Lily's chauffeur. She had not pursued a career of her own, preferring instead to look after the home.

In 1944 Lily became a DBE.

She died from coronary thrombosis on 20 May 1955, while on holiday at Hallsands, Devon.

Addresses

★*87 Kentish Town Road, NW1* – birthplace. She lived here until 1909.

★*6 Heath Drive, NW3* – her first home with Florence c1914.

★*Thames View, (at top of) Shooters Hill, SE18* – they lived here 1916–23.

Natalie Barney

(31 October 1876 – 2 February 1972)

"The most beautiful life," Natalie Barney wrote, "is the one spent in creating oneself, not in procreating." The self she created was that of an *Amazone,* boldly proclaiming and living her ideas on lesbianism and feminism. As a living advertisement for the abundant benefits of gay life, and the influential hostess of a famous literary salon which she established in Paris, she gave to generations of lesbians, gay men and writers enormous support and inspiration.

Natalie Clifford Barney was born into a wealthy family in Dayton, Ohio. She and her sister, Laura, first visited Paris as children when their mother, Alice Pike Barney, a patron of the arts, playwright and accomplished artist who studied under Whistler, took them with her when she went to study painting there.

Natalie had a French governess, attended a boarding school in Fontainebleu, and by her teens was completely bilingual. (The spirit of the language and culture of France were akin to her own, she later explained, and most of her writing is in French.) After finishing her education at a school for girls in New York she went on a European tour and studied the violin in Germany.

In 1898 she returned (with her sister and mother) to Paris, where the frankness and wit of her conversation and her independent manner caused as much comment as her beauty and extraordinary magnetism did.

Although she had become engaged to several eligible young men Natalie had at an early age realised that it was to women only that she was attracted. Her first lesbian affair, at the age of sixteen, was with Eva Palmer, whom she had met in Bar Harbor, Maine, where their families had summer homes.

Not long after her arrival in Paris she made the first of her many conquests by seducing the well-known courtesan, Liane de Pougy. Her father, Albert Clifford Barney, still reeling from Natalie's open declaration of her lesbianism in her love poems *Quelques portraits-sonnets des femmes,* published in 1900, was mortified when Liane de Pougy's autobiographical novel

Idylle saphique appeared in 1901. It was clear to many of its readers that Natalie was the original of Flossie, the young American woman who seduces the heroine. His efforts to get her to return to Washington society and respectability failed, and when he died the following year, Natalie, now financially independent and free to live as she wished, settled permanently in Paris.

The affair between Natalie and Renée Vivien, the poet, began in the winter of 1899, when Natalie was still involved with Liane. Their passion for each other, their pride in living openly as lesbians, the lesbian consciousness they developed together and the shared vision of a society in which women were emancipated and homosexuality not merely tolerated but honoured, made this the most intense relationship either woman would ever have.

All her life Natalie maintained that mutual independence, rather than dependence, should be the basis of a relationship and that love should not suffer the constraint of fidelity. Fidelity, she believed, meant that desire and love were dead. Yet she valued friendship above love and once said: "When it comes to friendship I am very lazy; once I confer friendship, I never take it back."

Romaine Brooks, who met Natalie around 1915, became her lover and remained faithful to her for over fifty years. She shared Natalie's perspective on relationships, and chose to live apart from her most of the time.

Natalie's other great love, "Lily", the duchesse de Clermont-Tonnerre, however, was less than pleased by Natalie's life of amorous intrigue and the many small *"affaires"* she was always embarking upon. The poet and novelist Lucie Delarue-Mardrus became one of Natalie's lovers, as did, briefly, Djuna Barnes, who remained a lifelong friend. A longer, traumatic relationship with Dolly Wilde, niece of Oscar Wilde, was reputedly terminated, with the cynicism verging on sadism which some of Natalie's lovers felt was typical of her treatment of them at times, by Natalie pointedly buying Dolly a one-way ticket to England.

Natalie's promiscuity was a subject much discussed by her friends and acquaintances. Alice B Toklas's cynical reply to Virgil Thomson's enquiry about Natalie, "Who does she do it with, and where does she get 'em?" was "I think from the toilets of the Louvre department store."

Her considerable charm was not only exercised on women. The elderly, reclusive scholar Rémy de Gourmont, friend and disciple of

Havelock Ellis, fell in love with her and became her close friend. He gave her the epithet *"l'Amazone"*, for her lesbianism and her love of horse-riding, and his "Lettres a l'Amazone" (published in *Mercure de France* during 1912–13) brought fame to her and the salon which she had established.

Her house at 20 rue Jacob, to which she moved in 1909 from the villa at Neuilly where Colette danced as a naked faun in the garden and Mata Hari portrayed Lady Godiva, became for some sixty years the setting for a justly renowned literary salon. Its habitués and visitors included Paul Valéry, Gertrude Stein, Harold Acton, Rainer Maria Rilke, Jean Cocteau, André Gide, Ezra Pound, Edith Sitwell, Janet Flanner, Ford Madox Ford and T S Eliot. A female equivalent of the Académie Française, the Académie des Femmes, was designed by Natalie and for years she awarded an annual prize to a woman writer in memory of Renée Vivien.

During the 1920s Radclyffe Hall and Una Troubridge were frequent visitors to Natalie's home, and in *The Well of Loneliness* Radclyffe Hall described its ambiance and Natalie's talent for making the many men and women "who must carry God's mark on their foreheads" feel "very normal and brave when they gathered together" there.

After so many years of their loving each other, the estrangement from Romaine Brooks in 1969 (because she refused to share Natalie's home and love with "Giselle", Jeanine Lahouvary), and Romaine's death the following year, left Natalie distraught and in ill-health. She died quietly two years later and, in deference to her paganism, was buried at Passy in a grave bearing no religious emblems or ornamentation.

Fictional portraits

She appears as Florence Temple Bradford (Flossie) in Liane de Pougy's *Idylle Saphique* (1901); as Vally (Lorely in the second version) of Renée Vivien's *A Woman Appeared to Me* (1904; 1905); Laurette in *L'Ange et les pervers* (1930) by Lucie Delarue-Mardrus; Dame Evangeline Musset in Djuna Barnes's *The Ladies Almanack* (1928); and Valerie Seymour in Radclyffe Hall's *The Well of Loneliness* (1928).

Address

★*97 Cadogan Gardens, SW3* – she stayed here in 1923.

Works include

Quelques portraits-sonnets des femmes (1900); *Je me souviens* (1910); *Pensées d'une Amazone* (1920); *The One who is Legion* (1930); *In Memory of Dorothy Ierne Wilde* (1951).

Memoirs: *Aventures de l'esprit* (1929); *Souvenirs indiscrets* (1960); *Traits et portraits* (1963).

Thomas Lovell Beddoes

(30 June 1803 – 26 January 1849)

The poet and dramatist Thomas Lovell Beddoes was born at Clifton, near Bristol. His father was a celebrated doctor and his mother was a sister of Maria Edgworth, the novelist.

Beddoes went to Charterhouse where he did well at his studies and was a ringleader in all sorts of escapades. His fag Charles Dacres Bevan recalled many years later that Beddoes "had a great knack at composition in prose and verse, generally burlesque, and a great notion of dramatic effect . . . I was pressed into the service as his accomplice, his enemy, or his love, with a due accompaniment of curses, caresses or kicks."

In 1822 while he was a student at Pembroke College, Oxford, Beddoes published his play *The Bride's Tragedy,* which received favourable reviews, and he met a young solicitor, Thomas Kelsall, who later became his biographer and editor.

Beddoes's closest friend at Oxford was John Bourne, a student younger than himself, who went on to become Chief Justice of Newfoundland. In a letter written to Beddoes after they had left Oxford, Bourne wrote: "If I am degenerate as you assert, it is partly your fault who have deserted your disciple so long. I miss you greatly and look back with regret to Pembroke and the joys of joy, lately bankrupt."

Having taken his degree, Beddoes left England and went to study at Göttingen. Here he wrote *Death's Jest Book, or The Fool's Tragedy,* in which he expressed his ideas about an intermediate existence between death and life, in marvellous Elizabethan blank verse, spoken prose and lyrical poetry.

The harsh criticism which the play received, when Beddoes sent the manuscript to his friends in England, contributed to a growing depression and to his slide into alcoholism. In 1829 he was ordered to leave Göttingen University for being drunk and disorderly.

John Bourne was the first to realise how wrong Beddoes's friends had been when they decided against publishing his play. "I regret now," he wrote, "the part I took in dissuading the publication of *The Fool's Tragedy* unless retouched, for I cannot but believe the reviewers would have done you wholesome service and stirred you up to better things."

At Würzburg in Bavaria Beddoes obtained his degree as doctor of medicine. He began taking an active part in Radical politics. After giving a fiery speech at a state banquet he was deported on the orders of the King.

He went next to Zurich where he remained for six years, moving restlessly from one lodging-house to another, still carrying around with him, and altering, his *Death's Jest Book.* In 1839 the Radical government of Zurich, to which Beddoes was closely allied, was overthrown and his friend Hegetschweiler, a government minister, was killed by rioters.

When his own life was threatened Beddoes fled from Zurich. He paid a brief visit to London, where he gave a lecture on drama at the Polytechnic Institute in Regent Street. So few people turned up to hear him that he suggested cancelling his lecture. He spent the next six years wandering around Europe, and came back to London in 1846.

His English friends were shocked by the alteration in his appearance and by his strange behaviour. He spent most of his time shut in his room, drinking and smoking "like Mount Etna". One evening he was arrested by the police for trying to set fire to Drury Lane Theatre with a £5 note.

From London he went to Frankfurt, where he lived for a year with a young baker named Conrad Degen (c1828–84), his closest friend, and perhaps his only lover. Beddoes taught him English and encouraged him to go on the stage. When Beddoes was ill Degen nursed him back to health.

For reasons which remain a mystery Beddoes suddenly left Frankfurt in July 1848 and went to Basle. A few weeks later he tried to kill himself by cutting open an artery in his leg. In Basle hospital he kept removing the bandages from his wound until gangrene set in and his leg had to be amputated. When he was well enough, he went to a chemist's shop, bought poison, returned to the hospital, and swallowed it. His lasts words were: "I am food for what I am good for – worms. I ought to have been among other things a good poet; life was too great a bore on one peg and that a bad one."

Nine years after Beddoes's death his cousin Zoë King went to Switzerland in search of his friends. She was told that Degen, now an actor, had been his closest friend. She wrote to Kelsall: "I saw Degen in his garret bedroom. A young man about thirty, nice looking, dressed in a blue blouse. At the mention of Beddoes's name Degen's face lit up. He said: 'He was my friend,' and could hardly speak for emotion."

Beddoes's brother and sister concealed the cause of his death and tried to stop the publication of his works. But they met their match in Kelsall, his literary executor, who published both *Death's Jest Book* and a collection of Beddoes's poems.

When he died in 1872 Kelsall left a box containing Beddoes's unpublished papers to Robert Browning. For eleven years the box remained locked and its contents unexamined. When Edmund Gosse asked Browning in 1883 if he might edit Beddoes's work Browning replied: "I mean to make a thorough examination of the contents of that dismal box and see how much of them I can give you with a free conscience . . . For the particular fact about which you enquire is painful enough, and must remain a secret, at least for some time longer."

Soon afterwards the "dismal box" with its secrets intact disappeared, and has never been found.

Addresses

★*2 Devereux Court, off Essex Street, WC2* – site of the house in which he stayed in 1824.
★*6 Devereux Court, off Essex Street, WC2* – site. He stayed here in 1825.

Works include

The Improvisatore (1821); *The Bride's Tragedy* (1822); *Death's Jest Book, or The Fool's Tragedy* (1850); *Poems Posthumous and Collected* (1851); *Poems* (1907).

Memorabilia

In the British Museum – a torn sheet of paper dating from 1830 and containing one of the songs which Beddoes added to the text of *Death's Jest Book*. On the other side of the sheet is written his most self-revealing poem. The *Oxford Book of English Verse* prudishly omitted the later stanzas of this poem, including this one:

If there were ghosts to raise
What shall I call
Out of Hell's murky haze,
Heaven's blue pall?
Raise my loved, long lost boy
To lead me to his joy?
There are no ghosts to raise;
Out of death lead no ways:
Vain is the call.

Benjamin Britten
(Lord Britten of Aldeburgh)

(22 November 1913 – 4 December 1976)

Edward Benjamin Britten, the foremost British composer of his time, was born, appropriately, on Saint Cecilia's Day, in Lowestoft, Suffolk. His father was a dental surgeon and his mother an amateur singer who came from a musical family. He was educated at Gresham's School where he captained the cricket eleven. He also became junior tennis champion of East Suffolk.

At the age of twelve Britten began studying music in the school holidays under the composer Frank Bridge. In 1930 he became a student at the Royal College of Music where he developed his impressive skills as a pianist under Arthur Benjamin, and studied composition under John Ireland.

He started his professional music career in 1935 when he joined the GPO Film Unit and wrote incidental music for documentary films, such as Night Mail which had a script by W H Auden who became a close friend.

In 1937 Britten began his lifelong relationship with the tenor Peter Pears (1910–86) They had first met three years before, but did not begin living together until after the death of Pears's friend Peter Burra in an air crash. In 1939 Britten and Pears went to live in America, where they gave recitals in aid of war charities and Britten wrote his operetta Paul Bunyan for which Auden wrote the libretto.

Two years later, after reading an article by E M Forster about the Suffolk poet George Crabbe, Britten decided to return to England and to write an opera based on Crabbe's poem about the "tortured idealist" Peter Grimes. "I soon realised where I belonged and what I lacked," he said later. "I had become without roots."

To celebrate their return home, Britten and Pears gave a recital at the Wigmore Hall of Britten's settings of seven sonnets by Michelangelo, the first of his compositions to be written for Pears.

Both men were pacifists and they were ordered to appear before a conscientious objectors tribunal which exempted them from military service. Britten's ardent pacifism is evident in many of his works, including the early song cycles, his short opera Owen Wingrave and the War Requiem.

His homosexuality also had an important effect upon his work as a composer. The musicologist Hans Keller referred to "the enormous creative advantage of Britten's homosexuality" which "placed him in the privileged position of discovering and musically defining new truths which otherwise might not have been accessible to him at all." An underlying theme of homoeroticism runs through his major operas, Peter Grimes, The Turn of the Screw, Billy Budd, and Death in Venice, and in many of his songs – the Michelangelo sonnets and the Canticles.

Peter Grimes was first performed in 1945 at the Sadler's Wells Theatre and was immediately hailed as the first indisputably great English opera since Purcell's Dido and Aeneas. From then on every new work by Britten was regarded as a major musical event.

After their return to England, Britten and Pears had settled in Aldeburgh, Suffolk, Crabbe's birthplace, and in 1948, at the suggestion of Pears, the first Aldeburgh Festival took place. They planned the early festivals themselves. Later they were joined by other artistic directors, but overall control remained with them. The scope of the festivals was much enlarged by the opening in 1967 of a concert hall, The Maltings at Snape. It burned down two years later, but was immediately rebuilt.

Britten reached his widest audience when his War Requiem, a large-scale choral work combining the Latin mass with war poems by Wilfred Owen, was performed in 1962 to mark the dedication of the new Coventry Cathedral.

In 1973 Britten underwent an operation to replace a heart valve. It was not wholly successful and for the last three years of his life he was an invalid. He continued working for short periods every day, but was no longer able to play the piano.

Six months before his death, Britten was created a life peer, the first musician to be so honoured.

Addresses

★*Burleigh House, 173 Cromwell Road, SW7* – a private boarding house at which Britten stayed while he was a student at the Royal College of Music.

★*2 West Cottages (formerly West Cottage Road), NW6* – he lived here in 1936. (See also *W H Auden*.)

★*559 Finchley Road, NW3* – he lived here 1936–37. (See also *W H Auden*.)

★*45a St John's Wood High Street, NW8* – he and Pears lived here 1943–46.

★*22 Melbury Road, W14* – they lived here 1948–53.

★*5 Chester Gate, NW1* – *site* of their home 1953–58.

★*59 Marlborough Place, NW8* – they lived here 1958–63.

★*99 Offord Road, N1* – they lived here 1965–70.

★*8 Halliford Street, N1* – they had a studio here 1970–76. (*Plaque*, 1985, unveiled by Sir Peter Pears.)

Works include

Operetta: *Paul Bunyan* (1941) (libretto by Auden).

Operas: *Peter Grimes* (1945); *Billy Budd* (1951) (from Melville's novella. Libretto by E M Forster and Eric Crozier); *The Turn of the Screw* (1954) (from a story by Henry James); *A Midsummer Night's Dream* (1960); *Owen Wingrave* (1970) (from a Henry James story); *Death in Venice* (1973) (from Thomas Mann's novella).

Ballet: *The Prince of the Pagodas* (choreographed by John Cranko) (1956).

Orchestral: *Variations on a Theme of Frank Bridge* (1937); *Piano Concerto* (1938); *The Young Person's Guide to the Orchestra* (1946).

Choral:*Hymn to Saint Cecilia* (text by Auden) (1942); *A Ceremony of Carols* (1942); *Saint Nicholas* (1948); *The War Requiem* (with settings of the war poems of Wilfred Owen) (1962).

Songs: *Our Hunting Fathers* (words by Auden) (1936); *On This Island* (words by Auden) (1937); *Les Illuminations* (settings of Rimbaud's masterpiece) (1939); *Seven Sonnets of Michelangelo* (1940).

Incidental Music: *The Ascent of F6* (play by Auden and Isherwood) (1937); *The Eagle Has Two Heads* (English production of Cocteau's play) (1946).

Portraits

Watercolour by Sarah Fanny Hockey (his aunt) (c1920) – National Portrait Gallery. Canvas – Britten and Pears, by Kenneth Green (1943) – N.P.G. Pencil drawing (undated) by Sir David Low – N.P.G. Working drawings by Sir David Low – N.P.G. (Archives). Photograph by Cecil Beaton (1945) – N.P.G. (Archives). Canvas by Jeffrey Spedding – Royal Festival Hall. Bronze cast head by Georg Ehrlich – Royal Festival Hall.

Memorial

Memorial stone (unveiled in 1978 by Lennox Berkeley) – Westminster Abbey.

Romaine Brooks

(1 May 1874 – 7 December 1970)

Many of the subjects of Romaine Brooks's portraits were lesbians and gay men; many of them were her friends. Her self-portrait and her paintings of, among others, Una Troubridge, Ida Rubinstein, Natalie Barney, Renata Borgatti and Elsie de Wolfe, have virtually become lesbian icons.

Beatrice Romaine Goddard was born in Rome. Not long after her birth her father, Major Harry Goddard, who was not at all interested in his son, St Mar, and his daughters, Maya and Romaine, left his wife, Ella Waterman Goddard.

Ella's love and attention were lavished on St Mar, who was incurably mentally ill; Maya was for the most part ignored by her mother, while Romaine was actively hated and persecuted for being that which St Mar was not – healthy, mentally alert and talented. Each of Romaine's drawings, which she had begun to do at the age of five, was destroyed upon discovery by her mother. "The atmosphere created," Romaine recalled, "was that of a court ruled over by a crazy queen."

The extremely wealthy Ella made no proper financial provision for the care of Romaine, who was left in New York at the age of six at the home of the family's laundress, when she took St Mar to Europe to seek treatment for his illness. Romaine became a street urchin, selling newspapers to help Mrs Hicky, the laundress, make ends meet.

After several months Romaine's aunt and grandfather intervened and arranged for her to be sent away to school.

Six years later, in 1886, she joined her mother and brother in London. She was next despatched to a convent school in Italy, and, later, to a private finishing school in Geneva. Somehow Romaine persuaded her irascible mother to allow her to go to Paris to study music and art.

She tried during these two years in Paris to support herself by working as a singer and as an artist's model, and then, having obtained a small allowance from her mother, went to study painting in Rome. She started painting portraits and making friends on Capri during the summer of 1899.

Romaine then entered into a marriage of convenience with John Ellingham Brooks, a dilettante pianist and writer, whom she had met on Capri. He, too, was homosexual.

The death of her mother in 1902 left Romaine very wealthy, and, free of the need to maintain the guise of married respectability, she separated from Brooks in London, whence he had followed her. She decided to retain her married name and arranged for Brooks to receive an annuity.

On the advice of an art donor friend, she followed Whistler's example by settling in St Ives, Cornwall, in order to refine her use of colour and treatment of landscape in her work. It was there that she developed her distinctive palette of greys, and there (and in the studio she took in Chelsea) that her first mature paintings were done.

By 1905 she felt ready to pursue a painting career, and went to Paris. There she was taken up as an inspired interior decorator by Parisian society, and when they learned that she painted portraits, they entreated her to let them sit for her.

In the introduction to the catalogue of her exhibition at the Galeries Durand-Ruel in 1910, Romaine was described by the aesthete Robert de Montesquiou as a "thief of souls". Perhaps the most notable portraits which she executed during the years between 1910 and 1920 are those of the androgynous Ida Rubinstein, Gabriel D'Annunzio, and Jean Cocteau.

D'Annunzio, with whom she had a brief affair, wrote of Romaine that she was "the most profound and wise orchestrator of greys in modern painting". She spent several years during the First World War in Venice, to be near D'Annunzio.

Neither Romaine nor Natalie Barney could later decide whether they had met in 1912 or in 1915, but they were in agreement that they were both about forty years old when their love began to grow to fullness. They shared their lives for over fifty years, but even though they enjoyed the comfort of staying for varying lengths of time in each other's several homes, each agreed upon the need for mutual independence and her own apartment. Natalie's seemingly insatiable desire to conquer and surround herself with beautiful young women caused Romaine to grow jealous, but she staunchly asserted that Natalie had a right to these adventures – as long as they were merely amorous dalliances and their own relationship remained the central one.

In 1920 Romaine received the Croix de la Légion d'Honneur, and in 1925 a comprehensive view of her achievement was given in three important exhibitions in Paris, London and New York.

She produced in 1923 and 1924 two of her most perceptive and introspective studies of personality and self-presentation: her self-portrait, in which she stands in coat and top hat, her shadowed and melancholy stare seeming reproachful towards life, and her gloved hand poised ready to fend off any further blows it may deal her; and the definitive portrait of Una Troubridge as a severe but sentimental woman with pin-striped suit, monocle, earrings and dachshunds.

From the mid-Twenties Romaine concentrated on producing her critically acclaimed drawings. She also began work on her memoirs, in an attempt to dispel her dead mother's still baleful influence on her life.

After her exhibition in Chicago in 1935 Romaine painted very little. She was drawn out of the retirement which she announced at the age of sixty-five with the words "I am dead" by the friendship of the portraitist Edouard MacAvoy to paint one more portrait, that of the Marchese Strozzi in 1961.

The tragic rupture of Romaine and Natalie's relationship came in 1969, when Romaine became convinced that she had been displaced from her central position in Natalie's love by Jeanine Lahouvary.

Bitter at what she perceived as Natalie's betrayal of their past years and their desire to share the ones remaining to them together, Romaine refused to have any further contact with Natalie, stating: "I am no longer 'My Angel' to her!"

She died peacefully in her sleep at the age of ninety-six. The epitaph she composed for herself reads: "Here remains Romaine, who Romaine remains." She also remained "My Angel" for Natalie: the photograph which was placed on Natalie's breast before her own funeral was that of Romaine.

Fictional portraits

Romaine Brooks and several other contemporary notable lesbians are portrayed (unsympathetically, as "odd women") in Compton Mackenzie's novel *Extraordinary Women* (1928); Olimpia Leigh is Romaine. Radclyffe Hall based Venetia Ford, the artist in *The Forge* (1924), on Romaine, who was so displeased with this "portrait" that she became a lifelong enemy of the author. In Djuna Barnes's *The Ladies Almanack* (1928) she appears as Cynic Sal.

Addresses

★ *50 (formerly 32) Tite Street, SW3* – Romaine's home and studio 1904–05.

★ *15 Cromwell Road, SW7* – she took a studio here (1924–26) where she painted Una Troubridge's portrait in 1924.

Bryher
(Winifred Ellerman)

*(2 September 1894 –
28 January 1983)*

She was the friend, confidante and adviser of many of the most celebrated writers of her time, though she herself preferred to remain out of the limelight: "I tried always to do what I could for the real artists, and especially the woman artist."

Bryher was born Annie Winifred Ellerman at Margate in Kent. When she was three months old the family returned to London. Her parents, the shipping magnate Sir John Ellerman and Hannah Glover, did not marry until the birth of their son John in 1909.

She was an intelligent and rebellious child and identified strongly with the heroes in boys' adventure stories. At the age of fourteen she was sent to Queenswood, a boarding school at Eastbourne. She hated school but made friends with several of the other girls. With the family of one of them she went on holiday to the Scilly Isles, and fell in love with the Isle of Bryher, which provided her in 1920 with the pen name for her first novel *Development*. Later she changed her name to Bryher by deed poll.

As soon as she was old enough to escape from the Victorian restraint and discipline of her family Bryher had her hair cut short and exchanged her floral-print dresses for tailor-made suits. In 1916 she read *Sea Gardens,* the first book of poems by H.D. (Hilda Doolittle). She was deeply affected by it and determined to meet the poet, having no idea that H.D. was really a young American woman. She found out through a friend that H.D. was living in a cottage at Zennor, Cornwall, and in July 1918 she called on her there. So began a relationship which was to last until H.D.'s death forty-three years later, and which gave to Bryher's life a new and clear direction.

In 1921, in order to become legally free from the dominance of her parents, Bryher married Robert McAlmon, a young American whom she and H.D. had met on holiday in New York. At that time he was working as a model, earning a dollar an hour in art classes. He was interested in modern writing and wanted to go to Paris to meet James Joyce. It was marriage in name only and apart from occasional joint visits to Bryher's parents they lived separate lives. Bryher paid all his living expenses and gave him a handsome allowance.

McAlmon became a leading figure of 1920s artistic life in Paris. With Bryher's money he was able to go into publishing. His Contact Press printed Gertrude Stein's *The Making of Americans* and H.D.'s *Palimpsest* (dedicated to Bryher). Eventually his heavy drinking and his refusal to comply with Bryher's rules for the marriage led, after six years, to divorce. He was given a generous settlement which led to his being known in Paris as Robert "McAlimony".

Within a few months of her divorce Bryher married twenty-four year old Kenneth Mac-Pherson, an aspiring writer. The same rules applied as with Bryher's first marriage. Mac-Pherson had briefly been H.D.'s lover and had a long affair with Jimmy Daniels, a popular black singer and cabaret entertainer in Paris.

In 1927 Bryher and MacPherson started a film magazine called *Close Up.* It was the first magazine devoted to film as an art form and among its contributors were Bryher's friends Gertrude Stein, Dorothy Richardson, Marianne Moore and Marc Allégret. At the suggestion of Allégret, who had once been tutor to her brother, Bryher bought MacPherson a film camera. They took a studio near Lausanne in Switzerland and began to make films. In 1930 MacPherson wrote and directed *Borderline,* which starred Paul Robeson and H.D. and featured Bryher as a cigar-smoking innkeeper.

Through both of Bryher's marriages the love and devotion of her relationship with H.D. remained constant. In 1927 she and MacPherson adopted H.D.'s eight year old daughter, Perdita, who became Bryher's heir.

During the 1930s Bryher divided her time between England and Switzerland, where she had built a house "Kenwin" (Kenneth-Winifred) above Lake Geneva. She spent several months each year in Berlin and witnessed Hitler's rise to power. She helped over a hundred refugees to escape from the Nazis and used her money to find them homes abroad.

Bryher returned to England in 1940 and spent the war years in London with H.D. while continuing her work with refugees. In 1946 she returned to Switzerland. The following year she divorced MacPherson who was living in America. Later Bryher bought him a villa on Capri when he went there to look after another of her dependants, the aging novelist Norman Douglas.

H.D. suffered a mental breakdown after the war from which she never fully recovered.

1 South Audley Street, W1

Bryher settled her into a hotel in Lausanne, close to her home. After H.D.'s death in 1961 Bryher stayed on at Kenwin, writing and giving practical help to other writers. She was always modest about her own work which received little critical attention until the series of historical novels, begun in 1952 with *The Fourteenth of October,* and her memoirs *The Heart to Artemis.*

Fictional portraits

She appears in many of H.D.'s stories and novels. Hilda Reid in *Lady Chatterley's Lover* (1928) by D H Lawrence is a composite of Bryher and H.D.

Addresses

★*1 South Audley Street, W1* – the family home. Bryher lived here 1909–21.

★ *2 Herbert Mansions, 35–36 Sloane Street, SW1* – she lived here 1925–28.

★*49 Lowndes Square, SW1* – she lived here with H.D. 1934–46.

Works include

Novels: *The Fourteenth of October* (1952); *The Player's Boy* (1953); *Roman Wall* (1954); *Gate to the Sea* (1958).

Memoirs: *The Heart to Artemis: A Writer's Memoirs* (1962); *The Days of Mars: A Memoir 1940–1946* (1972).

Samuel Butler

(4 December 1835 – 18 June 1902)

Samuel Butler, the supreme satirist of Victorian social mores, was born at Langar, Nottinghamshire, where his father was the rector. The Bishop of Lichfield was his grandfather and his namesake. At home his childhood was a lonely one, and while he balked initially at the strict regime at Shrewsbury School to which he was later sent, he welcomed the company of his fellow pupils. In 1854 he went up to St John's College, Cambridge, where he contributed to undergraduate newspapers.

In his youth he had planned to enter the church, and for a time served as lay assistant to a curate at St James's Church, Piccadilly, but on graduating from Cambridge he refused, on the ground of religious doubts, to continue the family tradition and take Orders.

His overbearing father was shocked and grieved by this and would not permit him to work as a teacher at Cambridge nor to adopt art as a profession. Instead, in 1859, Butler was sent to New Zealand to establish a sheep farm. So successful was he as a sheep-farmer that within five years he had practically doubled his initial capital of £4,000.

He began writing for the New Zealand press and producing articles and essays on the recently published theories of Charles Darwin. (Evolution and heredity are significant concerns in Butler's work, particularly in *Erewhon*; his other preoccupations were the criticism of orthodox Christianity and the examination, and undermining, of the Victorian virtues of ruthless ambition, competition and rapacity.)

When he returned to London in 1864 Butler invested his fortune and settled down to a life of painting, music and writing. He attended Heatherley's School of Painting in Newman Street, and later exhibited at the Royal Academy. At art school he met Eliza Mary Anne Savage, who became a close friend.

His richest, deepest friendship, however, was with Henry Festing Jones (1851–1928), a solicitor, whom he met in 1876. A devotion to music was one of the many interests they had in common: they jointly composed several musical works and greatly enjoyed playing piano duets. Another thing they had in common was their love for a Swiss youth, Hans Rudolph Faesch, whom they met in 1893. Each had a locket containing a lock of Faesch's hair; Festing Jones gave his locket to the young man's fiancée in 1898, and thenceforth he and Butler took turns in wearing Butler's locket suspended from their watch chains. (The occasion of Faesch's departure to Singapore, when he and Festing Jones saw him off from Holborn Viaduct Station, was recalled by Butler in his poem "In Memoriam H R F").

There were two other young men who figured largely in Butler's life: Alfred Emery Cathie, whom he engaged as his clerk and valet in 1887; and, especially, Charles Paine Pauli, whom he had met in New Zealand. Butler was so besotted with Pauli that he lent him funds for his passage home to England, and made him an annual allowance of £200 while he studied for the Bar. Pauli showed no compunction in continuing to accept this money throughout the twenty or so years of his successful career as a barrister, even though Butler was for a long time in dire financial straits.

Butler had invested all of his £8,000 from New Zealand in various companies promoted by a Mr Henry Hoare in 1873. Hoare's failure, and the loss of most of Butler's money, in the following year, led to Butler making two journeys to Canada to try to recover something from his lost fortune. It was only after the death of his father, in 1886, that Butler's financial embarrassment was eased.

Though painting had been initially his main business in London, Butler had begun, around 1869, to work on weaving a story around some of the articles and satirical sketches he had already written. The resulting book was published, anonymously and at his own expense, in 1872 as *Erewhon: or, Over the Range*. This, his most famous work and his only commercial success as an author, is regarded as one of the wittiest and most pungent satires in English since the days of Swift.

He was joined in his work and travels (chiefly in Italy, which he loved deeply) by Festing Jones after his retirement from law in 1887. His life was governed by what approached an obsession with routine and attention to detail: the certain hours in the day, and areas in his rooms, set aside for the activities of writing, painting and music-making; the mysterious weekly visits – his on Wednesdays, Festing Jones's on Thursdays – to Lucie Dumas, a Frenchwoman who lived in Handel Street and to whom they made a payment of £1 per week.

Butler's genius was never fully recognised during his lifetime, when the very diversity of his interests and his idiosyncratic theories resulted in his being regarded as a dilettante and a crank. (He regarded himself as "the enfant terrible of literature and science".) It was only after the posthumous publication of *The Way of All Flesh* and through the efforts of the self-appointed custodian of his memory, Festing Jones, who published selections from Butler's copious *Note-Books*, that his reputation began to grow to its present height.

Address

★*15 Clifford's Inn, EC4 – site*. In 1864 he took rooms here and occupied them until his death in 1902. (Pauli had his chambers in the same building.)

Works include

Books: *A First Year in Canterbury Settlement* (1863) – a selection from his letters from New Zealand to his father; *Erewhon: or, Over the Range* (1872); *The Fair Heaven* (1873); *Life and Habit* (1877); *Evolution Old and New* (1879); *Alps and Sanctuaries of Piedmont and the Canton Ticino* (1881); *Luck or Cunning as the Main Means of Organic Modification* (1886); *The Humour of Homer* (1892); *The Life and Letters of Dr Samuel Butler, Head-Master of Shrewsbury School* (1896); *The Authoress of the Odyssey* (1897); *Erewhon Revisited* (1901); *The Way of All Flesh* (1903); *Essays on Life, Art and Science* (1904); *The Note-Books of Samuel Butler* (1912) – edited by Henry Festing Jones; *Further Selections from the Note-Books of Samuel Butler* (1934) – edited by A T Bartholomew.

Music: *Gavottes, Minuets and Fugues* (1885) – with Henry Festing Jones; *Narcissus* (1888), a burlesque cantata – with Henry Festing Jones.

Painting: "Mr Heatherley's Holiday: an incident in Studio Life" (1874) – Tate Gallery.

Portraits

Canvas by Charles Gogin (1896) – National Portrait Gallery. Photograph (c1890, photographer unknown) – British Museum.

Fictional portraits

"Every man's work . . . is always a portrait of himself," wrote Butler. Ernest Pontifex in *The Way of All Flesh* is his alter-ego. Mr Emerson in E M Forster's *A Room with a View* (1908) is probably partly based on Butler.

Memorabilia

Holograph manuscript of *Erewhon* – British Museum.

Edward Carpenter

(29 August 1844 – 28 June 1929)

Edward Carpenter, social reformer and champion of homogenic love, was born in Brighton, into a wealthy middle-class family. After studying at Trinity Hall, Cambridge, he was ordained a deacon, and, in 1870, became curate at St Edward's Church, Cambridge. However, he soon began to feel at odds with his duties as a minister, which isolated him from the poor and gave him an "insuperable feeling of falsity and dislocation".

After two years he left the Church and also gave up the Fellowship which he had been awarded at Trinity. He became instead a travelling lecturer, in the North of England, for the University Extension Movement, and began writing about the poverty he saw around him and about the increasing alienation he felt from his own class. He was greatly influenced by Walt Whitman (they met in America for the first time in 1877) whose verse forms he followed in his long prose poem *Towards Democracy*.

In 1882 Carpenter's father died, leaving him £6,000, enough in those days to make him financially independent. He gave up lecturing and bought a smallholding at Millthorpe, near Sheffield, where he took up market gardening and learned to make sandals which he sent to his friends all over the world. He helped in the setting up of the socialist group in Sheffield, where he spoke in favour of nationalisation and communal farms. "We should not then work for profit, but because things required to be done."

His cottage at Millthorpe became a meeting place for the Sheffield socialists and radicals. There were visits also from like-minded middle-class friends, such as C R Ashbee, G L Dickinson and, later, Edith Lees Ellis and E M Forster. Music played an important part in these gatherings – Carpenter was an accomplished pianist – and the evenings often ended with the singing of his popular anthem "England Arise".

By 1888 Carpenter was so busy with his writing and with his political activities that he was forced to hand over the running of his market garden to his friend and former student

Albert Fearnehough, a scythe-maker. In 1893, when Fearnehough and his wife left Millthorpe, their place was taken by George Adams, a keen gardener and painter, and his wife Lucy.

In 1890 Carpenter went to Ceylon and India for a year, and meditated with a religious teacher. Soon after his return he began his lifelong relationship with a young working-class man, George Merrill, whom he met on a train. "We exchanged a few words and a look of recognition," Carpenter wrote. After they got off the train, Merrill followed Carpenter and gave him his address.

They were not able to live together until 1898 when the Adams's, with some bitterness, left Millthorpe. George Adams loved Carpenter and was filled with jealousy and hatred for Merrill.

The day after Adams's departure, Merrill arrived at Millthorpe, pushing all of his belongings in front of him on a handcart. His arrival upset many of Carpenter's friends in the neighbourhood. They were disturbed by Merrill's liking for housework, which they regarded as "woman's work", and by his frankness about his sexuality. One day a clergyman came to their door with a tract which he tried to hand to Merrill. "Keep your tract," said Merrill, "I don't want it." "But don't you wish to know the way to heaven?" asked the man. "No, I don't," was the reply. "Can't you see that we're in heaven here – We don't want any better than this, so go away." Merrill's ignorance of the Bible came as a surprise to Carpenter. When he heard that Gethsemane was the place where Jesus had spent his last night, Merrill enquired, "Who with?"

In 1914 Carpenter, with his friend Laurence Housman, founded the British Society for the Study of Sex Psychology. Their aim was to "question things that have not been questioned before," and talks were given on infantile sexuality, women's sexuality, and homosexuality. He also lectured at meetings of the Independent Labour Party and to the Fellowship of the New Life, the socialist group from which the Fabian Society grew.

Carpenter's books were translated into several languages and brought him friends and admirers from all over the world (particularly in the United States and in Germany, where *Love's Coming of Age* sold 40,000 copies.) His writings were regarded as the "bible" of British socialism, and on his eightieth birthday he received a greetings telegram signed by the entire Labour Cabinet.

Shortly after the First World War Carpenter

and Merrill had moved from Millthorpe to Guildford, Surrey. They lived together and loved and cared for each other for thirty years, and when Merrill died in 1928 Carpenter lived on for only a few months. They are buried together at Guildford.

Addresses

★*17 Osnaburgh Street, NW1* – *site* of the home of Carpenter's friend E R Pease and the first meeting-place of the Fellowship of the New Life. Carpenter attended some of the Fellowship's meetings here. (*Blue plaque* commemorating the founding of the Fabian Society, which grew out of the Fellowship.)
(See also *Edith Lees Ellis.*)
★*29 and 49 Doughty Street, WC1* – he gave several lectures at these Fellowship houses in the 1880s and early 1890s.
★*60 Myddelton Square, EC1* – he paid visits to Fenner Brockway and the Independent Labour Party community here c1908–10.

Works include

Towards Democracy (prose poem, 1883, ex-panded 1905); *England's Ideal* (1885); *Civilisation, its Cause and Cure* (1889, enlarged 1921); *From Adam's Peak to Elephanta* (1892) – part of which was reissued as *A Visit to a Gnani; Homogenic Love* (1895); *Love's Coming of Age* (1896); *Angel's Wings* (1898); *Iolaus* (1902); *The Art of Creation* (1904); *The Intermediate Sex* (1908); *My Days and Dreams* (autobiography, 1916).

Portraits

Canvas by Roger Fry (1894) – National Portrait Gallery. Canvas by Henry Bishop (1907) – N.P.G. Photograph by Alvin Langdon Coburn (1905) – N.P.G. Photograph by Elliott and Fry – N.P.G. (Archives). Photograph by Frederick Hollyer – in the Hollyer Albums, Victoria and Albert Museum.

Memorabilia

Archive material relating to Carpenter – National Museum of Labour History.

Emily Carr

(13 December 1871 – 2 March 1945)

Emily Carr, who ranks as one of Canada's greatest artists, struggled hard to follow her vocation, and she suffered a lifetime of obscurity and near-poverty before gaining recognition as a painter and a writer.

She was born of English parents in Victoria, British Columbia. At an early age she rebelled against her family's strictness and against the conservatism of the environment in which she grew up. Although her father encouraged her in art, she hated him. Equally despised was her sanctimonious and authoritarian elder sister who brought her up after their parents died (when Emily was in her early teens).

Emily's sisters regarded her determination to study art as yet another symptom of her "wild and shameful nature". At the age of eighteen she broke free from them and went to study at the San Francisco School of Art. On her return to Victoria five years later she began holding art classes for children. Visiting artists persuaded her that it was essential for her to study in Europe, and so, in 1899, she came to London and enrolled at the Westminster School of Art.

Before long she made friends with a fellow art student who lived in the same lodging house as her, Alice Watkins, nicknamed "Wattie". The other students called Emily "Motor", but to Wattie she was always "dear, dear Carlight". Emily disliked the noise and dirt of London and the snobbery she encountered here. "Do you know what hell would be like?" she once asked Wattie. "Hell would be London without you or Mrs Radcliffe." (Mrs Radcliffe, the aunt of friends in Victoria, had taken Emily under her wing, and later she found her and Wattie the rooms which they shared for a few months.) When Wattie graduated and left London, Emily transferred her affections to another young woman at the art school, Mildred Compton. She became ill around this time and spent eighteen months in a sanatorium, followed by a year in the artists' colony in St Ives and six months at a school in Hertfordshire.

Emily returned to Europe again (1910–11), to study at the Académie Colarossi in Paris. In the intervening years she had begun making visits to the Indian villages along the British Columbia coast, and had determined to record in paintings the people and their heritage, the totemic art which was rapidly vanishing. She began painting in a Fauvist style after her return to Canada, hoping that she might thereby express the vitality of the Indians and their culture, and the mighty, sweeping grandeur of the forests of the West Coast. The boldness of these paintings, however, brought her humiliating hostility: she could not sell her work; schools would not employ her; and her private pupils deserted her. Nevertheless, she refused to work in her old style again, insisting: "I would rather starve!"

In order to support herself she opened a boarding house (which acquired the name "The House of All Sorts"), made pottery and hooked rugs with Indian designs to sell to tourists, and bred bobtail sheepdogs. She came to prefer the company of animals to that of people. Her neighbours knew her by her menagerie rather than by her art, and local legends grew up about the eccentric middle-aged woman who once raised an abandoned vulture, tamed a maltreated racoon, kept parrots, and dressed her Javanese monkey, "Woo", in frocks and took her shopping in a baby-carriage.

During her years as a landlady Emily had little leisure or energy for painting, and for fifteen years she painted nothing at all. However, in the mid-1920s an ethnologist working among the Indians of the West Coast learned from them about a white woman who often sketched and painted in their villages. He eventually traced Emily and saw her work, which greatly impressed him. This led to her being introduced to the director of the National Gallery of Canada and to the inclusion of fifty of her early canvases in the "Northwest Coast Art" exhibition in Ottawa in 1927. Emily travelled east for the opening of the exhibition, and the appreciation of her fellow artists, particularly those in the Group of Seven, encouraged her to take up her brushes again with her old enthusiasm. (Her most characteristic work dates from this period.)

At the age of fifty-six Emily had begun to receive recognition as an artist: her works were being exhibited (and her style imitated) and many artists came to call at her studio. However, even with these callers and her friends surrounding her, she felt lonely and isolated. "Oh God, why did you make me a pelican and sit me down in a wilderness?" she wrote in her journal.

Emily's passion for telling the truth and

being entirely herself did not endear her to many. Admitting her tendency toward vituperation, she called herself "a spit-cat", but "Klee Wyck", the laughing one, was the Indians' name for her, because they early recognised her sense of humour. Laughter (usually at herself) and her rather self-conscious "cussedness" seem to have been salves for her despair of ever gaining recognition and acceptance.

Most of her work was done during trips to the forests, in which she lived in a "hideous but darling old caravan trailer" which she called "the Elephant". Occasionally Edythe Hembroff-Schleicher, one of her closest friends, would accompany her on these trips. Edythe, a portraitist, one day insisted that they should paint one another. With ill-concealed annoyance Emily set about the task, muttering: "How I wish you were a tree, Edythe!"

In 1937 Emily had her first heart attack, and as her health rapidly failed she was forced to curtail her outdoor sketching activities. She continued to paint, often while lying in her sickbed, but began to devote more of her time to her writing. Her first book, *Klee Wyck,* was an instant success when it was published in 1941 and it won the Governor-General's award for general literature for that year. In *Klee Wyck* she recalled some of her experiences with the Indians she loved so dearly; later she turned to recounting anecdotes of her childhood and womanhood, displaying the same integrity and great personal vision evident in her paintings.

Her books first brought popular attention to her paintings. International recognition came to her in her last years, and her work was shown in twenty-seven exhibitions in Europe and America.

She died at St Mary's Priory, Victoria, and was buried in her family's plot in the civic cemetery. A simple stone tablet, inscribed with the description "Artist and Author, Lover of Nature", was placed on her grave by her friends and admirers seventeen years later.

Works include

Books: *Klee Wyck* (1941); *Book of Small* (1942); *The House of All Sorts* (1944); *Growing Pains, the Autobiography of Emily Carr* (1946); *Hundreds and Thousands, the Journals of Emily Carr* (1966) – some editions contain colour plate reproductions of several of her paintings (none of which can be seen in public collections in London).

Addresses

★*Vincent Square, SW1* – c1900 she took a room in a house which stood here. Alice Watkins had the room next to hers. (*Site.*)

★*5 Bulstrode Street, W1* – she lived here in 1902 at "Mrs Mary Dodds's Home for Governesses and Ladies".

Elizabeth Carter

(16 December 1717 – 19 February 1806)

Elizabeth Carter, translator, poet and essayist, was born in Deal, Kent, the daughter of the Rev. Nicholas Carter and his first wife, Margaret Swayne, who died when Elizabeth was ten.

As the eldest child of the large family, Elizabeth became responsible for the running of the home, particularly after the death of her stepmother. She was educated at home by her father, and was so keen to learn Latin, Greek, Hebrew, French, Italian, Spanish and German that she would keep herself awake at night to study by chewing green tea and taking snuff. For relaxation she used to dance or play the German flute.

In February 1738 *The Gentleman's Magazine* published a riddle by Elizabeth. This was followed by other contributions from her, under the name "Eliza", and a pamphlet of her work entitled *Poems upon Particular Occasions*.

Through Edward Cave, the editor of *The Gentleman's Magazine,* she met Dr Johnson who published some of her essays in *The Rambler*. They remained friends for fifty years. He once declared that Elizabeth "could make a pudding as well as translate Epictetus from the Greek, and work a handkerchief as well as compose a poem."

Elizabeth was encouraged to publish her translation of the writings of the philosopher Epictetus by her closest friend, Catherine Talbot, with whom she carried on a passionate correspondence from their first meeting in 1741 until Catherine's death nearly thirty years later. Catherine was an invalid and was looked after by her mother, so she and Elizabeth never lived together.

The Epictetus translation established Elizabeth's reputation as a Greek scholar, with four editions of the work being produced in her lifetime, and gave her financial independence from her family. She began to divide her time between Deal and London, where she took rooms in Piccadilly.

After Catherine's death in 1770, Elizabeth became friendly with a group of intellectual women led by Elizabeth Montagu, and including Elizabeth Vesey and Frances Boscowan, who were known as the Bluestockings. She also knew Horace Walpole, Fanny Burney, and Samuel Richardson (who included Elizabeth's best known verse, "Ode to Wisdom", without acknowledgement, in his novel *Clarissa*).

The success of her writings and the generosity of her friends (Elizabeth Montagu gave her an annual allowance and Catherine Talbot's mother left her a legacy) enabled Elizabeth to travel. In 1763 she went to France, the Low Countries and the Rhineland, and wrote letters to her friends giving her reactions to the places she saw and the people she met. She disapproved of the governments and religious customs of the largely Roman Catholic regions which she visited, but enjoyed exploring the cities and looking at old buildings. She particularly admired Gothic architecture, both in Britain and on the Continent; as she wrote to Elizabeth Montagu, "I have, at least, as much of the Goth as of the Athenian, in my composition."

Elizabeth was described in her old age by Fanny Burney as "really a noble looking woman; I never saw age so graceful in the female sex yet; her whole face seems to beam with goodness, piety and philanthropy."

She died in London and was buried in the grounds of the Grosvenor Chapel, Mayfair, where her epitaph notes her "deep learning and extensive knowledge".

Addresses

★*20 Clarges Street, W1* – site of her first London home. She lived here from 1762.
★*21 Clarges Street, W1* – site of her home during the last years of her life. (Died here.)

Works include

Translations: *Sir Isaac Newton's philosophy explained, for the use of ladies* (1739) – from the Italian of Algarotti; *All the Works of Epictetus* (1758).
Poetry: *Poems upon Particular Occasions* (1738); *Poems upon Several Occasions* (1762).

Portraits

Pastel by Sir Thomas Lawrence (exh. 1790) – National Portrait Gallery. Drawing "The Nine Living Muses of Great Britain" by Richard Samuel (1779) – N.P.G. Oil by Catherine Read (c1765) – Dr Johnson's House, Gough Square, EC4. Print by J R Smith (1781) – British Museum. Print by Mackenzie (1807) – British Museum.

Memorabilia

Her bureau, armchair, two books which belonged to her, and a locket (containing a portrait of her as a young woman, by an unknown artist) – Dr Johnson's House.

Constantine Cavafy

(29 April 1863 – 29 April 1933)

The poems of Constantine Cavafy, whether dealing with the history and incidents of the ancient world or reflecting upon his own life in modern Alexandria, illuminate aspects of homosexual experience and feelings that exist in any time or place.

He was born in Alexandria into a wealthy Greek family of textile merchants. His father died when he was seven and his mother took the family to England, where they stayed for seven years, first in Liverpool and then in London.

In 1877 the family export company failed. They lost most of their money and returned to Alexandria, where Cavafy went to a school for children of the Greek community. Then in 1882, before the British bombardment of Alexandria, they moved to Constantinople. Here Cavafy, a gifted linguist, wrote his first poems in English and French and evolved his highly individual style of writing in a mixture of classical and demotic Greek. He also had his first love affair, with his cousin, George Psilliary.

Cavafy returned to Alexandria with his mother in 1885 and found work as a clerk in the Department of Irrigation. As a Greek citizen he was not eligible for promotion, but despite that he remained there until his retirement over thirty years later. At night he would rumple his bedclothes so that his mother would think that he had slept at home and gone out early, and make his way to a male brothel and the arms of the young men of his poems.

He was reticent about his poetry and sensitive to criticism. No volume of his poems was published during his lifetime. Instead he had them printed privately and distributed them among his friends and relatives. Fortunately his close friend Pericles Anastassiades collected together everything that Cavafy wrote and was able eventually to bring his work to a wider audience.

After his mother's death in 1899 Cavafy took a flat above a brothel on the Rue Lepsius in the old Greek quarter. His rooms were filled with ornate Byzantine furniture and lit by candles. He was usally at home to friends between the hours of five and seven, when he would serve ouzo or whisky, hard-boiled eggs, cheese and olives. He always sat in the shadows, gazing intently at his guests. Occasionally he would move about the room, opening or closing shutters or rearranging the candles, hastily lighting more whenever a beautiful youth arrived.

Cavafy was a familiar figure in the neighbourhood bars and cafes. A small, rather timid man with round tortoise-shell spectacles, he dressed in a shabby suit and a straw hat. As he grew older he curled and dyed his hair. He had the appearance, someone observed, not of an old man trying to stay young, but of "a boy who had aged". He used to go sometimes to the Cafe Al Salam where he could always be sure of the company of young men. His favourite was Toto, a handsome motor mechanic, who would often return with him at the end of the evening to the Rue Lepsius. As far as is known, Cavafy's only long-term sexual relationship was with Alexander Singopoulos, whom he made his heir and literary executor. He wept when Alexander married in 1926. Later he became fond of Rika, Alexander's wife, and she helped him distribute his work.

Cavafy's fame began to grow as magazines published more and more of his poems, mostly supplied by his friend Anastassiades. Literary visitors to the city began to seek him out. E M Forster, an early admirer of his work, was the first to introduce him to English readers in his essays *Pharos and Pharillon,* describing him as "a Greek gentleman in a straw hat, standing absolutely motionless at a slight angle to the universe".

In 1932 Cavafy became ill and cancer of the throat was diagnosed. He suffered a great deal of pain and could not speak at all. For a time he was looked after at home by Alexander, but when he grew weaker he was taken into hospital, where he died on his seventieth birthday. His last act was to draw a circle on a blank piece of paper, in the centre of which he placed a full stop.

In his poem "Hidden Things", Cavafy predicted:

> Later, in a more perfect society,
> Someone else made just like me
> Is certain to appear and act freely.

Address

★ *15 Queensborough Terrace, W2* – he lived here 1873–76. (*Plaque,* unveiled by Lawrence Durrell, was erected by the London Hellenic Society in 1974.)

Works include

Poems by C P Cavafy, translated by John Mavrogordato, with an introduction by Rex Warner (1951).

Charlotte Charke

(13 January 1713 – 6 April 1760)

Charlotte Charke was the youngest of the twelve children of Colley Cibber, the Poet Laureate. In her memoirs she described how at the age of three she took to wearing her brother's clothes and boots and her father's periwig, and to swaggering about the house with a brace of pistols tied around her waist. These she would fire unexpectedly, while her poor asthmatic mother "lay half expiring with dreadful imaginations". Besides becoming a good shot, her other early interests were in horse-riding and gardening. She was educated at "a famous school in Park Street, Westminster" run by a Mrs Draper, where she learned French, Italian and Latin.

In February 1729 Charlotte married Richard Charke, a violinist with the Drury Lane Theatre Company. "To be sure," she wrote, "I thought it gave me an air of more consequence to be called Mrs Charke than Miss Charlotte. My spouse on his part, I believe, thought it a fine feather in his cap to be Mr Cibber's son-in-law." The marriage was not a success. Charke spent all his wife's money on the upkeep of his mistress. Within a year of the wedding, and shortly after the birth of their daughter Katherine, Charlotte left him and, forced to earn a living, she began her career as an actress. Thereafter she always dressed as a man.

Her first appearance on the stage was as Mademoiselle in *The Provok'd Wife* in April 1730 at Drury Lane. Then she moved to the Haymarket Theatre where she played Roderigo in *Othello* for £3 a week.

Charlotte's relationship with her father had never been close and they quarrelled bitterly after she appeared as Fopling Fribble, intended as a satire on Cibber, in Fielding's *Battle of the Poets, or The Contention for the Laurel,* produced at the Haymarket Theatre in January 1731. Cibber never forgave her and ignored all of her subsequent pleas for help.

After her season at the Haymarket, she went into business as a grocer and oil seller in a shop in Long Acre. "When I first went into my shop," she wrote, "I was horribly puzzled for the means of securing my efforts from the power of my husband, who though he did not live with me, I knew had a right to make bold with any thing that was mine, as there was no formal article of separation between us, and I could not easily brook his taking any thing from me to be profusely expended on his mistress." At about this time, however, Richard Charke went to Jamaica where, shortly afterwards, he died.

When the shop failed to make a profit Charlotte, ever resourceful, set up a puppet show in St James Street. This venture also failed and she was forced to sell the puppets at a considerable loss. Finding it increasingly difficult to support herself and her daughter, she took on several jobs: she made sausages in Red Lion Square, became a waiter at the King's Head tavern in Marylebone, was valet to an Irish peer, ran a tavern in Drury Lane and pulled the wires for Punch in Mr Russell's Italian Puppet Opera in Brewer Street.

Then she was arrested for debt and spent a night in a sponging house. Her friends, the women who kept the "coffee houses" (a euphemism for brothels) around Covent Garden, came to visit "poor Sir Charles" as they called her. Between them they raised enough money to pay off the debt and secure Charlotte's release.

Returning to the stage Charlotte played a variety of masculine roles, including Hamlet, Mercury and Captain Plume. Her Hamlet was especially well received because she "so frequently broke out in fresh places". In 1744 she went back to the Haymarket Theatre to play MacHeath in *The Threepenny Opera*. When her brother, Theophilus Cibber, resigned as manager of the Haymarket, Charlotte tried to manage the company herself, but without success. One wonders at this point why all of Charlotte's various attempts to earn a living failed. There is evidence to suggest that, at least in the case of her attempt to manage the Haymarket company, her father's substantial influence was brought to bear against her.

Charlotte wrote two novels and had two of her plays produced. In 1755 she published her memoirs in which she wrote of her relationships with, and conquests of, women, and how she would "creep out by owl-light in search of adventures". Her closest and most enduring relationship was with the actress who played the Queen to Charlotte's Lorenzo in *The Spanish Fryar*. She is referred to in the book as "Mrs Brown" to Charlotte's "Mr Brown". They went to live for a time in a village near Bristol, where Charlotte passed as a man and they were thought of as a married couple. Charlotte set up as "Brown, Pastry

Cook of London", but as usual all her efforts went unrewarded and they returned to London.

A visit to Charlotte's daughter, recently married to a strolling player, did not end happily. The son-in-law, whom Charlotte described as "the little incompetent", was rude to "Mrs Brown", so they left hurriedly and found lodgings in Islington.

The last years of "Mr and Mrs Brown" were spent in abject poverty. Charlotte earned very little from her writings and they were reduced to relying on the generosity of friends and, finally, on parish relief.

Charlotte's obituary in *The Gentleman's Magazine* states:

Death to you is profitable:
Now you need nor pot nor table;
And what you never had before,
You've a house for ever more.

Addresses

★*37 Wellington Street (formerly 3 Charles Street), WC2* – she lived here 1721–29. (The Transport Museum stands on the *site* of the house.)

★*Oxendon Street, SW1* – *site* of the house which she took lodgings in 1731.

★*Marsham Street, SW1* – *site* of her lodgings in the early 1730s.

★*Great Queen Street, WC2* – she lived here with her daughter in the 1740s in what she described as "a most dismal mansion". (*Site*.)

★*Little Turnstile, WC1* – *site* of the house in which she had lodgings in the 1740s.

Works

Plays: *The Art of Management* (never performed); *The Carnival, or Harlequin Blunderer* (1735); *Tit for Tat, or Comedy and Tragedy at War* (1743).

Novels: *The History of Henry Dumont, Esq. and Miss Charlotte Evelyn, with Some Critical Remarks on Comic Actors* (1756) (the critical remarks were omitted); *The Lovers' Treat, or Unnatural Hatred* (1758).

Memoirs: *A Narrative of the Life of Mrs Charlotte Charke, Youngest Daughter of Colley Cibber, Esq, as told by Herself* (1755).

Portraits

Print by F Garden – "Aged four, dressed as a gentleman, walking in a ditch" (1755) – British Museum. Print by Dandridge – British Museum. Print (full length) by unknown artist – National Portrait Gallery. Print (¾ length) by unknown artist – N.P.G. Woodcut for *The Table Book* (unknown artist) – N.P.G.

Memorabilia

Material relating to the Cibber family – Theatre Museum.

Frances Power Cobbe

(4 December 1822 – 5 April 1904)

In what the *Athenaeum* called "a long, combative and in many ways useful career" Frances Power Cobbe, a forceful, witty and compassionate woman with radical ideas about society and religion, progressed from writing about religion and moral philosophy, through philanthropy, to active social reform. Her chief interests were, in her own words, "everything concerning women" and "looking after the interests of animals".

She was born into a landowning Anglo-Irish family who were strict Evangelical Protestants. Frances, however, was "heretical" from girlhood. She was educated at home by governesses and then attended a boarding school in Brighton, which specialised in "female accomplishments". Her real education came from private studies and lessons from a local clergyman on her return to the family home, Newbridge House, in 1838.

Following the death of her beloved mother in 1847 Frances took her place as head of the household, and was proud to be an able housekeeper who "also knew a little Greek and geometry". For eight years she kept house for her father and brothers, "all the time in a sort of moral Coventry", the result of "abandoning the creed of my youth". Her spare time was spent in studying and in receiving visitors, particularly her friend Harriet St Leger, who brought Fanny Kemble with her on one occasion. (Fanny Kemble, whom Frances regarded as the most remarkable woman she had known, later became a close friend).

After an attack of bronchitis from which she nearly died, at the age of thirty, Frances resolved to write a book to help others with religious doubts. *The Theory of Intuitive Morals* (1855) took her three years to write and was published anonymously. When it was rumoured that the author was a woman "the criticisms were barbed with sharper teeth". Nevertheless, the book was a *succès d'estime*.

The death of her father in 1857 left Frances with £100 in cash and £200 a year, and for eleven months she travelled alone in the Holy Land and Europe.

In 1858, shortly after her return to England,

her "independent life as I had planned it" began with her cooperation with Mary Carpenter in the work of the Red Lodge Reformatory and "ragged schools" at Bristol. The following year she became a pioneer in workhouse visiting. (The first money she earned from journalism – £14 – was spent on providing a splendid tea for the elderly women in one of these workhouses.)

Frances took up journalism professionally after her active work in Bristol ended, chiefly through her becoming crippled (for nearly four years) by her doctor's incorrect treatment of a sprained ankle. (This, and their involvement in vivisection, left her with an abiding hatred of the medical profession.)

In 1860 Charlotte Cushman introduced Frances to Mary Charlotte Lloyd, a friend of Mary Somerville, with whom Frances had become friends in Rome. The friendship between Frances and Mary Lloyd deepened when Mary joined her in Italy two years later. On their return to London Mary bought the house in South Kensington which became their home for a quarter of a century. "My lonely wanderings were over," Frances wrote in her autobiography. Mary resumed her sculpting and painting while Frances, with her friend's steadfast support and encouragement, began using her journalism as a means of campaigning for various social reforms.

She continued to publish works on the subject of religion and morality, but a great deal of her writing and lecturing, during the 1860s especially, was on women's rights and their obligations to society. The part of her work to which she looked back with most satisfaction was that concerning battered wives. She obtained the release of a woman who had killed her husband in self-defence and been sentenced to hang; and legislation was initiated by her which empowered women to gain legal separation from battering husbands and to retain custody of their children. She was an early suffragist, and in addition to votes for women, she called for the right of married women to hold property. In 1862 she read before the Social Science Congress at the Guildhall a paper advocating the admission of women to university degrees. For some time afterwards she was "the butt of universal ridicule", but seventeen years later she had the satisfaction of being invited to join the deputation to thank the President of London University for finally doing this.

Frances met, and often gained the friendship of, many of the leading figures of her day, such as Gladstone, Cardinal Manning and John Stuart Mill; many happy hours were spent "talking dogs" with Charles Darwin and Matthew Arnold, and she knew "nearly all the more gifted Englishwomen". All of her friends and acquaintances were pressed by her to lend their support and influence to the campaigns she undertook.

Although Frances remained active in feminist work, the last thirty years of her life were largely devoted to the anti-vivisection crusade. She founded, in 1875, the Victoria Street Society for the Protection of Animals and, until 1884, acted as its joint secretary and editor of its publication, *The Zoophilist*. In 1898 she founded the British Society for the Abolition of Vivisection.

Poor health and "the strain of London life" had led to her move in 1884 to North Wales with Mary, "the friend who made my life so happy . . . for thirty-four blessed years". She still worked tirelessly for the feminist and anti-vivisectionist causes, and made several trips around Britain to give lectures and visit friends.

After Mary's death Frances enjoyed spending her leisure time reading the records of their life together. In her autobiography she paid splendid tribute to Mary and their love: she thanked God for "two priceless benedictions in life; – in my youth, a perfect Mother; in my later years, a perfect Friend", and reproduced a poem she had written to Mary in 1873. The poem, which begins "Friend of my life!", contains the glorious stanza:

> Now, – while the vigorous pulses leap
> Still strong within my spirits deep,
> Now, while my yet unwearied brain
> Weaves its thick web of thoughts amain,
>   I want you – Mary.

("I want you – Mary" is the refrain of all eight stanzas of the poem.)

In 1902 Frances joined the Women's Liberal Federation. A few days before her death she was asked to serve as Honorary Vice-President of the National Union of Women Workers of Great Britain and Ireland.

She was buried, as she wished, next to Mary in Llanelltyd churchyard.

Addresses

★*15 Connaught Square, W2* – she completed work on *The Theory of Intuitive Morals* during her stay here, while on holiday with her father during the summer of 1855.

★*26 Hereford Square, SW7* – site. She and Mary Lloyd lived here 1862–84. In the garden Mary built a studio, and in the "Boundless Prairie", the vacant lot behind the house, they

gave "teaparties beneath the limeblossoms" for their many distinguished friends and acquaintances. (When they moved to Hengwrt they let the house to Fanny Kemble.)

Works include

The Theory of Intuitive Morals (1855) – her "magnum opus"; *Friendless Girls, and How to Help Them* (1861); *Broken Lights* (1864); *Studies of Ethical and Social Subjects* (1865); *The Confessions of a Lost Dog* (1867); *Dawning Lights* (1868); *Criminals, Idiots, Women and Minors* (1868); *The Final Cause of Women* (1869); *Re-Echoes* (1876) – collected articles for the *Echo*; *Why Women Desire the Franchise* (1877); *The Duties of Women* (1881); *The Scientific Spirit of the Age* (1888); *Life of Frances Power Cobbe, as told by herself* (1894; 1904 edition with an introduction by Blanche Atkinson).

Portrait

Photograph (undated, unknown photographer) – Fawcett Library.

Memorabilia

Several autograph letters (including one, c1879, to Geraldine Jewsbury, inviting her to come to a party at her home) – Fawcett Library.

Robert Colquhoun
(22 December 1914 –
20 September 1962)
&
Robert MacBryde
(5 December 1913 – 15 May 1966)

"The Roberts", as they were known, hailed from Ayrshire: MacBryde from Maybole and Colquhoun from Kilmarnock. They became lovers after meeting at Glasgow School of Art, where they began studying in 1932, and for the rest of their lives they were inseparable. Their first joint exhibition was held in Kilmarnock in 1938. Both won scholarships which enabled them to visit Italy and France together during 1938–39.

Upon the outbreak of the war they returned to Scotland and Colquhoun began serving as an ambulance driver with the Royal Army Medical Corps in Edinburgh. MacBryde was exempt from war service due to a tubercular condition, and when Colquhoun was invalided out of the army in 1941 after collapsing from heart trouble they settled in London. During the day Colquhoun drove an ambulance in the Civil Defence Corps and at night he painted; MacBryde, when not painting, took pride in being, as he called it, "the servant of a great master", organising their domestic and professional lives. (Both Roberts were fastidious about their appearance: MacBryde was once observed using a heated teaspoon to iron a shirt for Colquhoun.)

MacBryde always referred to Colquhoun as "ma lover" and they were regarded as a devoted, inseparable couple. Although they displayed great loyalty and were extremely solicitous of each other's comfort and welfare, they sometimes had violent quarrels, usually in pubs and usually about Colquhoun's attraction to other men.

Both Roberts enjoyed singing, their repertoire comprising chiefly Scots songs, and both tended to be rude and aggressive when drunk. Colquhoun was the more inhibited of the two: MacBryde called him a "Presbyterian puritan". He was tall and thin and his passivity and shyness gave many acquaintances a misleading impression of extreme lethargy and inarticulateness. MacBryde, on the other hand, was a short, wiry man with boundless verve and energy. He wore a kilt around town as much out of flamboyance as national pride and did not need much persuading to do a sword dance on the pavement.

They were both successes during the 1940s, with Colquhoun reaching the peak of his powers about the middle of the decade, and were among the most praised of the Neo-Romantics, a group of artists for many of whom the Roberts' studio had become a centre. They included John Minton, Keith Vaughan, Michael Ayrton, John Craxton and Prunella Clough. (Other friends and visitors to the studio were Rodrigo Moynihan, Sidney Graham, Dylan Thomas and George Barker.)

Colquhoun's painting was influenced and much admired by Wyndham Lewis. His draughtsmanship was much better than MacBryde's and he was early recognised as an artist "with something to say". MacBryde, whose work was influenced by the Surrealists and the Polish artist Jankel Adler, displayed the finer sense of colour but contemporary critics considered that much of his work tended towards the decorative. His artistic reputation suffered too through his insistence on always placing Colquhoun's work above his own. (The works of Colquhoun and MacBryde are now being reappraised and the more subtle qualities of MacBryde's are beginning to be acknowledged and appreciated.)

The decline in their artistic powers and the crumbling of their lives dates from the Roberts' eviction from their studio in 1947. (The landlord told them that they had been let the studio for painting in by day, not for having "drunken orgies" by night.) Displaced from their home and the centre of their artistic and social lives, they found it increasingly difficult to regain their earlier momentum and to work at full stretch. They found that, with the shift of critical attention from Neo-Romanticism to the burgeoning of Abstract Expressionism in England and to a more extreme realism in painting, by the 1950s few people wanted their work. Their friends noted with distress their increased addiction to drink, their evident despair and deteriorating health and confidence.

Between 1947 and 1949 they lived in Lewes, Sussex, where Frances Byng Stamper and Caroline Lucas, who commissioned from them drawings and lithographs for their Miller's Press, put a studio at their disposal. On their return from a trip to Italy with their close friend George Barker they went to live with him and his wife Elizabeth Smart at Tilty Mill, near Dunmow, Essex, and remained there for four years.

MacBryde had his first one-man exhibition at the Lefevre Gallery in 1943; Colquhoun exhibited there in 1943, 1944 and 1947. The death in 1950 of Duncan Macdonald, a director of the gallery, deprived them of a friend, supporter, dealer and banker, and was a further blow to their assurance. (Colquhoun was given another exhibition at the gallery in 1951, but then the connection fell away.)

They were commissioned by Massine to design the costumes and decor for his new Scottish ballet *Donald of the Burthens* which was produced in 1951 at Covent Garden. They also designed the sets and costumes for George Devine's production of *King Lear* at Stratford in 1953.

A Colquhoun retrospective, organised by Bryan Robertson, was held at the Whitechapel Gallery in 1958 and the Roberts went to Spain on the proceeds of this.

Restless and lacking application to their work, they spent the next few years living in a succession of rooms in London. The offer of an exhibition at the Museum Galleries in Bloomsbury provided Colquhoun with the incentive he needed. Whilst working hard for this exhibition he suffered a seizure and died shortly afterwards in MacBryde's arms. The drawing he had been working on was of a man in space, dying.

MacBryde was inconsolable after Colquhoun's death. He was seldom sober, he neglected his appearance and his talk was only of Colquhoun. At a summer school of painting at Kinsale, Co. Cork, which he had been asked to supervise by Louis MacNeice's widow, Hedli Anderson, he disgraced himself by stealing wine from the restaurant and drinking it in the henhouse, and by taking a handbag from a guest's car and spending the money he found in it on whiskey.

For a time MacBryde stayed in Dublin with a doctor whom he had met shortly after Colquhoun's death. He later moved into the Dublin home of the poet Leland Bardwell, with whom he and Colquhoun had stayed in Holloway, London. Returning home from a pub late one night he was knocked down by a car and killed.

MacBryde is buried at Maybole and Colquhoun at Kilmarnock, where a Colquhoun Memorial Gallery with an annual Colquhoun Art Prize opened in 1972. George Barker, to whom MacBryde had once said, "We must be certain to create our legends before we die," wrote "Funeral Elegy for Robert Colquhoun" and "In Memory of Robert MacBryde".

The Roberts' last joint exhibition had been at the Kaplan Gallery in 1960; there was a posthumous Colquhoun exhibition at the Douglas and Foulis Gallery, Edinburgh, in 1963, and in 1977 an exhibition of both artists' work was given at the Mayor Gallery.

Addresses

★*77 Bedford Gardens, W8* – their studio and home 1941–47. Jankel Adler took a studio in the house in 1943. (See also *John Minton*.)

★*47 Gibson Square, N1* – they had rooms here in 1958.

★*9 Westbourne Terrace, W2*, and

★*8 Norland Square, W11* – they had rooms in these two houses c1958–59.

★*14a Addison Crescent, W14* – Elizabeth Smart's flat, where MacBryde stayed for a time after Colquhoun's death.

Works include

Colquhoun: Canvas "Woman with Leaping Cat" (1945) – Tate Gallery. Watercolour and chalks "Two Sisters" (1945) – Tate Gallery. Canvas "Woman with Still Life" (1958) – Tate Gallery. Studies for his canvas "Drawing War Threads" (1945) – Imperial War Museum.

MacBryde: Canvas "Woman with Paper Flowers" (1944) – Tate Gallery. Canvas "Performing Clown" (1946) – Tate Gallery. Colour prints "Still Life I" (1960) and "Still Life II" (1960) – Tate Gallery.

Portraits

MacBryde: Ink drawing by Colquhoun (1938) – National Portrait Gallery.

Colquhoun: Pencil self-portrait (1940) – N.P.G.

Memorabilia

Theatre designs, etc. – Theatre Museum.

Sir Noel Coward

(16 December 1899 – 26 March 1973)

Noel Coward, playwright, composer, lyricist, actor, singer and wit, the most versatile of all the great figures of the English theatre, was born at Teddington, Middlesex, the son of Arthur Sabin Coward, a piano salesman, and his wife Violet Veitch, a naval captain's daughter.

He made his acting debut at the age of ten in a children's play, *The Goldfish*, at Crystal Palace. He continued playing small parts in undistinguished plays until 1918, when he spent nine months in the army, an experience he did not enjoy.

In 1920 Coward's first comedy *I Leave It To You* was produced. He appeared in it too, a habit he was rarely to break. His first big success was in André Charlot's revue *London Calling* in 1923, in which he starred with Gertrude Lawrence. He also wrote the book, lyrics and music. During the run of *London Calling* he wrote *The Vortex*, a play about drug addiction, which opened on his birthday in 1924 and in which he appeared with Lilian Braithwaite. It shocked some of the critics but brought him the success he had always longed for.

He became a star overnight, was invited to all the smart parties, and was much photographed in silk dressing-gowns, with a cigarette poised elegantly between two fingers. He worked hard to live up to his glamorous image and vied with the Prince of Wales in setting the fashion for men's clothes.

At the same time he was busily writing and composing, and by 1928 he had two other plays besides *The Vortex* in the West End: *Fallen Angels*, which starred Tallulah Bankhead, and *Hay Fever*, which he wrote in a weekend; as well as the revue *On With The Dance*.

Coward first developed his clipped manner of speaking in an effort to communicate with his mother who had become deaf after falling out of a porthole in Madeira and landing on her head. Despite his efforts she never managed to lip-read what he was saying.

In 1926 Coward met with failure and unpopularity. His play *The Rat Trap* closed after only twelve performances, and he was booed and spat at as he left Daly's Theatre after the disastrous first night of *Sirocco* in which Ivor Novello played the leading role. He made a comeback in 1928 with his operetta *Bitter Sweet* which was a huge success both in the West End and on Broadway. (He wrote the hit song from the show, "I'll See You Again", in twenty minutes while his taxi was stuck in a traffic jam.)

This was followed by his sophisticated comedy *Private Lives* in which he and Gertrude Lawrence starred as the divorced couple reunited in adultery, perfectly embodying Coward's ideals of wit, suavity and romance. He claimed to have written the play in a mere four days while recovering from flu in Shanghai.

Most of Coward's spare time was spent at his farm Goldenhurst in Kent, where he entertained innumerable weekend guests. In the Thirties he went into management partnership with Jack Wilson, an American with whom he was in love. However, in 1940, Wilson went back to live in the States and they began to lead increasingly separate lives.

During the war Coward toured America, Australia and New Zealand with shows for the British war effort, and went on a troop show tour of the Middle East. After the war, in the period of austerity and social change in Britain, he found that his own individual style was out of tune with the times and he had to compete with the new "kitchen sink" school of playwrights.

Short of money after the failure of three expensive musicals, Coward began a new, highly paid career as a cabaret artiste, singing in his distinctive way his own songs at the Café de Paris and at nightclubs in New York and Las Vegas. He also began accepting film roles, starting with *Our Man in Havana*.

In 1948 he built a house in Jamaica where he lived with his friend Graham Payn, who appeared in many of his shows. Later they moved to Bermuda and finally to Switzerland.

Coward's later stage shows, mostly premiered in America, could not always recapture the wit and spontaneity of his earlier works. In 1964 he directed Dame Edith Evans in *Hay Fever* at the National Theatre, the first play ever to be directed there by its author. This was followed by revivals of several of his plays. In 1966 he made his last stage appearance in London in the three plays he had written to make up *Suite in Three Keys*.

In 1969 Coward received his knighthood, and his seventieth birthday was celebrated with a charity midnight matinee at the

Phoenix Theatre, which had opened in 1930 with the first night of *Private Lives*. There were also celebrations at the Savoy Hotel where he received tributes from many of his friends and admirers. In America he was given a special award for his services to the theatre.

He died four years later at his home in Switzerland.

Addresses

★*Helmsdale, 5 Waldegrave Road, Teddington* – Coward's birthplace and childhood home.

★*70 Prince of Wales Mansions, (Chelsea Bridge end of) Prince of Wales Drive, SW11* – he lived here 1908–13.

★*111 Ebury Street, SW1* – a guest house run by his mother. He lived here 1917–c1926.

★*17 Gerald Road, SW1* – he lived in the upper part of the house known as The Studio 1935–56. (Privately erected *plaque*.)

★*37 Chesham Place, SW1* – he stayed here in 1966 while giving his last stage performances, in *Suite for Three Keys*.

Works include

Stage Works: *The Vortex* (1924); *Hay Fever* (1925); *Bitter Sweet* (1929); *Private Lives* (1930); *Cavalcade* (1931); *Blithe Spirit* (1941); *Present Laughter* (1942).

Screenplays: *In Which We Serve* (1942) – starred in and co-directed; *Brief Encounter* (1944) – based on "Still Life" from his stage show *Tonight at 8.30*.

Short stories: "Star Quality" (1951); "Bon Voyage" (1967).

Songs: "Mad Dogs and Englishmen" (1930); "Mad about the Boy" (1932); "Don't put your Daughter on the Stage Mrs Worthington" (1933); "The Stately Homes of England" (1937); "Marvellous Party" (1938); "London Pride" (1941); "Matelot" (1945).

Autobiographies: *Present Indicative* (1937); *Future Indefinite* (1954).

Diaries: *Diaries*, edited by Graham Payn and Sheridan Morley (1982).

Portraits

Bronze head by Paul Hamann (1930) – National Portrait Gallery. Photograph by Norman Parkinson (1936) – N.P.G. Painting by Clemence Dane (c1945) – N.P.G. Bronze bust by Clemence Dane (after 1945) – N.P.G.

Memorial

Memorial tablet in St Paul's Church, Covent Garden, WC2.

Memorabilia

Photographs, playbills, programmes, etc. – Theatre Museum.

Edith Craig

(9 December 1869 – 27 March 1947)

Much of Edy Craig's childhood was spent in the wings, listening to the rapturous applause which greeted her mother, Ellen Terry, whenever she appeared on stage. Her parents never married, and separated while Edy was still a child. She and her brother, Edward Gordon Craig (later to become the celebrated theatre designer and director), saw little of their father, the architect Edward Godwin.

It was taken for granted that Edy would follow in the Terry tradition by becoming an actress. Her mother gave her the name Ailsa Craig (after a Scottish island) because she thought it would make a good stage name.

For a while Edy went to a boarding school in Gloucestershire, run by Mrs Malleson, a pioneer of women's suffrage; but when she was nine her godfather, Sir Henry Irving (her mother's supposed lover), decided that it was time for her to begin her career. She made her debut in *Olivia* by W G Wills at the Court Theatre.

Edy realised that, as an actress of limited range, she would always live in her mother's shadow and never achieve recognition in her own right. She managed eventually to persuade Ellen to let her go to Berlin to train as a concert pianist. After a year, however, she was forced to give up her studies because of chronic rheumatism in the joints of her fingers, and returned to London and the theatre. She joined Irving's Lyceum Theatre Company and played a number of character roles.

It was in 1899 that Edy first met Christopher St John (Christabel Marshall), backstage after a performance. "She gave me a welcome I cannot truthfully describe as cordial," Chris wrote. "She was busy mending a mitten (for her part in *Olivia* I suppose) and did not put it down before shaking hands. With the result that I was pricked by the needle."

Christopher St John, who had changed her name when she became a Roman Catholic, was at that time working as secretary to Winston Churchill. Later she would write a biography of Ethel Smyth and "ghost" Ellen Terry's *Story of My Life*. Within a few weeks of their first meeting Edy and Chris were living together. They became suffragettes and their home became a "safe house" for women on the run from the police or just out of prison.

Edy rented a studio in Henrietta Street and set up as a theatrical costumier. Her costumes for Irving's production of Sardou's *Robespierre* were a great success and, although her business lost money, she gained high praise as a designer.

In 1909 Edy produced *How the Vote Was Won*, a play by Christopher St John and Cicely Hamilton, and the following year staged *The Pageant of Great Women*, also by Cicely Hamilton. Encouraged by the success of these productions, Edy founded, in 1911, a feminist theatre group, The Pioneer Players. Edy was in charge of production and set and costume design, and Chris and Cicely wrote plays for the company. Over one hundred and fifty plays were produced over the next ten years. Sybil Thorndike gave a memorable performance for them in Claudel's *The Hostage*.

At the outbreak of the war Edy and Chris moved to The Priest's House, a cottage on Ellen Terry's estate at Smallhythe, Kent. They were joined in 1916 by Clare Atwood, the painter, who was known as "Tony". Clare Atwood, one of the few women to receive official commissions during the First World War, was a member of the New English Art Club, exhibited at the Royal Academy, and painted portraits of several members of the Terry family.

Edy was concerned at first that the new arrival might cause problems in her relationship with Chris. She told Tony, "I must warn you that if Chris does not like your being here, and feels you are interfering with our friendship, out you go." However, Chris reported that "the bond between Edy and me was strengthened not weakened by Tony's association with us." Friends such as Vita Sackville-West remarked on the calm, happy atmosphere of life at The Priest's House. Other visitors included Radclyffe Hall and Una Troubridge, who sought refuge there after the *Well of Loneliness* trial.

After the war Edy tried without success to find work as a freelance director in London. "We don't want another woman here," declared Lilian Baylis, "and anyhow we don't want Edy, she would upset the staff." So instead Edy worked with amateur groups and organised pageants in towns and villages all over the country.

When Ellen Terry died in 1928 Edy converted the farmhouse at Smallhythe into the Ellen Terry Museum and the Elizabethan barn into a theatre in memory of her mother. She produced four or five plays there every year until the Second World War.

In 1938 Edy's services to the English theatre were finally recognised by the theatrical establishment. She was given a dinner at the Savoy Hotel, presided over by Sybil Thorndike, who presented her with a cheque and a scroll inscribed with the names of all those present. She also received a message of congratulations from Queen Mary.

During the last few months of Edy's life, despite failing health, she was able to attend a service at St Paul's Cathedral commemorating the centenary of her mother's birth. Arrangements were made with the National Trust for the Ellen Terry Museum to be preserved for the nation.

Edy was lying on her chaise-longue chatting about the theatre with Chris and Tony when she suddenly cried out, "It's all black . . . Who's put out the light?" and died. Her obituary in *The Times* said, "Her devotion to her mother shone out more brightly than the remarkable theatrical talent which never perhaps received its due attention."

7 Smith Square, SW1

Addresses

★*20 Taviton Street, W1* – she lived here with her parents and brother c1874–75.

★*221 Camden Road, NW1* – site of the villa where she lived with her parents and brother in 1875.

★*33 Longridge Road, SW5* – she lived here with her mother and brother in 1876.

★*22 Barkston Gardens, SW5* – she lived here with her mother c1892–99.

★*7 Smith Square, SW1* – her first home with Christopher St John, in 1899.

★*31–32 Bedford Street, WC2* – the "safe house" where she lived with Christopher St John and where Clare Atwood later joined them. (Pre-WW1 – c1940.)

★*Burleigh Mansions, 96 St Martin's Lane, WC2* – her home during the 1940s.

Portraits

Photograph – National Portrait Gallery. Photographs (including one of her, Cicely Hamilton and Christopher St John) – Fawcett Library. *Portrait on p. 52.*

Fictional Portraits

Edith Craig appears as the pageant producer Miss La Trobe in *Between the Acts* (1941) by Virginia Woolf. In 1915 Christopher St John published, anonymously, a semi-autobiographical novel *Hungerheart*, in which she appears as John and Edith as Sally.

Memorabilia

Material relating to the Terry family – Theatre Museum.

Edith Craig

John Cranko

(15 August 1927 – 26 June 1973)

John Cyril Cranko was born at Rustenburg in the Transvaal. When he was ten his parents were divorced, and he went to live with his father in Johannesburg. His parents used to tell him about the ballets they had seen the Diaghilev company perform in London, and he spent his pocket-money on gramophone records of *Scheherezade* and *The Firebird*, inventing stories and dances to go with the music.

When he was fourteen Cranko was given a puppet theatre. He learned how to carve marionettes from wood and gave shows at local schools and garden fêtes. Then he started going to ballet classes, not because he particularly wanted to be a dancer, but because he realised that he needed a knowledge of dancing in order to be able to create ballets.

The University of Cape Town Ballet Company came to Johannesburg for a season in 1943. Cranko got a job working backstage and made his stage debut as an attendant to a goddess in *Pastoral*, a ballet to Beethoven's Sixth Symphony. A year later he began training at the University of Cape Town Ballet School, where he created his first ballet, *The Soldier's Tale*, using Stravinsky's music to a story he had devised himself. It was premiered at the Alhambra, Cape Town, and proved so popular that it was performed again the following year.

By now Cranko was beginning to feel restless. He knew that he had gone as far as he could professionally in South Africa and that his future lay overseas. In February 1946 he sailed for England. His hatred of apartheid meant that he would never return.

In London he enrolled at the Sadler's Wells School and danced in the corps de ballet at Covent Garden, before joining the Sadler's Wells Ballet. He was keen to work with other choreographers and to perform in new works, which was essential for him in learning his craft. He danced small parts in ballets by Ashton and de Valois, but in 1950, at the age of twenty-three, gave up dancing completely to concentrate on choreography. At about that time he met a young Australian psychiatrist, Frank Tait, and they bought a house together.

In 1951 Cranko created *Pineapple Poll* to music by Arthur Sullivan. It was a great popular success, demonstrating his marvellous gift for comedy, and made his reputation with the British public. In 1955 he wrote a revue *Cranks* which opened at the New Watergate Theatre Club in Buckingham Street. At first it played to only a small cult audience, but after it was reported that Princess Margaret had been to see it three times it began to attract wider interest and transferred to the West End. It won a Best Musical of the Year award and excerpts from it were shown on television.

In the early hours of 8 April 1959, Cranko was walking home from a friend's house in Chelsea when he was arrested by a plainclothes policeman in Britten Street and charged with "persistently importuning men for an immoral purpose". Later that day, at Marlborough Street Police Court, he was fined £10 after pleading guilty. The magistrate warned him, "If you do anything of this sort again, you will most certainly land in prison." The *Daily Express*, which was campaigning against the proposed reform of the law relating to homosexuality recommended in the 1957 Wolfenden Report, carried a long article about Cranko's "crime". Homosexuals, it said, "do not want psychiatric treatment or cures. They live complacently in their own remote world with its shrill enthusiasms, but they are evil."

The adverse publicity does not seem to have affected Cranko's work opportunities. His new ballet *Antigone*, with music by Mikis Theodorakis, was well received, though his second revue *New Cranks* was a dismal flop.

Cranko went to Stuttgart in 1960 to mount his ballet *The Prince of the Pagodas*. It was so successful that he was invited to become director of the ballet company, and he accepted the offer without hesitation.

With hard work, dedication and flair, Cranko transformed a small provincial dance group into one of the world's top ballet companies, and during the last years of his life he created over fifty new works. Among the dancers he discovered and who joined his company were Marcia Haydee (who later succeeded him as director), Richard Cragun, Egon Madsen and Birgit Keil.

Cranko died on a plane taking him and members of his company back to Stuttgart after a triumphant American tour. He had been prescribed a supposedly safe drug, chloral hydrate, to help him sleep. Very rarely it can cause vomiting, which is what happened to Cranko. He lost consciousness so rapidly that he choked on the vomit. The aircraft made an

6 Montpelier Walk, SW7

emergency landing at Dublin but he was dead before they touched down.

He is buried on a hillside overlooking Stuttgart.

Addresses

★46 Belsize Square, NW3 – he lived here in 1946.

★Upper Berkeley Street, W1 – he had lodgings here in 1947.

★6 Montpelier Walk, SW7 – he lived here with his father and stepmother c1947–1950.

★19 Alderney Street, SW1 – he lived here from 1950 with Frank Tait. It remained his London home until his death.

Ballets include

Tritsch Tratsch (1946); Beauty and the Beast (1949); Pineapple Poll (1951); Harlequin in April (1951); The Lady and the Fool (1954); The Prince of the Pagodas (1957); Romeo and Juliet (1958); Daphnis and Chloe (1962); The Firebird (1964); Onegin (1965); The Taming of the Shrew (1969); Brouillards (1970); Ami Yam Ami Ya'ar (Song of my people) (1971).

Memorial

A ballet studio, named the John Cranko Room, was opened by Princess Margaret on 22 September 1977 at the Sadler's Wells Theatre.

Charlotte Cushman

(23 July 1816 – 18 February 1876)

Charlotte Saunders Cushman was born in Boston, Massachusetts. When her father, a merchant in the West Indies trade, died, the Cushmans were forced to support themselves. Charlotte's mother ran a boarding house, and Charlotte herself, at the age of thirteen, ended her education to take a job as a domestic. She later trained for the operatic stage and made her debut as Countess Almaviva in *The Marriage of Figaro* in 1835.

Although her voice was pleasing it did not live up to its early promise, and Charlotte was advised to turn to acting. In New Orleans in 1836 she made her debut as an actress, playing Lady Macbeth, and during the next six years, working chiefly in New York, she gained valuable experience in dozens of roles. Her first appearance as the gypsy Meg Merrilies in a stage adaptation of *Guy Mannering*, which was to become a favourite with her audiences, was not greatly acclaimed; as Nancy in *Oliver Twist*, however, she made an instant hit.

From 1842 to 1844 she was stage manager of the Walnut Street Theatre in Philadelphia, and in the 1843–44 season she played Lady Macbeth opposite William Macready. Through performing with the great Shakespearean on alternate nights in Philadelphia and New York and through experiment and constant study of her craft, Charlotte developed her talent as an actress.

She was not content with being merely a local success, but was filled with an ambition to act in London. In the winter of 1844 she took the plunge and arrived in England with scores of letters of recommendation but with very little money and no firm prospects. Nevertheless, within a few months she was given the chance of playing a strong supporting role, that of Bianca in *Fazio*, opposite Edwin Forrest at the Princess's Theatre. The press hailed her as "a great acquisition to the London stage" and compared her triumphal English debut with Edmund Kean's first appearance thirty years earlier.

She appeared again as Lady Macbeth and added the role of Rosalind to her repertoire. On the strength of a successful tour of the provinces she arranged for her family to join her in London. The stage career of her sister, Susan, was launched towards the end of 1845 when she appeared as Juliet to Charlotte's Romeo.

Charlotte showed a fondness for playing masculine roles, which caused a good deal of comment. However much audiences may have been shocked by her vigorous portrayals of Romeo, Hamlet, Claude Melnotte and Cardinal Wolsey, Charlotte's well-known solicitude for her family ensured that her public was never scandalised. (Nevertheless, she was not above dragging off the stage, by his hair, a leading man who had dared to suggest that she did not physically resemble his idea of a Lady Macbeth.)

She was described as having "a shade too exuberant" a figure and plain features, but her great energy, dark and versatile voice, piercing eyes and hair the colour of mahogany, made her a compelling presence on the stage. In her private life she tended to affect many of the qualities of the vivid characters she portrayed on the stage, and although extremely generous to friends and family and helpful in advancing the careers of aspiring young artists, she was also rather possessive and domineering.

Even though the critics soon began pointing out her limitations as an actress (which she herself recognised), Charlotte's success continued to grow. A performance before Queen Victoria in 1848 was followed by a tour of America between 1849 and 1852, when she was hailed by the critics and public alike as "without dispute the leading actress of our stage".

In 1852, when she was at the height of her fame and only thirty-six years old, she announced her retirement from the stage. She had carefully invested the fortune she had made during her career, and she spent the next five years living in London and wintering in Rome. There, during the winter of 1852–53, she met the American sculptor Emma Stebbins (1815–82). They became lovers, and after 1857, when Charlotte settled in Rome, they were inseparable. Charlotte, however, also spent much time then and in later years with the poet Eliza Cook, many of whose sonnets were about Charlotte, with whom she had fallen deeply in love. Two other of Charlotte's lovers, Matilda Hays, an English actress, and Harriet Hosmer, lived for a time in the Cushman-Stebbins residence at 38 via Gregoriana, which became a meeting-place for theatre people, artists, writers and many of the lesbian and gay members of Italian society and Rome's British and American expatriate colonies.

Despite the announcement of her retirement, Charlotte continued to make a good many stage appearances. She was sometimes criticised for her numerous "farewell performances" and "comebacks", but her popularity remained undiminished during her American tours of 1857–58 and 1860, her benefit performances (in aid of the U.S. Sanitary Commission in 1863) and, after 1870, her public readings of famous plays.

She returned permanently to America in 1870 with Emma Stebbins. They established a home in Boston, Charlotte's birthplace, and had a summer residence in Newport, Rhode Island. Charlotte's last major engagement was at Booth's Theatre in New York in October and November 1874, when she acted three of her greatest roles – Queen Katharine (in *Henry VIII*), Meg Merrilies and Lady Macbeth. After the last performance of the season she was presented with a laurel crown and later that evening a crowd of more than 20,000 of her fans gathered in front of her Madison Square hotel to accord her an ovation. She last appeared on any stage in June 1875.

Charlotte's constitution had long been undermined by cancer (she had had an operation for the removal of a tumour in Edinburgh in 1869), but despite the pain she suffered and the bouts of depression to which she was prone, she honoured all of her professional engagements – even seeking new ones – and neither showed self-pity nor stinted in her energetic performances and powerful readings.

She died at her home in Boston, cared for by Emma Stebbins to the end.

Portraits

Lithograph of Charlotte Cushman as "Mrs Maller" – National Portrait Gallery (Archives). Various engravings and prints – N.P.G. (Archives). Drawing by Rudolph Lehmann – British Museum.

Fictional portrait

The heroine Bianca Pazzi (a talented actress) of Geraldine Jewsbury's novel *The Half-Sisters* (1848) is modelled on Charlotte Cushman.

Address

★*1 Bolton Row (now part of Curzon Street, Berkley Square end), W1 – site.* Charlotte took a house here in 1853 and maintained it until early in 1858.

Works include

Charlotte Cushman: Her Letters and Memories of Her Life, edited by Emma Stebbins (1878).

Memorabilia

Prints, playbills, programmes, etc. – Theatre Museum.

Anne Damer

(1749 – 28 May 1828)

Anne Seymour Damer was the only British woman sculptor of note until the twentieth century. She was the daughter of Field-Marshal Henry Seymour Conway and his wife, Lady Caroline Campbell. As a child she saw an Italian pavement artist modelling a head in wax and declared that she could do better herself. She began practising with wax and quickly progressed to carving terracotta. Later, with the help and encouragement of her father's cousin, Horace Walpole, she was allowed to work in the studio of John Bacon (the sculptor of Dr Johnson's statue in St Paul's Cathedral) and to take lessons from Joseph Ceracchi.

When she was eighteen Anne married John Damer, the twenty-three year old son of Lord Milton (afterwards Earl of Dorchester) and heir to a fortune of £30,000. It was an arranged marriage and unhappy from the start, with little if any affection between them. Damer was a fop and a spendthrift and by 1776 he had run up debts amounting to £70,000 which his father refused to pay. On 15 August he shot himself in an upstairs room of the Bedford Arms in Covent Garden. In a note found near his body he had written, "The people of this house are not to blame for what has happened, which is my own act."

Anne had to sell her jewels to help pay the debts (the sale of Damer's clothes raised £1,500) but was left with a yearly allowance of £2,500 which enabled her to devote herself to sculpture. She divided her time between England, Italy and Portugal. On one occasion the mail boat on which she was a passenger was captured by a privateer, but she was released and permitted to go to Jersey where her father was Governor.

Among her best known works are the stone heads of the rivers Thames and Isis sculpted in 1785 for the bridge at Henley which had been chiefly designed by her father. She produced some wonderfully naturalistic animal studies and several busts, including those of George III, Napoleon and Nelson. "She models like Bernini," wrote Horace Walpole, "[and] has excelled moderns in the similitudes of her busts."

Anne was a staunch supporter of Charles James Fox and his Whig policies and canvassed for him in the 1780 election. She was opposed to George III's colonial policies and was in sympathy with the American colonists' struggle for independence. Her friendship with the Empress Josephine led to a meeting with Napoleon. She presented him with a bust of Fox and in return was given a gold snuff-box, set in diamonds, containing a miniature portrait of the Emperor.

In 1797 Horace Walpole died and left Anne his magnificent villa, Strawberry Hill, and £2,000 a year for its upkeep. She entertained on a lavish scale and gave garden parties at which she would appear in the man's coat, hat and shoes which she habitually wore. Among her closest friends were Mary Berry (1763–1852) and her sister Agnes. They lived nearby at Little Strawberry Hill, Walpole's second house in Twickenham, which he had left to them in his will. Anne fell in love with Mary but was never allowed beyond the bounds of friendship. In 1800 Mary wrote a comedy play *Fashionable Friends*. Anne produced it for a private performance at Strawberry Hill and recited the epilogue written by Joanna Baillie. It was performed at Drury Lane two years later, but was withdrawn after three nights because of its "lax morality".

Anne's relationship with the actress Elizabeth Farren (1759?–1829), who later became Countess of Derby, was the cause of much gossip and speculation. A pamphlet called *The Whig Club, or a Sketch of Modern Patriotism* reported of Elizabeth that "she is supposed to feel more exquisite delight from the touch of the cheek of Mrs D–r than the fancy of any novelties which the wedding night can promise with such a partner as His Lordship."

Towards the end of her life Anne left Strawberry Hill and moved to York House. She built a studio there and, watched by her friend Queen Caroline, "she chipped away all summer." The winters were spent at her house in Mayfair.

When she died Anne left instructions that all her papers, including letters from Horace Walpole, were to be burnt, and that her working tools, apron and the ashes of her favourite dog were to be placed in her coffin. She was buried at Sundridge in Kent. The church contains monuments by her to her mother and other members of her family.

York House, Richmond Road (cnr Church Street), Twickenham

Addresses

★*18 Dunraven (formerly Norfolk) Street, W1* – she lived here in the 1780s.

★*18 Sackville Street, W1* – she lived here c1792.

★*8 Grosvenor Square, W1* – *site* of her home 1795–1800.

★*Strawberry Hill, Waldegrave Road, Twickenham* – her home 1797–1811. (Now St Mary's RC Training College. Admission only by prior application to the Principal.) (See also *Horace Walpole.*)

★*18 Upper Brook Street, W1* – her town house 1800–28. (Died here.)

★*York House, Richmond Road (cnr Church Street), Twickenham* – her home 1818–28. (It was also the home of James II when he was Duke of York. His daughter Queen Anne was born here in 1664. Since 1925 it has been the Municipal Offices of the London Borough of Richmond-upon-Thames. The gardens are open to the public.)

Works include

Marble bust of Elizabeth Farren, Countess of Derby, as Thalia, Muse of Comedy (c1789) – National Portrait Gallery. Marble bust of Lord Nelson – Council Chamber at the Guildhall, EC4. Marble bust of Mrs Freeman as Isis – Victoria and Albert Museum. Bronze bust of Sir Joseph Banks – British Museum.

Portraits

Canvas by studio of Sir Joshua Reynolds (1772) – National Portrait Gallery. Miniature on ivory oval by Richard Cosway (1785) – N.P.G. Print by L Schiavonetti (1791) – N.P.G. (Archives) and British Museum. Print by T Ryder (1792) – N.P.G. (Archives) and British Museum. Print by J Hopwood (1812) – N.P.G. (Archives) and British Museum. Statue of Anne Damer as the Muse of Sculpture by Ceracchi (c1777) – British Museum. Print by J.R. Smith after Reynolds (1774) – Victoria and Albert Museum. *Portrait on p. 53.*

Memorabilia

The snuff-box which Napoleon presented to her – British Museum.

59

Goldsworthy Lowes Dickinson

(6 August 1862 – 3 August 1932)

"It is difficult to think of a life where so little happened outwardly," wrote E M Forster of his friend, the humanist and historian, Goldsworthy Lowes Dickinson. Most of Dickinson's life was spent as a typical Cambridge don – so far as outward appearances went. His inner character was revealed only in his autobiography (which was not published until forty years after his death) and to the men with whom he fell in love.

He was born in London, the son of Lowes Cato Dickinson, the portrait painter, and Margaret Williams Dickinson. After his schooldays at Charterhouse, he went up to King's College, Cambridge, from where he graduated in 1884 with a First in Classics and the Chancellor's English Medal.

One of Dickinson's closest friends was C R Ashbee, who had been a fellow student at Cambridge. They took several holidays together over the years and Dickinson became a regular visitor to Ashbee's Guild of Handicrafts at Chipping Campden. For Ashbee he embodied "the ultimate and perfect type of friendship – the friend always at hand, from whom nothing is hid".

Dickinson's first sexual feelings had been connected with boots, and the fetishism accompanied him throughout his life. As a child he used to get his brother or his sisters to tread on him. Later, through a succession of intense love affairs with young men (none of whom was homosexual) his greatest pleasure came from being trodden upon. "I liked him to stand upon me when we met. I think this rather bothered him, though he used not to seem to object," he wrote in his autobiography. "I used to lie on the floor and get him to put his feet on me." His first love affair was with the artist Roger Fry, whom he came to know through his membership of the Society of Apostles at Cambridge.

In 1887 Dickinson was elected a Fellow of King's College. He went on lecture tours of America and visited India, Japan and China. He brought back a mandarin's cap from China and wore it as indoor headgear for the rest of his life as a symbol of his affection for that country, second only to his love for Greece.

At the outbreak of the First World War Dickinson was fifty-two and therefore too old to enlist. He was not a conscientious objector and he did not believe that the war could have been avoided, yet he devoted himself at once to the task of trying to prevent future wars. He drew up plans for a "league of nations" (a phrase which he probably invented) and played the leading part in founding the group of international pacifists which later formed an important part of the League of Nations Union. He wrote a large number of books and pamphlets putting forward his ideas for world peace, and toured America in 1916 (as did Ashbee) campaigning for disarmament. Throughout the war he continued, despite his other activities, to work at Cambridge, lecturing twice a week to a class which now consisted almost entirely of women.

In appearance he was thin, bespectacled, stooped and shabbily dressed, but with a sudden smile "which for the moment", said Forster, "made him indescribably beautiful." He was known for his illegible handwriting: he once wrote "Good" on a student's essay and she asked him indignantly why he had called her a fool!

Dickinson's friendships, especially with younger men, the new generation of undergraduates growing up after the war, were the greatest comfort of his last years. He continued to write, and gave radio talks on Goethe and Plato. His last work, "The Contribution of Ancient Greece to Modern Life", was a lecture which he gave a few weeks before his death. He died after an operation, three days short of his seventieth birthday. "If anyone values anything I have done," he once wrote, "they should value also the passions that have alone made it possible".

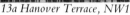
13a Hanover Terrace, NW1

Addresses

★*1 All Souls Place, W1 – site* of his childhood home.

★*11 Edwardes Square, W8* – he lived here 1912–20. (*Plaque* erected by public subscription in 1956.)

★*13a Hanover Terrace, NW1* – he lived here c1930–32.

Works include

The Greek View of Life (1896); *Letters from John Chinaman* (1901); *The European Anarchy* (1916); *The International Anarchy: 1904–1914* (1926); *After Two Thousand Years: A Dialogue between Plato and a Modern Young Man* (1930); *Autobiography* (1973).

Portraits

Canvas by L C Dickinson (his father) (1869) – National Portrait Gallery. Chalk by Roger Fry (1893) – N.P.G. Photograph by A Boughton (c1916) – N.P.G. Photograph by Walter Stoneman (1931) – N.P.G. (Archives). Two photographs (undated; photographer unknown) – N.P.G. (Archives)

Menlove Edwards

(18 June 1910 – 2 February 1958)

A brilliant cragsman, generally regarded as the father of the modern sport of rock-climbing, Menlove Edwards was renowned for his exploration of Welsh rock-faces. He was one of the greatest pioneers and innovators, and his essays on climbing are considered to be the finest ever written. In daring feats of endurance on water, he swam down the Linn of Dee, crossed from the Isle of Man to the Cumberland coast at night in a canoe and rowed across the Minch to the Outer Hebrides in an open rowing-boat.

John Menlove Edwards was the fourth and youngest child of the Reverend George Edwards and his wife Helen, and was born at Crossens, near Southport, Lancashire, where his father was the Vicar. He was educated at Fettes College and at Liverpool University where he studied medicine. He was rather shy and did not immediately get involved in student social life, although he played hockey for the university and was a keen cricketer.

Menlove began climbing in 1930, initially with his brothers, and within a few weeks he was scaling the Welsh cliffs around Helyg and had climbed his first new route on Lliwedd. He exercised daily at his local gymnasium, doing circuit training to improve balance and strengthen muscles. In a remarkably short time he established himself as one of the great rock-climbers of his day. He was a founder member in 1930 of the Liverpool University Rock-Climbing Club, the first of its kind in the country. Until then the sport had had no separate identity, being thought of as merely a part of the training for mountaineering.

He graduated in 1933 and a year later gained his diploma in psychological medicine. He set up in psychiatric practice and was appointed psychiatrist to the Liverpool Child Guidance Clinic.

In 1935 at Stokesay Church in Shropshire, where his brother Stephen was Vicar, Menlove courageously delivered a sermon in which he called for the recognition and understanding of homosexuals, maintaining that Christianity and homosexuality are not incompatible.

A group of love poems which Menlove wrote at about this time are addressed to someone called "Jimmy", but it seems that by the summer of 1935 their relationship had ended.

A few weeks after the sermon he went to Helyg and stayed at the Climbers' Club hut. Also staying there was a seventeen year old Charterhouse schoolboy, Wilfred Noyce. Menlove invited him to climb on Clogwyn Y Grochan and they made the first ascent of Long Tree Gate. From the first Noyce was infatuated with Menlove, but Menlove's poems suggest that he was still preoccupied with Jimmy. However, he was soon in love with Noyce and spending every possible moment with him. In 1936 they worked together on a guidebook for the Climbers' Club.

Noyce went up to Cambridge and was taken up by the man he was to call his "fairy godfather". Arthur Cecil Pigou (1877–1959), the economist and Fellow of King's – Noyce's college – was captivated by the beautiful young man. He had himself been a keen climber in his younger days. He took Noyce to the Alps and introduced him to mountaineering. Noyce began to spend most of his free time at Pigou's country home at Buttermere in the Lake District, and he and Menlove began to drift apart. The "golden lad" of Charterhouse and Cambridge and the burly North Country socialist found less and less common ground.

Nevertheless Menlove tried to keep them together. There were occasional meetings and talk of collaboration on a new guidebook. Climbing together on Scafell in 1937, Noyce slipped and fell 180 feet. Menlove brilliantly held him on a rope on which two of the three strands had parted. Noyce was badly injured, but Menlove's immense physical strength and skills as a doctor saved his life.

When the war came Noyce and Pigou joined the Friends' Ambulance Corps, although Noyce later went into the army as an instructor in mountain warfare. Menlove registered as a conscientious objector. The war closed down his clinic so he rented a cottage, Hafod Owen, in a secluded area of Wales and concentrated on his psychiatric research work.

In 1942 Menlove came to London and worked at the Great Ormond Street Children's Hospital and at the Tavistock Clinic. He considered his academic work to be more important than his clinical work and suffered a cruel blow when J T MacCurdy, in his book *The Structure of Morale*, cut across most of the areas of research which he had been working on for the last eight years.

Increasingly, Menlove suffered from bouts of depression and paranoia, and during 1944 his mental deterioration became more apparent. He had to give up his work at the clinics and went to live in Kent with his sister Nowell and her husband Hewlett Johnson, the so-called "Red Dean of Canterbury". There were attempts at suicide followed by periods in hospital, but he still went climbing occasionally, and on Noyce's recommendation he was made an Honorary Member of the Climbers' Club.

Noyce married in 1950 and had two sons. He was a member of the 1953 Everest expedition, becoming the first man to reach the South Col.

For Menlove, now living alone in a house on the North Downs, there was a growing feeling of isolation as he rejected and felt rejected by his family and friends. "I'm not frightened of being alone, but I do not like not being anything else ever." He ended his life by swallowing potassium cyanide. He was cremated at Ashford and his ashes were scattered on a hillside above Hafod Owen.

In 1962 Wilfred Noyce was killed in a fall while climbing in the Pamirs.

Addresses

★8 Meadow Road, SW8 – his home 1942–44.
★Pattison Road, NW2 – he stayed here in 1944.

Works include

Guidebooks: *Cwm Idwal* (Climbers' Club, 1936); *Tryfan* (with C W F Noyce – Climbers' Club, 1937); *Lliwedd* (with C W F Noyce – Climbers' Club, 1939); *Clogwyn Du'r Arddu* (with J E Q Barford – Climbers' Club, 1942).

Articles, poems and reviews appeared in *The Climbers' Club Journal, The Wayfarers' Journal* and *The British Mountaineering Journal* between 1932 and 1941. His major prose pieces have been frequently anthologised.

Samson: The life and writings of J Menlove Edwards by C W F Noyce and Geoffrey Sutton was privately printed in 1960.

Edith Lees Ellis

(9 March 1861 – 13 September 1916)

Edith Mary Oldham Lees, novelist, feminist and pioneer socialist, was born at Clayton Bridge, Newton, in Cheshire. Her mother died shortly after Edith's birth, and she was brought up by her father who tried to break her spirit by force and brutal punishment. When he remarried she was sent away to a convent school in Manchester and then to a school near London. There she developed a talent for acting and appeared in student plays, always playing the leading male roles.

When she left school Edith went to live with her grandmother and started to work as a teacher. Soon afterwards she heard, with feelings more of relief than remorse, that her father had died.

Shortly after her twenty-first birthday Edith moved to London and opened a girls' school in Sydenham called Girton House. She rushed into the venture with her usual enthusiasm and boundless energy but with very little money. After two years she ran into debt and suffered a nervous breakdown.

She was nursed back to health by her friend Honor Brooke. While staying at the home of Honor and her father, Stopford Brooke, a socialist clergyman, she met Percival Chubb, a founder member of a socialist community called The Fellowship of the New Life.

Edith moved into the Fellowship's house, became joint secretary with Ramsay Macdonald, and contributed to the New Lifers' journal, *Seedtime*.

Through the Fellowship of the New Life Edith met, in 1887, her future husband, the psychologist and sexologist Havelock Ellis. He described her as "a small compact, active person, scarcely five feet in height, with a fine skin, a singularly well-shaped head with curly hair, square powerful hands, very small feet – large rather pale blue eyes".

They were married in 1891 and spent their honeymoon in Paris. When they returned to London he went back to his flat in Paddington and she returned to the Fellowship house. They agreed that they would spend the winter months together in Cornwall and the summers apart.

Soon after her marriage Edith fell in love with a woman named Claire. It came as a surprise to Ellis, but after Edith had written to him telling him how much she loved him, he was able to accept the situation. She was less understanding when he told her of his attractions to other women. Edith had several passionate affairs. In 1900 she fell in love with "Lily", an artist who lived at St Ives. Two years later Lily died at the age of thirty-six. For the rest of her life Edith kept a portrait of Lily beside her and communicated with her through a medium.

Edith and her husband grew closer as the years passed, and he nursed her devotedly through her frequent illnesses. "I am his champagne," she said, "and he is my opium."

Edward Carpenter, whom she met through the Fellowship, was one of Edith's closest friends. She visited him at Millthorpe, and he took her to his local pub. He wrote of the impression she made: "Her at-homeness among that company was most refreshing . . . Later they would ask 'When is that little lady coming again, with that curly hair like a lad's and them blue eyes, what talked about pigs and cows?' "

In 1914 Edith went on a lecture tour of the United States. It was a great success and she won many admirers. They praised her voice, saying it held them spellbound, and warmly applauded her lectures on Ellis. However, she received some surprising compliments: one chairman introduced her as "a prophetess from the wilderness, neither wholly woman nor wholly man but wholly human". She made headlines in the Chicago press when she spoke in favour of lesbian relationships.

Soon after returning from a second American lecture tour Edith had another nervous breakdown. She developed persecution mania and imagined that her neighbours were plotting against her. Eventually she was taken to hospital, where she tried to commit suicide by throwing herself out of a window.

After a while she began to recover, but then a woman friend came to visit and Edith invited her to stay the night. When she was told that this was against the hospital rules Edith flew into a rage, gathered together her belongings, and left.

She went to Cornwall, taking with her an orphaned youth whom she had met on a bus. She was not made welcome by her friends, who considered her "dangerous" and kept her away from their children.

Believing that Ellis was planning to have her committed to an asylum, Edith hurried back to London, still accompanied by the young man, whom she now called her adopted son. She went to see her lawyer and arranged for a legal separation from Ellis.

Edith now seemed to regain some of her old energy, and she began planning a season of plays based on her novels, to be put on at the Little Theater in Chicago during the winter.

On the night of 3 September 1916 there was a Zeppelin raid over London. Edith went out into the street to watch, with only a coat thrown over her pyjamas. When a woman in the crowd complained of the cold Edith took off her coat and handed it to her. This brought on a chill which led, ten days later, to her death.

Edith had expressed the wish that her old friend Edward Carpenter should speak at her funeral. Unfortunately he was ill and could not attend, but he did read a paper about her at the first meeting of the Edith Ellis Fellowship, a little group which met occasionally for several years.

Addresses

★ *1 Manchester Square, W1* – she stayed here c1885 at the home of Honor Brooke.

★ *Wigmore Mansion, 90 Wigmore Street, W1* – she lived here c1889.

★ *29 and 49 Doughty St, WC1* – the "Fellowship houses". She lived here c1890–92. (see also *Edward Carpenter*.)

★ *Harley Street, W1* – she had a room over a doctor's surgery, c1909.

★ *14 Dover Mansions, Canterbury Crescent (formerly Canterbury Road), SW9* – she had a room in Havelock Ellis's flat, c1909–15.

★ *Sandringham Court, Maida Vale, W9* – her home in 1916. (Died here.)

Works include

Novels: *Kit's Woman* (1907); *Attainment* (1909); *Love Acre* (1914).

Short stories: *My Cornish Neighbours* (1906).

Biography: *Three Modern Seers* (Nietzche, Carpenter & Hinton) (1910).

"Heaven's Jester", an allegory on her love for women, was published in America in the *Little Review* (1914).

Her last book, *The New Horizon in Love and Life*, was published posthumously in 1921. It contains, as a preface, the speech about her which Edward Carpenter delivered at the first meeting of the Edith Ellis Fellowship.

Desiderius Erasmus

(27 October 1469 – 12 July 1536)

The great Dutch Humanist and scholar was born in Gouda, Holland, the illegitimate son of Roger Gerard, a priest, and Margaret, a washerwoman. He was christened Erasmus, the Greek form of Gerard. His first nine years were spent with his parents and his older brother, Peter, at the rectory in Gouda. They were not happy years. The priest's living openly with a woman must have caused a scandal in the parish and the parishioners probably treated the children with contempt.

In later years Erasmus tried to hide the circumstances of his birth by maintaining that he had been born in Rotterdam, the home of his grandparents. He never used his father's name, but instead called himself Desiderius, the Latin form of Erasmus, which means "the desired one".

In about 1478 Margaret left Gouda with the children and went to live in Deventer, where the boys attended school. When Erasmus was about fifteen both of his parents died of the plague. His father had appointed guardians to care for his sons and they persuaded Erasmus, much against his will, to enter a monastery. When he was eighteen he became a novice in the Augustinian monastery at Steyn. In many ways he was unsuited to monastic life, his interests being more secular than ascetic, but he was able to study classical literature and to write the first of his poems.

Erasmus also spent a lot of time writing letters to a tall handsome monk, Servatius Roger, with whom he had fallen in love. "I place my hopes in you alone", he wrote to Servatius, "I have become yours so completely that you have left me naught of myself," and he cited the friendships of Orestes and Pylades, Theseus and Pirithous, and Damon and Pythias, as examples for them to follow. "But since lovers find nothing so distressing as not being allowed to meet one another . . . I long . . . to see you face to face as often as we please. That joy is denied us. I cannot think of it without tears . . . Farewell my soul, and if there is anything human in you, return the love of him who loves you." Servatius was aghast at these outpourings and cautioned Erasmus to be more discreet.

In 1492 Erasmus was ordained a priest and became secretary to a bishop. This enabled him to leave the monastery, although he was still bound to his monastic vows. After three years the bishop sent him to Paris to study theology at the Sorbonne.

While in Paris Erasmus became tutor to a young Englishman, Thomas Grey, later Marquis of Dorset. Their attachment to each other alarmed Grey's guardian, who accused Erasmus of seducing his young pupil. However his remonstrations were ignored and the relationship continued until Grey returned to England.

Another of Erasmus's English pupils was William Blount, Lord Mountjoy, who became his patron and arranged, in 1499, the first of his many visits to England. Here he became a friend of Sir Thomas More, with whom he stayed on several occasions, and he got to know the English Humanists, especially John Colet. Colet hailed him as the future leader of European Humanism and influenced him to make the study of theology the main purpose of his life.

Meanwhile Servatius had become the Prior at Steyn, and he wrote to Erasmus demanding an account of his life since leaving Paris and accusing him of squandering the years spent outside the monastery. Erasmus was naturally upset by the letter and, with the help of his English friends, applied to the Pope for a dispensation from his vows. When a second letter from Servatius arrived, asking him to return to Steyn, Erasmus replied, "Whenever I have thought of rejoining your society I have been reminded of the jealousy of many, the contempt of all, the coldness and silliness of the conversations, utterly lacking any savour of Christ." After many passages in Greek, which he knew Servatius would not understand, he expressed the wish that one day he might meet again his "once sweetest companion" to discuss "all the secrets which cannot be dealt with in letters". Servatius did not bother him again and eventually Erasmus received the dispensation from Rome, which released him from his monastic vows, although he remained a priest.

In 1511 Erasmus went to Queen's College, Cambridge, to lecture in Greek. The post had been created for him as until then Greek had never been taught there. However, he soon became ill with kidney trouble, which he attributed to English beer, and decided to leave England. Although he came back for short visits, he never lived here again.

During his last years Erasmus became half-crippled with syphilis of the bones, but he continued to travel about Europe preaching pacifism and tolerance; and to write, often standing at a lectern for up to sixteen hours a day. He became a citizen of the free city of Basle, where he died and is buried.

Addresses

★*15 Cheyne Walk, SW3 – site* of Sir Thomas More's house. Erasmus stayed here. (On the outer wall of the house now occupying the *site* there is a medallion showing Erasmus facing More.)

★*Knightrider Street, EC4 – site* of Lord Mountjoy's house where Erasmus stayed in 1499.

★*Bucklersbury, EC4 – site* of Sir Thomas More's house. Erasmus wrote *Moriae Encomium* – the title is a play upon More's name – here in 1509. (In 1863 the street was cut in half by Queen Victoria Street.)

Works include

The Adages (1500) – dedicated to Lord Mountjoy; *The Praise of Folly (Moriae Encomium)* (1509) – his most popular work; *Julius Shut Out* (1513); *Colloquia* (1516).

Portraits

Various prints, engravings and facsimiles (of portraits elsewhere) – National Portrait Gallery.

Fictional portrait

Charles Reade's novel *The Cloister and the Hearth* (1861) was based on Erasmus's own fanciful account of his family background.

Memorials

Commemorative window in St Margaret's Church, Westminster. Figure in stained glass window in library of Sion College, Victoria Embankment, EC4.

Memorabilia

Copy of *Novum Testamentum* (1518) – Gray's Inn library. Several editions of his work – British Museum. Erasmus Street, SW1, is named after him.

Emily Faithfull

(27 May 1835 – 31 May 1895)

Emily Faithfull, pioneer in the promotion of employment for women, was born at Headley, Surrey. Her parents, Reverend Ferdinand Faithfull and Elizabeth (Timberlake) Faithfull, saw to it that Emily received a conventional, albeit liberal, "lady's education".

Recognising the lack of career openings for women and the poor treatment of women in the areas of employment deemed suitable for them, Emily set about tackling the problem in a typically practical manner: she started her own printing house in Edinburgh in 1857 where the printing work was done by women. Undaunted by the commercial failure of this venture, Emily came to London to join forces with a group of women who were similarly concerned with the issues of women's education and training and the problem of finding suitable work for women of all classes.

In 1859 Emily, together with several members of this group of concerned women, including her friend Bessie Rayner Parkes, her "adopted aunt" Anna Jameson and Adelaide Procter, was appointed to a committee of the National Association for the Promotion of the Social Sciences. The committee's task was to investigate certain jobs which might prove suitable for women. (It later merged with the first Society for Promoting the Employment of Women, of which Emily became Secretary.)

Emily's investigation into the printing trade, together with her earlier work in helping women gain the necessary skills and experience in printing and her observations on the relative ease and speed with which Bessie Parkes learned to print on a press bought for this purpose, confirmed her belief that it would be appropriate for women to pursue careers in this trade.

In March 1860, Emily opened The Victoria Press to women workers. There were sixteen female compositors and several men to do the heavy lifting work. The printing unions were hostile, maintaining that a mixed workshop would encourage immorality. Despite this opposition The Victoria Press rapidly became a commercial success and provided exemplary work conditions for its employees. Notable among the chiefly feminist material it published was *The English Woman's Journal*, which Barbara Bodichon and Bessie Parkes had acquired in 1858. In 1861 Emily published *The Victoria Regia* as "a choice specimen of the skill of my compositors". Queen Victoria was so impressed by the quality of the work produced by The Victoria Press that in June 1862 she presented a warrant to Emily appointing her "Publisher and Printer-in-Ordinary to the Queen".

The following year Emily began the publication of *The Victoria Magazine*, which served to inform women about training and job opportunities, as well as ensuring that the general public was made aware of the growing range of jobs in which women were proving themselves proficient. With working-class women in mind, Emily launched a complementary weekly, *Work and Women*, in 1865.

Such was the strength of Emily's personality and the respect she commanded that her involvement in a highly publicised divorce case in 1864 caused no lasting damage to her reputation and did not hinder her activities on behalf of women's claims for independence through remunerative employment. The divorce action was between Admiral Henry Codrington and Helen Jane Codrington, with whom Emily had, at the age of nineteen, begun a friendship which grew into a love affair. Emily moved into the Codrington home in 1854 while the Admiral was in the Crimea, and even after his return two years later, she continued to share Helen Jane's bed. It was alleged later that Admiral Codrington had attempted to rape Emily. Since Helen Jane refused to "perform her wifely duties", he ejected Emily from the house and deposited with his brother a sealed package which is believed to have contained either his own account of what had taken place or such "incriminating" material as the women's letters to each other. It was perhaps fear of the disclosure of the contents of this package that led Emily, when called later as a witness during the Codringtons' divorce proceedings, to refuse to confirm that the Admiral had sexually assaulted her.

Emily kept the Victoria Press imprint when she set up a steam printing firm in Farringdon Street (in 1862) and (later) editorial offices in Praed Street, and she remained editor of *The Victoria Magazine* for seventeen years.

In addition to her practical involvement in printing and publishing, Emily was an effective and popular lecturer in the cause of women's rights in employment. She was an active supporter of the suffrage movement, but it was chiefly through her tireless efforts to change attitudes toward women working and toward the education and training for work of women that she contributed to the struggle for the attainment of the vote for women.

On her tour of the United States in 1872–73 Emily lectured to large and appreciative audiences. She was very well received by the leaders of the American women's emancipation movement, upon whose activities she reported in *The Lady's Pictorial* (whose staff she had joined). During this and two further tours (1882–83 and 1883–84) she also reported on the establishment of kindergartens, the variety of jobs which American women did and advances in women's education and vocational training.

From the time of her first lecture at Hanover Square (which included dramatic readings and occasional verse which she had written) Emily was a celebrity, and she was much admired for her commonsense, the soundness of her initiatives and her spirit of cooperation with others involved in the cause of women's employment and suffrage.

Between about 1870 and 1881 she founded the Victorian Discussion Society "to give the ladies an increased opportunity for oral utterance"; organised the Ladies' Work Society (for "reduced gentlewomen"); helped establish the National Association for the Formation of Industrial Homes (ie. training schools for domestic servants) Throughout the Country; opened the Industrial and Educational Bureau; became one of the first members of the Women's Trades Union League, which her friend Emma Paterson founded in 1875; was closely involved in the establishment of the Women's Printing Society (concerned with finding apprenticeships and skilled work for women); started the *West London Express* (another successful publishing venture); and organised the International Musical, Dramatic and Literary Association (to secure protection of the rights of artists and composers).

In 1881, after having transferred The Victoria Press to the Queen Printing and Publishing Company, Emily moved to Manchester. She spent most of the remaining years of her life working to improve the lot of dressmakers and female cotton operatives and campaigning for reforms in industrial employment and women's education.

Official recognition of Emily Faithfull's hard work and splendid achievements came late: from the Royal Bounty she received £100 in 1886 and a Civil List Pension of £50 per year was awarded to her in 1889. For her "thirty years dedication to the interests of her sex" she received a signed photograph of Queen Victoria in 1892.

Addresses

★*82 Eccleston Square, SW1* – the home of Admiral and Mrs Codrington, where Emily lived 1854–56. (Now part of the Eccleston Hotel.)

★*9 Coram Street (formerly Great Coram Street), WC1* – site of her home c1861.

★*Harp Alley (between Farringdon and St Bride Streets), EC4* – site of the Victoria Press premises.

Works include:

Novel: *Change upon Change – A love story* (1868) (in US, *A Reed Shaken with the Wind*, 1873), the message of which is a plea for the education of women and the creation of career opportunities which would afford them economic and political independence.

Non-fiction: *Three Visits to America* (1884).

Pamphlets: *On Some of the Drawbacks Connected with the Present Employment of Women* (1862); *Woman's Work, with special reference to industrial employments* (1871).

Portraits

Photograph (undated; unknown photographer) – Fawcett Library. Reproduction of engraving (from *Illustrated London News*, 30/11/1861) – National Portrait Gallery (Archives). *Portrait on p. 70.*

Memorabilia

Several autograph letters – Fawcett Library.

Emily Faithfull

'Michael Field'

*Katherine Bradley (27 October 1848 –
26 September 1914)*

&

*Edith Cooper (12 January 1862 –
13 December 1913)*

Michael Field was the joint pseudonym of the passionately loving partnership of Katherine Harris Bradley, who was known as Michael, and her niece Edith Emma Cooper, known as Field or more intimately as Henry. They always used the masculine pronoun when referring to each other.

Katherine, the daughter of a tobacco manufacturer, was born in Birmingham. Edith was born in Kenilworth, Warwickshire. Her mother (who was Katherine's elder sister) became a permanent invalid after the birth of her second child, and Katherine, who was then sixteen, joined the household to help look after the children.

Edith was educated at home by Katherine until 1878, when they both enrolled as students at University College, Bristol, where they studied classics and philosophy together and took an active part in the students' debating society.

From Bristol they moved to Reigate in Surrey and began to devote themselves to writing. They adopted a pagan attitude to life, perhaps as a reaction against their strict Protestant upbringing, and built an altar to Dionysus in their garden.

They worked in separate rooms and seldom spoke to each other between nine o'clock in the morning and two in the afternoon, yet the style of writing of one is indistinguishable from that of the other. Altogether they produced twenty-seven tragedies, eight volumes of poetry (including love poems addressed by Katherine to Edith) and a masque.

Katherine was a small, vivacious and quick-tempered woman, with a sharp wit and a gift for mimicry. She had a dread of draughts and wore a fur wrap around her neck, even in the height of summer. Edith was tall and pale and gentler in manner than Katherine. She was very shy and had a wistful air about her, perhaps because of her almost continuous ill-health.

Their first tragedy *Callirrhoë*, which was published in 1884, received high praise from the reviewers, and there was much speculation as to who the mysterious Michael Field really was. For some time only Robert Browning, a staunch supporter of their work, knew their real identity. When it was eventually revealed that the "male" poet was really two women, interest in their writings faded and their later works were ignored by the critics. The comparative success of *Borgia* which they published anonymously in 1905 confirmed their suspicions that it had been the disclosure of the true identity of Michael Field rather than literary judgement of their writings which had led to their critical neglect.

In 1898 they moved into an eighteenth-century house in Richmond, Surrey, which they shared with a pair of doves and their adored dog Whym Chow. Edith was suffering increasingly from rheumatism, and they withdrew more and more into their small circle of close friends.

The painters Charles Ricketts and Charles Shannon, whom the poets had first met in 1894, were neighbours of theirs in Richmond and among their closest friends. They called Ricketts "Fay" and Shannon "Rox" and made a practice over several years of entertaining them on Thursdays to exquisite dinners. Ricketts designed elaborate jewellery for them and decorated the bindings of their books. Both artists presented them with their paintings.

In 1907 Katherine and Edith visited their friends John Gray and André Raffalovich in Edinburgh, and they were present at the official opening of St Peter's Church, Morningside, which Raffalovich built for Gray. Shortly afterwards Gray received Katherine into the Catholic Church. Later in the year Edith also became a Catholic. Their writings, which had hitherto taken their inspiration from classical sources, now took on a religious tone.

Both women died of cancer, within a year of each other. Katherine nursed Edith through her fatal illness, never revealing that she was suffering from the same disease.

Addresses

★ *1 Paragon Row, Petersham Road, Richmond* – their home 1898–1913. (Now the Bingham Hotel.)
★ *13 Well Walk, NW3* – their home 1913–14.

Works include

Tragedies: *Callirrhoë* (1884); *Canute the Great* (1887); *The Tragic Mary* (about Mary Stuart) (1890); *Borgia* (1905).
Masque: *Noontide Branches* (1899).
Collected Poems: *Long Ago* (inspired by fragments of Sappho) (1889); *Poems of Adoration* (1912); *A Selection from the Poems of Michael Field* (1923).
Journals: *Works and Days from the Journals of Michael Field* (1933).

Memorial

Charles Ricketts made a gift of Rossetti's portrait of Lucrezia Borgia to the Tate Gallery as a memorial to Michael Field.

Ronald Firbank

(17 January 1886 – 21 May 1926)

The world of Firbank's novels is that of doting duchesses having their puppies baptised in liqueur, of birds shrieking "Tiara! Tiara! Tiara!", of naked cardinals pursuing choirboys around the altar: novels in which yet another exploding jewelled handbagful of aphorisms and epigrams awaits you just over the page.

Arthur Annesley Ronald Firbank was the grandson of a self-made railway millionaire and son of Sir Thomas Firbank MP and Harriet Jane Garrett, a society beauty. As "Artie" was a sickly child his doting mother, "Baba", insisted that he be educated at home. At the age of fourteen, however, he was sent away to school. Later he was sent to France to study French in preparation for a career in the diplomatic service.

In 1905 Firbank published privately a volume of two stories, *Odette d'Antrevernes* and *A Study in Temperament*. The following year he went up to Trinity Hall, Cambridge, where he stayed just five terms and sat no examinations. For Firbank, Cambridge was the scene of two significant meetings: with Vyvyan Holland, son of Oscar Wilde, and with R H Benson, who received him into the Roman Catholic Church in 1907. His interest in Christian mysticism was short-lived, but he retained his passion for Roman Catholic ritual. For a time he fancied he might serve in some capacity at the Vatican, but as he later admitted to Lord Berners, "The Church of Rome wouldn't have me, and so I laugh at her."

Whilst at Cambridge Firbank developed a style and manner based nostalgically and self-consciously on the aestheticism and fin de siècle decadence of Wilde and Beardsley. Around this tall, thin, chronically ill man with a morbid fear that eating hastened the process of aging there arose a legend that his diet consisted of champagne and a few flower petals or, occasionally, a single grape "forced down" at the Cafe Royal.

He dressed in dark, softly draped lounge suits, wore a bowler hat, and always carried a cane and gloves. His hands, which he was constantly fluttering and admiring, were white and on his long fingers were many jewelled Oriental rings. His finger-nails he stained crimson. With pomander he sleeked his fine, dark hair close to his head, accentuating the profile which Osbert Sitwell described as being "like a coastline". A light dusting of powder on his cheeks covered the consumptive's blush of seeming good health.

Mrs Shamefoot, in *Vainglory* (1915), his first fully Firbankian novel, declared, "The world is disgracefully managed, one hardly knows to whom to complain." Firbank himself deciding the world to be mismanaged, and not knowing to which agency, temporal or spiritual, to address his complaints, reacted by withdrawing from it, refusing to engage in "this shabby thing, real life". At Cambridge his red silk-draped room, filled with candles, lilies and portraits of his mother and royalty, was his sanctuary; during the war his retreat was to the quiet of Oxford, and later, it was into the surreally ordered world of his novels. Nevertheless, he was no retiring hermit: his large private income enabled him to flit, like the butterfly always found in his novels, around Europe, North Africa, the Middle East and the Caribbean.

His metamorphosis into brilliant butterfly novelist demanded a change of name, Firbank felt. "Arthur is such a horrid name!" he insisted. He was now Ronald Firbank, and it irked him when his beloved Baba continued to call him Arthur or Artie.

Although he had many acquaintances, he had no close friends. At the Cafe Royal or the Eiffel Tower restaurant in Soho he sat on his own. Visitors invited to his home would find him alone in a darkened, incense-filled room, silhouetted against the light of dozens of candles. He would writhe about in his seat, talking nervously in a high-pitched voice, often breaking into hysterical laughter, the cause of which was seldom evident to the visitor.

Carl Van Vechten was one of the few who appreciated the joke, and was also, for a long time, virtually the only wholehearted literary champion Firbank had. They never met, but corresponded regularly, Van Vechten often addressing Firbank as "Dear gay genius".

Sexual attraction and love, particularly homosexual love, in Firbank's work is treated characteristically with cynicism and camp humour. Of himself, Firbank wrote to Van Vechten, "I am a spinster sir, & by God's grace intend to stay so," and he saw no contradiction between this declaration and his pursuit of Arab youths or the disclosure that "I have found a most beautiful creature about sixteen with eyes like a gazelle, digging up a road. I took a taxi each morning at six to look at it."

His mother's death in 1924 heightened his sense that his own death was imminent and he made efforts to put in order his oeuvre, which he hoped would serve as his monument. At the time of his death in Rome two years later he was working on *The New Rythum* and awaiting the appearance of *Concerning the Eccentricities of Cardinal Pirelli*.

Firbank would not have been surprised that, owing either to the disgraceful management of the world or simply to the disbelief that someone with his decidedly heretical attitude to the Church of Rome could be a Catholic, he was buried in the Protestant cemetery in Rome before being transferred to the Catholic one.

During Firbank's lifetime his work, when it did receive any critical attention, was dismissed as the obscure, albeit amusing, nonsense of a literary exquisite. Only recently have his role in the invention of the modern comic novel and the pervasiveness of his stylistic influence been generally acknowledged by the critical establishment.

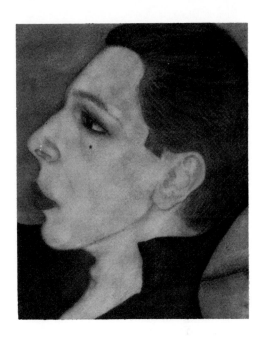

Addresses

★*40 Clarges Street, W1 (now Fleming's Hotel)* – birthplace.

★*49 Nevern Square, SW5* – he lived here 1905–06 in the home of Mr De V Payen-Payne, a tutor, while studying for the diplomatic service.

★*33 Curzon Street, W1* – he lived here for a short time with his mother c1911–12.

★*102 Queen's Gate, SW7 (now part of the Regency Hotel)* – he lived here with his mother in 1912.

★*44 Sloane Street, SW1* – his mother's flat, where he often stayed during 1913 and 1914.

★*48 Jermyn Street, SW1* – *site* of the house in which he had rooms in 1914. He took rooms elsewhere in this street c1919.

★*19 Old Square, WC2* – he had a flat here 1914–15.

★*28 Pall Mall, SW1* – he kept rooms here, as a London address, during his "retreat" to Oxford.

★*78 Brook Street, W1* – he lived here c1919.

★*49a Pall Mall, SW1* – he lived here in 1922.

Works include

A Study in Temperament & Odette d'Antrevernes: A Fairy Tale for Weary People (1905; latter story revised in 1916); *Vainglory* (1915); *Inclinations* (1916); *Caprice* (1917); *Valmouth* (1919); *The Princess Zoubaroff* (1920) – a play; *Santal* (1921); *The Flower Beneath the Foot* (1923); *Sorrow in Sunlight* (in US *Prancing Nigger*) (1924); *Concerning the Eccentricities of Cardinal Pirelli* (1926); *The Artificial Princess* (1934); *The New Rythum, and Other Pieces* (1962).

Portrait

Pencil drawing by Augustus John (c1915) – National Portrait Gallery.

Fictional portraits

He is portrayed as Lambert Orme in Harold Nicolson's *Some People* (1927). It is believed that Cardinal Pirelli in *The Princess Zoubaroff* is a composite of Firbank himself and Oscar Wilde.

Edward FitzGerald

(31 March 1809 – 14 June 1883)

When Edward Purcell was nine years old his mother, who was already very wealthy, inherited her father's fortune and became a millionaire. Her husband promptly changed his name to hers and young Edward Purcell became Edward FitzGerald. He was the seventh of the eight children of Mary Frances FitzGerald and John Purcell, and was born at Bredfield, near Woodbridge, in Suffolk.

When he came down from Trinity College, Cambridge, FitzGerald, with more than enough money to meet his requirements and no need or inclination to earn a living, had no idea what to do next.

His parents were living apart: his father on the family estate in Suffolk and his mother in London. She lived there in solitary grandeur, dining off gold plate and driving about in a glittering yellow coach drawn by four black horses. FitzGerald was expected to act as his mother's escort on her endless round of dinners and dances and visits to the opera. He hated that kind of life and chose instead to live alone in a succession of shabby lodging-houses.

As his Cambridge friends entered into careers and marriages FitzGerald felt increasingly shut out of their lives. As a way of putting off his own future he took to travelling around the country, sometimes visiting old friends en route. On one such journey, in 1832, he fell in love with a young man he met on a steamship going to Tenby. Sixteen year old William Kenworthy Browne was the first of the two great loves of FitzGerald's life. They would seem to have had very little in common: Browne's interests were in hunting, shooting and fishing (which FitzGerald would have found distasteful in anyone else) and he had scant knowledge of books or music. On the other hand, he was young, uncomplicated and very attractive. They saw each other every day for the remainder of the holiday, and for many years after spent idyllic summers fishing from the banks of the Ouse. Then in 1844 Browne married and FitzGerald wrote, "I have laid my rod and line by the willows of the Ouse forever. He is married and cannot come."

In 1856 FitzGerald married Lucy Barton, the daughter of his friend, the poet Bernard Barton, who on his deathbed had asked him to take care of her. It was a brief, disastrous episode, and they separated after less than a year.

During 1857 FitzGerald began his translation of *The Rubaiyat* (quatrains) *of Omar Khayyam* from a pencil copy made for him by a young protégé of his, Edward Cowell, in the Bodleian Library. It is an unashamedly free translation, true to the spirit rather than the letter of the original, and the image of the Persian garden is FitzGerald's own. It is interesting to note that although illustrators have made the Beloved female, the sex is, in fact, unspecified. FitzGerald's hymn to sensual appetite expresses emotions and realises dreams that he was never able to acknowledge in his life.

In 1859, the year that the *Rubaiyat* was first published, Kenworthy Browne was fatally injured in a riding accident, and FitzGerald rushed to his bedside. Browne, unable to speak, scrawled a note to FitzGerald: "I love you very – whenever – WKB." They were the last words he ever wrote.

After Browne's death FitzGerald went to live in Lowestoft. He described in a letter to Browne's widow how he used to walk along the beach at night "longing for some fellow to accost me who might give me some promise of filling up a very vacant place in my heart".

His last attachment was to a handsome fisherman, Joseph "Posh" Fletcher, who was, wrote FitzGerald, "broader and taller than all the rest" and "like one of the Elgin marbles in a guernsey". FitzGerald had a boat built for him, the Meum & Tuum, and settled all his debts. He also had a portrait painted of Posh by Samuel Laurence, which he hung beside those of Tennyson and Thackeray. Although Posh exploited and cheated him FitzGerald considered him to be "the greatest man I have ever known". Eventually FitzGerald tired of his drunkenness and constant demands for money, and their relationship ended, but his feelings for Posh never changed.

During his last years FitzGerald did several more translations, particularly of the dramas of Aeschylus and Sophocles. He lived alone, quite contentedly, on a diet of bread, fruit and tea. When his eyesight began to fail he employed local boys to read to him. There were visits to old friends and he in turn was visited by new friends who, through their love of the *Rubaiyat*, sought him out.

He died while on a visit to Merton in Norfolk, and was buried in the churchyard at

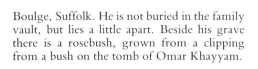
60 Lincoln's Inn Fields, WC2

Boulge, Suffolk. He is not buried in the family vault, but lies a little apart. Beside his grave there is a rosebush, grown from a clipping from a bush on the tomb of Omar Khayyam.

Addresses

★*39 Portland Place, W1* – he spent his childhood here.

★*7 Southampton Row, WC1* – he lived here in 1833.

★*19 Charlotte Street, W1* – he stayed here several times between 1841–51.

★*24 Greenberry Street, NW8* – *site* of his home in 1843.

★*60 Charlotte Street, W1* – *site* of the house in which he stayed several times between 1844–48.

★*Terrace House, Richmond Hill, Richmond* – he lived here with his mother in 1849.

★*39 Bolsover Street, W1* – *site* of his home 1848–50.

★*60 Lincoln's Inn Fields, WC2* – he lived here in 1851.

★*17 Old Gloucester Street, WC1* – *site* of the house in which he lived in 1854.

★*31 Great Portland Street, W1* – he lived here between 1855–57.

★*88 Great Portland Street, W1* – he stayed here in 1859.

Works include

Euphranor: A Dialogue on Youth (1851) – a glorification of William Kenworthy Browne; *Polonius: A Collection of Wise Saws and Modern Instances* (1852); *The Rubaiyat of Omar Khayyam* (1859); *Letters to Fanny Kemble* (1895); *Collected Letters* (1901).

Portrait

Miniature on ivory by Eva, Lady Rivett-Carnac, after a photograph of 1873 – National Portrait Gallery.

Fictional portrait

George Warrington in *The History of Pendennis* (1848–50) by William Makepeace Thackeray is partly based on FitzGerald.

Memorial

Plaque, designed by Frank Brangwyn and sculpted by Joseph Cribb (1946) – School of Oriental and African Studies, Malet Street, WC1.

Memorabilia

FitzGerald's letters and the manuscript of *The Rubaiyat of Omar Khayyam* – British Museum.

E M Forster

(1 January 1879 – 7 June 1970)

The novelist and writer Edward Morgan Forster was born in London. Soon after his birth, his father died, and Forster, an only child, was brought up by his mother and various aunts.

He went as a day boy to Tonbridge School, and then to King's College, Cambridge, where he began his close friendship with the unconventional don, Goldsworthy Lowes Dickinson.

After graduating from Cambridge with a degree in Classics and History, Forster began writing short stories, some of which appeared in the *Independent Review*. His style was influenced mostly, he said, by the writings of Jane Austen and Samuel Butler.

He had a small private income and was able to travel in Europe and settle in Italy, where he wrote the novels *Where Angels Fear to Tread* and *A Room with a View*. Between these Italian novels came *The Longest Journey*, his own favourite among his works, which dealt with his schooldays at Tonbridge and student life at Cambridge. In 1907, after his return to England, he wrote *Howards End*, his most mature work thus far, which established his reputation as a major novelist.

In 1912 Forster went to India with Dickinson, where he gathered material for what, twelve years later, would become his greatest novel.

Shortly after his return from India, Forster visited Edward Carpenter at Millthorpe and was given the inspiration to write his novel about homosexual love, *Maurice*. In a terminal note to the novel, he wrote, "George Merrill . . . touched my backside – gently and just above the buttocks. I believe he touched most people's. The sensation was unusual and I still remember it . . . It seemed to go straight through the small of my back into my ideas without involving my thoughts." Convinced that "at that precise moment I had conceived", Forster huried away and began at once to write. He did not intend publishing the novel – his mother would never have approved – but he felt the overwhelming necessity to write it.

During the First World War, Forster served with the Red Cross in Alexandria, where he had his first love affair, with Mohammed el Adi, a young Egyptian tram driver, and a momentous meeting with Constantine Cavafy.

In 1921 he returned to India and became private secretary to the Maharajah of Dewas. Over the next two years he wrote *A Passage to India*, for which he was awarded the Femina-Vie Heureuse and James Tait Black Memorial prizes in 1925.

Since his university days Forster had taken a keen interest in the Working Men's College, and over the years he gave several lectures there. He was twice President of the National Council for Civil Liberties, a cause to which he was deeply attached.

In 1946 Forster was invited to return to Cambridge as an honorary Fellow of King's College. This was the beginning of a new life for him. He made many friends among the undergraduates, who entertained him and gave him their confidence. To some he gave generous financial help. He refused a knighthood, but in 1953 became a Companion of Honour, and on his ninetieth birthday he was admitted to the Order of Merit.

Many years before, in 1930, at a party given by his friend Joe Ackerley, Forster had met a policeman, Bob Buckingham. Forster was partial to policemen – he used to wave to them from his window – and had only recently ended an affair with one, Harry Daley, who had become "indiscreet". With Buckingham he formed a deep and lasting relationship. Soon he was writing to a friend, "I'm quite sure that his [Buckingham's] feeling for me is something he has never had before. It's a spiritual feeling which has extended to my physique."

Although Buckingham married and later denied that he and Forster had been lovers – he even claimed not to have known that Forster was homosexual – they remained close friends. It was at the Buckinghams' home in Coventry that Forster died, and his ashes were scattered over a rose bed in their garden.

Addresses

★6 *Melcombe Place (cnr Boston Place), NW1* – site of his birthplace.

★11 *Drayton Court, Drayton Gardens, SW10* – he lived here in 1904.

★5 *Raymond Buildings, WC1* – Sir Edward Marsh's flat. Forster used it as a pied-à-terre in 1909.

★27 *Brunswick Square, WC1* – *site* of his home 1925–30.

★26 *Brunswick Square, WC1* – *site* of his home 1930–40.

★9 *Arlington Park Mansions, Sutton Lane, W4* – his home 1940–c1946.

Works include

Novels: *Where Angels Fear to Tread* (1905); *The Longest Journey* (1907); *A Room with a View* (1908); *Howards End* (1910); *Maurice* (published posthumously 1971); *A Passage to India* (1924).

Essays: *Pharos and Pharillon* (1923) – in which he introduced Cavafy's poems to English readers; *Abinger Harvest* (1936); *Two Cheers for Democracy* (1951).

Letters from India: *The Hill of Devi* (1953).

Portraits

Canvas by Dora Carrington (after 1924) – National Portrait Gallery. Photographs by Cecil Beaton, Bill Brandt (1947), and Howard Coster (1930s) – N.P.G.

Fictional portrait

He appears as the writer Benjamin Dexter in *The Third Man* (1950) by Graham Greene.

Memorabilia

Several autograph letters – Fawcett Library.

André Gide

(22 November 1869 –
19 February 1951)

"My function is to disturb," Gide often stated, and disturb he certainly did, whether as an outspoken critic of colonialism, bureaucracy and dogma, or as an advocate, not merely a defender, of homosexuality.

André Paul Guillaume Gide was born in Paris. After his father, who was Professor of Law at the Sorbonne, died in 1880, he was brought up by his mother and her ex-governess. A delicate child, he had an irregular schooling, mainly at the Protestant École Alsacienne. In his last years at school he began writing, and met Pierre Louÿs, who introduced him to the Symbolists and their doctrine. In 1891 he published a first book at his own expense.

Two years later, after an attack of tuberculosis, and in a state of profound moral uncertainty, Gide went for the first time to North Africa. He had been introduced to Oscar Wilde by Rémy de Gourmont, and it was Wilde who is reputed to have forced the issue of Gide's hidden homosexuality during a visit to Algiers, which led to his enjoying his first sexual encounters. He fell in love with an Algerian youth, Athman, and arranged for him to go to Paris. Gide returned to France with his health restored and his outlook much altered by the revelations his experiences in North Africa had brought.

In 1895 he married his cousin, Madeleine Rondeaux, whom he regarded as his "spiritual pole". It was a marriage of convenience: Madeleine had a horror of sex, while Gide's sexual interests lay elsewhere. Nevertheless, conflicts arose between her strict Christian values and his desire for freedom and his homosexuality.

By now an established literary figure, Gide embarked on the most fruitful period of his career, producing much of his best work during the years leading up to the First World War. Les Nourritures terrestres propounded his new-found belief in the need for personal liberation and moral individualism; L'Immoraliste, which traced the career of the "immoralist" from conformity to hedonism and self-fulfilment, developed this concern. In La Porte étroite Gide analysed the deleterious effects of French Protestantism on personal relationships and spiritual growth. Corydon, his "gay manifesto", was written during the pre-war years, but he did not feel self-assured enough to publish it until the 1920s.

In 1917 he met Marc Allégret (1900–73), whose father had been best man at Gide's wedding. The long and close relationship with Allégret, whom he virtually adopted as his nephew, was the most significant of Gide's life. "It was for him," Gide later explained, "that I wrote Les Faux-Monnayeurs," the complex work in the guise of fiction which he called his first novel.

Allégret became a prolific film-maker, who in the 1930s gave their first major screen roles to Simone Simon and Jean-Pierre Aumont, and later discovered other stars such as Michelle Morgan, Gerard Philipe, and Brigitte Bardot. His first film, a documentary on the Belgian Congo, which he made while accompanying Gide on his West African expedition in 1925, is generally regarded as his best. Gide's own account of their journey shared the title Voyage au Congo with the film.

During the 1920s Gide came to wide public attention with Corydon, his autobiography Si le grain ne meurt, and Les Faux-Monnayeurs. The very image of the free man (as the historian Jean Touchard described him), he was a signatory to many petitions and was a popular speaker at numerous meetings in the Anti-Fascist Campaign. His conversion to Communism in 1932 was much publicised. He was adopted by many young intellectuals as a father confessor and his "carnets", which were published regularly, were held to be the left-wing conscience of an entire generation. However, his expression of profound disenchantment with the Soviet scheme of things, in Retour de l'URRS in 1936, following a visit to Russia as a correspondent for the Nouvelle Revue Française (which he had helped to found in 1909), led to his being accused of treachery by the Communist Party. He came to realise that his vision of society was essentially humanist, and that his own doctrines of moral individualism and personal liberation were equally incompatible with those of the extreme Left and with those of the Fascists.

In 1939, the year of his wife's death, Gide undertook further extensive travel. Through most of the war he lived in North Africa.

Several of his plays had been well received in Paris during the two decades before the war, but probably his greatest successes in the theatre came through the Renaud-Barrault Company's productions in the 1940s of his translation of *Hamlet* and his adaptation of Kafka's *The Trial*. There was also an acclaimed production of his *Les Caves du Vatican* in 1950.

Gide valued highly the friendship of women. Dorothy Bussy, a sister of Lytton Strachey, was a close friend and confidante for thirty years, and it was largely through her translations of his work that he gained his large readership in Britain and America. Maria van Rysselberghe, the daughter of another woman friend, bore him a daughter, Catherine, in 1923.

In 1947 Gide received an honorary degree from Oxford, and in the same year he won the Nobel Prize for Literature.

Many great thinkers and writers, such as Sartre and Camus, have acknowledged their debt to Gide. Sartre's tribute to his courage, generosity and vision did much to counteract the vicious comments made by the Communist Party after his death, typical of which were, "A corpse has died" and references to his having "lived dangerously, wrapped in three layers of flannel".

Address

★*51 Gordon Square, WC1* – the home of Dorothy and Simon Bussy. Gide stayed here with Allégret in August 1920; he stayed here again in June 1947. (See also *Lytton Strachey*.)

Works include

Fiction: *Le traité du Narcisse* (1891); *Paludes* (1896; translation by G Painter *Marshlands*, 1953); *Les Nourritures terrestres* (1897; tr. D Bussy, *Fruits of the Earth*, 1949); *L'Immoraliste* (1902; tr. D Bussy, *The Immoralist*, 1930); *La Porte étroite* (1909; tr. D Bussy, *Strait is the Gate*, 1924); *Les Caves du Vatican* (1914; tr. D Bussy, *The Vatican Cellars*, 1927); *La Symphonie pastorale* (1919; tr. D Bussy, 1931); *Les Faux-Monnayeurs* (1926; tr. D Bussy, *The Coiners*, 1950); *Thésée* (1946).

Drama: *Le Roi Candaule* (1901).

Non-fiction: *Prétextes* (1903); *Souvenirs de la cours d'assise* (1914; tr. D Bussy, *Recollections of the Assize Court*, 1941); *Dostoïevsky* (1923; tr. D Bussy, 1949); *Corydon* (1923; tr. H Gibb, 1950); *Voyage au Congo* (1928) & *Le Retour du Tchad* (1928) – (both tr. D Bussy, *Travels in the Congo*, 1930); *Retour de l'URSS* (1936); *Retouches à mon Retour de l'URSS* (1937).

Autobiography: *Si le grain ne meurt* (1926; tr. D Bussy, *If It die . . .*, 1950); *Et nunc manet in te* (1951; tr. J O'Brien, *Madeleine*, 1953).

Journals: *The Journals of André Gide, 1889–1949*, tr. J O'Brien, 1953.

Gluck

(13 August 1895 – 10 January 1978)

Born Hannah Gluckstein, she was the daughter of Joseph Gluckstein, one of the founders of J Lyons & Co (the chain of restaurants and teashops), and Francesca Halle Gluckstein, an opera singer. Although a talented and dominant personality, Francesca submitted to the conventions of her husband's family and gave up her career in music. Nevertheless, she maintained her interest and encouraged it in her daughter, who had inherited a fine singing voice.

After attending St Paul's Girls' School, Gluck was enrolled at the St John's Wood School of Art, presumably to give her something to do until a suitable husband turned up, because she certainly had no great interest in art then. Rather, her ambition was to become an opera singer. However, a portrait by Sargent (of the violinist Joachim) was to alter the course of her life. In this painting, a photograph of which she saw in the artists' room of the Wigmore Hall whilst waiting to make her appearance at her first Pupil's Concert, "there was a great whirl of paint . . . this hit me plumb in my solar plexus, all thoughts of being a singer vanished."

She determined to paint and, fortunately, her family permitted her to spend a month in Cornwall with three other students in a house rented by a friend of the artist Alfred Munnings. Her parents and her teachers had shown little interest in her artistic abilities, and the fact that such "genuine artists" as Dod and Ernest Proctor, Harold and Laura Knight and Lamorna Birch should take her work and ambitions seriously gave her self-confidence an enormous boost.

To return from the bohemian life of the artists' colony in Cornwall, where her burgeoning talents were so agreeably nurtured, to the confines of the family home in St John's Wood and the expectations of her marrying and settling down, was frustrating and she felt the need to rebel.

She later recalled, "I ran away with 2s.6d. in my pocket and no food card, a necessity during the war." Munnings had offered to help her if she left home, but it appears that financial support came from her family, once they had accepted her determination to become an artist. Nonetheless, Gluck's assertion of her individuality and personal independence was uncompromising: by calling herself "Gluck" and insisting that neither "Miss" nor her first name should be a spoken or written prefix to this, she rejected her family name and background; she cropped her hair; and she began wearing men's clothes.

Gordon Selfridge took an interest in her career and gave her space in his store in Oxford Street, where she did "instant portraits" (done in one sitting). However, fearing that this approach to portraiture would make her work slick, and preferring to choose the subjects of her portraits herself, she left to establish her own studio. "I never 'pose' a sitter," she wrote. "I spend much time watching them at work and at ease, then seize that split second when the whole personality is involved, and thereafter everything else comes into being at the dictation of what I have felt and seen." She was a most versatile painter: apart from her splendid portraits, she painted sea- and landscapes, theatrical and court scenes, still lifes (especially of flowers) and genre pictures. She observed, "I only respond to a vision from wherever it comes and whatever its form. The vision once received becomes a tyrant."

Her first exhibition was held at the Dorien Gallery in 1924 and was organized by the photographer Emil Otto Hoppé, a friend and admirer of her work. Around this time (1923–24) she met Romaine Brooks and they arranged to paint each other's portrait. Romaine called her portrait of Gluck "Peter - a young English Girl"; her own portrait was never completed, as she took against the sketch Gluck made for this during a brief, late night sitting at Gluck's studio in Chelsea.

For her 1932 exhibition at the Fine Arts Society (which gave her one-artist shows in 1926, 1932, 1937, a retrospective in 1973 and a memorial exhibition in 1980), Gluck decorated the gallery as a "Gluck room", with white panelled walls, modern furniture and flower-and-vegetable arrangements by Constance Spry. All of the paintings on show were in the three-tier, stepped "Gluck" frames which she designed (and patented that year).

Gluck's flair for "setting off" beautiful things was the theme of a *Homes and Gardens* article, in July 1935, about her home in Hampstead. The journalist was greatly taken with the effect of the display of Gluck's paintings, collection of seashells, Rockingham and Worcester china, and even larger collection of glass walking-sticks, against the white walls of her living room and "completely modern and efficient" studio. (Gluck had had an old stable behind the house pulled down and a studio built to the design of Edward Maufe, who, with his wife Prudence, also promoted her career.) When her home was requisitioned by the War Office early in the war she went to Sussex where she had friends.

Between 1937 and 1964 Gluck was engaged in research into oil paint quality and she waged a campaign against the paint industry on the grounds that the frequent changes in the composition of artists' materials over the years created difficulties for the artists and imperilled the life of their paintings. On this matter she addressed such bodies as the Museums Association (of which she was a member) and the Royal Society of Arts (of which she was awarded a Life Fellowship in 1951). She later admitted that with these activities and engagements as visiting lecturer at art clubs and colleges, she had perhaps diverted too much time and energy from her painting.

Although friendly and sociable, Gluck was happiest of all in her own studio, just painting, and living quietly with her lover and companion of many years, the critic and journalist Edith Shackleton Heald (? - 1976), and Edith's older sister, Nora, at The Chantry House in Steyning, Sussex. Occasionally she would venture up to London when her work required her to do so.

Her retrospective exhibition in 1973 made up for the long period in which she felt she had been artistically neglected. The public's response to the memorial exhibition for her in 1980 confirmed a renewal of interest in Gluck's work and life.

Bolton House, Windmill Hill, NW3

Publications: "The Dilemma of the Painter and Conservator in the Synthetic Age", in *Museums Journal* (1954, London); "The Impermanency of Paintings in Relation to Artists' Materials", in *Royal Society of Arts Journal* (February 1964, London); "Artists vis-à-vis the Paint Industry", in *Journal of the Oil and Colour Chemists Association* (July 1967, London); "On the Quality of Paint", in *Tempera* (July 1969, London).

Addresses

★*32 Compayne Gardens, NW6* – birthplace. The Glucksteins lived here until 1905.

★*73 Avenue Road, NW8* – site of the family home (from 1906) which she fled from during the First World War.

★*48 (formerly 30) Tite Street, SW3* – she had a studio here during the 1920s.

★*Bolton House, Windmill Hill, NW3* – her home c1934–40.

Works include

Painting: Canvas – Portrait of Sir James Crichton-Browne (1928) – National Portrait Gallery.

Portraits

Canvas – self-portrait (1942) – National Portrait Gallery. Photographs – Fine Arts Society Ltd. *Portrait on p. 71.*

Memorabilia

Exhibition catalogues – Fine Arts Society Ltd.

Eva Gore-Booth

(1870 – 30 June 1926)

Eva Selina Gore-Booth came from a wealthy landowning family and was born at Lissadell House in Co. Sligo. Both she and her sister, Constance, reacted against their privileged background and devoted themselves to helping the poor and the disadvantaged. Eva became especially involved in campaigning for women's rights and in the 1890s she founded, with Constance's help, a suffrage society in Sligo.

The poet W B Yeats visited Lissadell in 1894 and was immediately attracted by Eva's "delicate gazelle-like beauty". She listened sympathetically as he told her of his unhappiness in love, and he felt encouraged to declare his feelings for her. However, being unsure of her response, he consulted the Tarot. "And when The Fool came up, which means that nothing at all would happen, I turned my mind away."

In 1895 Eva became seriously ill with tuberculosis and took many months to recover. The following year, while convalescing in Italy, the most important event in her life took place. She met and fell in love with a young Englishwoman, Esther Roper (1868–1938), who was at that time the secretary of the North of England Society for Women's Suffrage. Instead of returning to Ireland as planned, Eva went to live in Manchester with Esther. From now on they worked together to further the aims of the women's movement by peaceful means. They became joint secretaries of the Women's Textile and Other Workers Representation Committee and edited the *Women's Labour News*. Their main concern was for the plight of working women. They organized special suffrage campaigns for them and visited them in their homes and at the factory gate. In 1908 they started the Manchester Barmaids Association, to protect barmaids' jobs against attempts being made to prevent women from working in bars.

In the midst of all this activity Eva was also busy writing poetry. Her first published volume was highly praised by Yeats.

One day while out shopping the two women came upon the young Christabel Pankhurst repining in a curio shop. Her mother, the redoubtable Emmeline, had set up the business in an effort to improve the family fortune. Christabel, however, did not have the inclination, nor the shop sufficient customers, to make a success of the venture. Eva and Esther befriended Christabel. With their help and guidance she gave up the shop and began to study law. Through them also, she began her association with the suffrage movement, proving herself to be a tireless worker for the cause and a fiery orator. For a time the friendship prospered. Christabel was particularly fond of Eva and would sit for hours massaging her head, to soothe away frequent bouts of neuralgia.

Emmeline was alarmed by the unexpected turn of events and jealous of Eva's place in Christabel's affections. She was involved in campaigning for workhouse reform and had not hitherto concentrated on votes for women. One of her main reasons for founding the Women's Social and Political Union in 1903 was to prise her daughter away from Eva. The plan worked well. Christabel dutifully joined her mother at the head of the new militant group. Her feelings for Eva and Esther cooled when they disagreed with her militant tactics, and their friendship ended when the WSPU pulled away from the Independent Labour Party and the Labour movement.

In 1913 Eva's health deteriorated and she and Esther moved to London. During the war they worked for the Women's Peace Crusade and the No-Conscription Fellowship. Despite Eva's illness they travelled around the country attending courts-martial and tribunals in support of conscientious objectors.

Meanwhile Eva's sister Constance had married and become Countess Markievicz. She was deeply committed to the cause of Ireland and commanded the revolutionary forces which held St Stephen's Green in Dublin during the 1916 rebellion. She was arrested and served a period in prison. In 1918 she became the first woman elected to the House of Commons, but did not take her seat.

After the war Eva and Esther became members of the Committee for the Abolition of Capital Punishment and worked for prison reform. As she grew weaker Eva was forced to give up active work, but continued writing poetry. Esther took care of her throughout her long illness and they were together at the end.

After Eva's death Esther collected together many of her poems for publication and wrote a biographical introduction to them. Esther was an extremely reticent person and little is known of her last years. Constance wrote of her, "The more one knows her, the more one

loves her, and I feel so glad Eva and she were together, and so thankful that her love was with Eva to the end."

Address

★*14 Frognal Gardens, NW3 – (now Frognal Lodge Hotel).* She lived here with Esther from 1913 until her death in 1926. After Eva's death Constance wrote, "I feel very sad leaving this house . . . Every corner in it speaks of Eva and her lovely spirit of peace and love is here just the same as ever, and Esther too, who is her spiritual sister, I hate leaving."

Works include

Poetry: *The Collected Poems of Eva Gore-Booth,* edited with a biographical introduction by Esther Roper (1929).
Pamphlets: *Women's Right to Work* and *Women Workers and Parliamentary Representation.*
Journalism: Articles in *Women's Labour News* and *The Common Cause.*

Memorabilia

A poem by W B Yeats "In Memory of Eva Gore-Booth and Con Markievicz", in his collection *The Winding Stair, and Other Poems* (1933). Several autograph letters – Fawcett Library.

Duncan Grant

(21 January 1885 – 9 May 1978)

Duncan James Corrowr Grant was born at The Doune, Inverness. He spent his early life in India and Burma where his father, an army officer, was posted. During the years that he attended St Paul's School in London he lived with his cousins, the Stracheys. His aunt, Lady Jane Strachey, recognising that he was wasting his time at school and was quite unsuited for a career in the army for which he was destined, persuaded his parents to let him leave St Paul's, and enrol, in 1902, at the Westminster School of Art.

In 1906 he spent a year studying with Jacques-Emile Blanche in Paris. There he was captivated by the Impressionists, many of whose paintings he saw for the first time in the salon of Gertrude and Leo Stein. (He became friendly with Gertrude Stein, as well as with Pablo Picasso.)

By 1908 Grant had begun to paint professionally. He started making a name for himself with the paintings he showed over the next two years at the Friday Club, a studio in Chelsea where the Bloomsbury Group met; in the atmosphere created by the first Post-Impressionist Exhibition (in London) organised by Roger Fry in 1910 his reputation grew until he was widely regarded as the leader of the English Post-Impressionists.

He had been introduced to the Bloomsbury Group by his cousin Lytton Strachey, with whom he had had an affair. The affair, which began in 1905, had been conducted in a desultory manner: "There's distinctly something of the lovee about his affection if not about his lust," Strachey once complained to his friend John Maynard Keynes; it was interrupted by a brief liaison between Grant and Harold Hobhouse in Paris in 1906, and came to an end when, in 1908, Grant and Keynes became lovers. Perhaps the most significant of Grant's homosexual relationships was the one with Keynes, who was to become the most influential economist of the twentieth century. It was certainly the strongest attachment Keynes ever formed. Their sexual relationship ended around 1912 but they remained the closest of friends until Keynes's death in 1946.

If Lytton Strachey was the intellectual focus of the Bloomsbury Group, Duncan Grant was its emotional lynch-pin. He was charming, kind and sympathetic, and his casual attitude to life and his carefree behaviour endeared him to the "Bloomsberries". "Anyone could fall in love with Duncan if he wanted to," Keynes wrote. Strachey described him thus: "His face is outspoken, bold and not just rough. It's the full, aquiline type, with frank grey-blue eyes and incomparably lascivious lips."

For Vanessa Bell (the sister of Virginia Woolf and Adrian Stephen – with whom Grant had a brief affair) his attractions were that he was fun to be with, was homosexual and, like her, a painter. She had recently ended her affair with Roger Fry when she invited Grant and his current companion David Garnett to come and work on the land (as they were required to do as conscientious objectors during the First World War) at Charleston, the house in Sussex which she and her husband, the art critic Clive Bell, owned.

Although Grant took homes and studios in London, Charleston became his real home for the rest of his life, and it was there that his and Vanessa Bell's daughter, Angelica, was born in 1918. Garnett, known to the Bloomsbury Group as "Bunny", continued to live at Charleston for some time, and was to marry Angelica (in 1942). Clive Bell came often to visit his and Vanessa's sons Julian and Quentin, usually bringing with him one of his mistresses.

By the end of the 1920s Grant and Vanessa Bell each had a secure place in the London art world. They made annual visits to Europe and divided their time in England between London and Charleston. Together they undertook several commissions for the interior decorations of the houses of family and friends (including that of Ethel Sands). The decorations of Charleston were added to constantly, with paintings of fruit, flowers and nude figures, both male and female, covering every annexable surface, from ashtrays to walls, doors, chairs and table tops. They had been directors of the Omega Workshops (1913–19), which were started by Roger Fry with the aim of producing decorated objects in the spirit of the Post-Impressionists, and their decorative work and designs for book jackets, pottery, tiles, carpets, needlework, fabrics, and costumes and sets for the stage during the following two decades or so continued to reflect the Omega principles.

During the Second World War Grant served as a War Artist. He also carried out, with Vanessa and Quentin Bell, decorations at the parish church of Berwick, in Sussex. In the late 1950s he decorated the Russell Chantry of Lincoln Cathedral.

He was a prolific artist and had many exhibitions of his work (all of which has a strong decorative element), but he remained a figure outside the popular art establishment. He turned down invitations to join the Royal Academy or to show work in the Academy's exhibitions, disliking the snobbery of artistic society and institutions. The formal teaching of art was also something he hated, but he graciously accepted the honorary doctorate awarded to him by the Royal College of Art in 1970.

In the years following the death (in 1961) of Vanessa Bell, who had been his faithful companion for nearly half a century and who had rarely objected to the sometimes lengthy visits of his boyfriends to their homes, Grant continued to paint, decorate ceramics, and exhibit his work. Remaining remarkably fit and active until well into his eighties, he particularly enjoyed travelling. He made many friends during his trips abroad and at Charleston, where art students sought him out. With his legendary charm, gentle humour and striking good looks he continued to make many conquests in his last years.

He died in Aldermaston at the home of a friend and model, Paul Roche, and is buried next to Vanessa Bell in the churchyard at Thirle, Sussex.

Addresses

★*69 Lancaster Gate, W2* (now part of the Charles Dickens Hotel). He lived here, with his uncle and aunt Sir Richard and Lady Jane Strachey, while a day scholar at Westminster School. (See also *Lytton Strachey*.)

★*143 Fellows Road, NW3 – site*. He lived here with his parents c1905–09.

★*(27?) Belgrave Gardens (formerly Belgrave Road), NW8* – he and Keynes had rooms here October–November 1909.

★*21 Fitzroy Square, W1* – he took the ground floor flat in December 1909. It was his home and studio (and Keynes's pied-à-terre) until 1911.

★*38 Brunswick Square, WC1 – site* of the home of Adrian and Virginia Stephen (later Woolf), where Grant and Keynes rented rooms 1911–14.

★*46 Gordon Square, WC1* – he moved into the Bells' home in October 1914. (*Plaque* – Keynes.)

★*22 Fitzroy Street, W1 – site* of the studio he took in October 1914.

★*18 Fitzroy Street, W1 – site* of the studio he took early in 1919.

★*8 Fitzroy Street, W1 – site* of his studio from 1920–c1940.

★*1 Taviton Street, WC1* – he had a room in his cousin Marjorie Strachey's flat 1946–48.

★*26a Canonbury Square, N1* – he and Vanessa Bell had a flat here 1949–55.

★*28 Percy Street, W1* – he and Vanessa Bell had a flat here 1955–1961.

★*24 Victoria Square, SW1* – from 1961 the top flat was his pied-à-terre. (He rented it from Leonard Woolf.)

★*3 Park Square West, NW1* – his London home from 1970.

★*(33 Fitzroy Square, W1* – the premises of the Omega Workshops 1913–19).

Works include

"Vanessa Bell" (c1918) – National Portrait Gallery. Portraits of Sir Desmond McCarthy (c1938; c1942; 1944) – N.P.G. "Group of Male Nudes" (c1911) – verso "Studland Beach" by Vanessa Bell (c1912) – Tate Gallery. "Interior at Gordon Square" (c1915) – Tate Gallery. "Venus and Adonis" (c1919) – Tate Gallery. "Abstract kinetic collage painting with sound (1914) – Tate Gallery. Sketches and designs for Omega Workshops and interior decorating commissions – Victoria and Albert Museum. Shop signboard for the Omega Workshops (1913) – V & A Museum. Examples of ceramics, furniture, textiles, etc. – V & A Museum. Canvas "St Paul's Cathedral" (1941) – Imperial War Museum.

Portraits

Canvas self-portrait (c1909) – National Portrait Gallery. Photographs by Cecil Beaton and by Godfrey Argent (1968) – N.P.G. (Archives).

Fictional portrait

Duncan Forbes in *Lady Chatterley's Lover* (1928) by D H Lawrence is modelled on Duncan Grant – "that dark-skinned taciturn Hamlet of a fellow with straight black hair and a weird Celtic conceit of himself".

Memorabilia

Autograph letter from Duncan Grant to Pippa Strachey (1951) – Fawcett Library.

John Gray
(2 March 1866 –14 June 1934)
&
André Raffalovich
(11 September 1864–
14 February 1934)

John Henry Gray was born in Bethnal Green, the first of nine children of Scottish parents, John Gray, a carpenter and wheelwright at Woolwich Dockyard, and his wife, Hannah Williamson.

When he was thirteen Gray went to work as an apprentice metal turner at Woolwich Arsenal. In his spare time he studied Latin, French and German. He also learned to play the violin and taught himself to draw and paint. In 1882 he passed a civil service examination and became a clerk at the London General Post Office. Five years later he progressed to a job as a librarian at the Foreign Office – then quite an achievement for someone without a public-school background.

At last, at the age of twenty-four, Gray was able to afford to leave home and start leading his own life. He took a room in The Temple and began to frequent bars and music halls. It is not known when or where he first met Oscar Wilde, but they were both guests at a dinner party given by Ricketts and Shannon early in 1889, the year that *The Picture of Dorian Gray* was written.

Wilde took a delight in showing off his young friend at the theatre and at the Cafe Royal. He also helped to further Gray's literary aspirations. Ricketts and Shannon accepted a story entitled "The Great Worm" and an article on the Goncourt brothers for the first number of their literary journal *The Dial.* Gray was a regular contributor to the journal over the next ten years. His first book of poems, *Silverpoints,* was designed by Ricketts. Wilde paid for its publication.

In the summer of 1889 Gray was invited to spend a holiday in Brittany with the family of his friend Marmaduke Langdale. The Langdales were fervent Catholics and made a strong impression on the hitherto nonconformist Gray, which led a year later to his conversion to Roman Catholicism.

When *The Picture of Dorian Gray* was published in 1891 many people were struck by the resemblance between Gray and the protagonist of Wilde's novel, "a young man of extraordinary personal beauty . . . who looks as if he was made out of ivory and rose leaves . . . with his finely curved scarlet lips, his frank blue eyes, his crisp gold hair". Gray objected to the comparison and when the *Star* newspaper declared that "Mr Gray, who has cultivated his manner to the highest pitch of langour yet attained," was the original Dorian, he sued them for libel. The *Star* apologised and the matter was settled out of court. Seventy years later, in 1961, a first edition of *The Picture of Dorian Gray* came up for sale in New York. Inside was found an autograph letter from Gray to Wilde signed, "Yours ever, Dorian."

In November 1892, in the poet Arthur Symons's rooms in The Temple, Gray met the man with whom he was to share the rest of his life. Marc-André Raffalovich was born in Paris a year after his wealthy Russian-Jewish family had been forced by pogroms to flee from their home in Odessa. When he was eighteen Raffalovich came to London and bought a house in Mayfair, where he founded a literary and artistic salon. However, his extravagance and his flamboyant manner made an unfavourable impression on some of his guests, who thought him rather vulgar, and prompted Wilde's epigram "Dear André! He came to London to found a salon and only succeeded in opening a saloon."

Raffalovich fell instantly in love with Gray, whose relationship with Wilde had recently ended, and began showering him with expensive gifts. He gave him the keys of a luxury flat in Park Lane and took him sailing in the Mediterranean on his black-painted yacht "Iniquity". They became well known as bejewelled and overdressed men–about–town, attending first nights and going to Covent Garden twice a week during the opera season. They were ambitious to succeed as playwrights. In 1894 their play *The Blackmailers,* about the blackmail of a homosexual, was performed at the Prince of Wales Theatre. Unfortunately it was never printed and no copy of the text is known to exist.

Three months after Wilde's conviction Raffalovich published in Paris an essay "L'Affaire Oscar Wilde", the first printed account of the trials. He wrote about Wilde in a spiteful and disparaging manner. Wilde had never taken Raffalovich seriously either as an aesthete or as a writer and perhaps there was some lingering jealousy regarding Wilde's earlier involvement with Gray. In another article on Wilde which Raffalovich wrote in 1927 for the Dominican monthly *Blackfriars* he was less harsh: "Much as I grew to dislike him I cannot remember his ever giving me bad advice. It is to his credit that he never did me any harm . . . For years

I detested him and his presence and traces of his influence."

In 1896 Raffalovich became a Roman Catholic (six years after Gray) and a Dominican lay brother, taking the name of Brother Sebastian. Two years later Gray went to Rome and entered the Scots College as a candidate for the priesthood. Raffalovich visited him regularly in Rome and was present at his ordination there in 1901.

Gray was sent as a curate to St Patrick's Church in the Cowgate, a poor area of Edinburgh. Raffalovich bought a house in the Morningside district of South Edinburgh. Here he built a church for Gray, St Peter's Morningside. Raffalovich gave affectionate and financial support to many people. In 1897 when he heard that Aubrey Beardsley was ill and penniless he immediately made arrangements for him to receive a yearly allowance of £400; and it was Raffalovich who built St Sebastian's Priory for the Dominicans, at Pendleton, Manchester.

Every morning at 7.20 Raffalovich drove in a hansom cab the short distance from his house to St Peter's Church to hear mass celebrated by Gray. He spent the rest of the day reading, dealing with financial matters and cultivating his roses. His Sunday luncheons and Tuesday dinner parties were attended by many literary and artistic celebrities, including Henry James, Max Beerbohm, Robert Hugh Benson, Eric Gill and of course, John Gray.

Gray, who became a canon in 1930, visited Raffalovich every day. They affected a restrained formality in front of strangers which gave no indication of the intimacy of their relationship. Whenever Gray was announced by the parlour-maid Raffalovich would jump to his feet, grasp his visitor's hand and exclaim in a tone of surprise, "Dear Canon, how kind of you to call." When Gray went on walking expeditions in the Highlands or Cotswolds he kept in touch with Raffalovich by sending him a telegram every day. They usually went on holiday together in the summer.

On the morning of Ash Wednesday 1934, when the taxi arrived to take him as usual to early mass at St Peter's, Raffalovich was found dead in his room. Gray was sent for at once and was heard to say, "I'm the saddest man in Edinburgh. My friend has gone to heaven." The funeral took place on a bitterly cold day. The mourners were wrapped up in overcoats and scarves, but Gray, who officiated, stood beside his friend's grave impervious to the freezing weather. He refused to put a cloak over his thin vestments and remained bareheaded. As a result he caught a severe chill which led to his death four months later.

Gray and Raffalovich are buried, some distance apart, in Mount Vernon Cemetery on the outskirts of Edinburgh.

Addresses

Gray:
★*2 Vivian Road, E3* – birthplace.
★*96 Eglinton Road, SE18* – his home from childhood until 1890.
★*No. 1 Cloister, The Temple, EC4* – he lived here 1890–91.
★*62 Chancery Lane, WC2* – *site* of his home 1891–92.
★*No. 3, Plowden Buildings, The Temple, EC4* – he lived here 1892–93.
★*43 Park Lane, W1* – *site* of his home 1893–98.
Raffalovich:
★*72 South Audley Street, W1* – he lived here 1882–98.
★*11 Egerton Gardens, SW3* – his home 1898–1905. (Gray stayed here during his holidays while studying for the priesthood.)

Works include

Gray: *Silverpoints* (1893) – poems; *Poems* (1931) – dedicated to Charles Ricketts; *Park: a Fantastic Story* (1932).
Raffalovich: Uranisme et Unisexualité – includes his essay "L'Affaire Oscar Wilde" (published in France, 1896).

Portrait

Gray: Lithograph of Gray by Raymond Savage (undated) – National Portrait Gallery.
Portrait on p. 94.

Fictional portrait

Gray is thought to have been the model for Wilde's Dorian Gray. Father Brown in Ronald Firbank's *Inclinations* (1916) is Gray.

Memorabilia

Rickett's bookbinding for *Silverpoints* – Victoria and Albert Museum. Letters of Gray to various correspondents – British Museum and Victoria and Albert Museum.

Thomas Gray

(26 December 1716 – 30 July 1771)

Thomas Gray, the poet and man of letters whose "Elegy Written in a Country Church-yard" remains one of the most popular poems in the English language, was born over his mother's millinery shop in Cornhill. All of his eleven brothers and sisters died in infancy. His mother saved his life by opening one of his veins with her scissors when he was in a fit. Gray's father was a money-broker and a violent alcoholic who beat his wife and squandered his money. He showed little interest in his son and refused to contribute towards the cost of his education. Dorothy Gray alone paid the school fees with money from the shop.

At Eton Gray showed great promise. He particularly enjoyed the classics and began composing Latin verse. Among his school-friends was Horace Walpole, the witty, urbane son of the Prime Minister. Gray became infatuated with Walpole and remained so throughout their school and undergraduate days.

In 1734 Gray went up to Peterhouse College, Cambridge. He was unhappy there at first, bored and at odds with the rough, loutish behaviour of most of the other students. They scoffed at his small, frail physique, his effeminate manner and short, mincing steps, and called him "Miss Gray". William Cole, a contemporary at Eton, described him as being "nice and elegant in his person, dress, and behaviour, even to a degree of finicalness and effeminacy".

"Everything is so tediously regular," Gray wrote to Walpole. "So samish that I expire for want of a little variety." He was existing, he said, on Walpole's letters "and a few mince-pyes". However, in 1736 something happened which changed all that. One of Gray's aunts died and left him enough money to give him financial independence. He was now able to indulge his passion for good food and books. He bought a harpsichord on which he learned to play pieces by Pergolesi and Scarlatti, and filled his rooms with flowers and jars of potpourri. No longer feeling the pressure on him to do well academically he abandoned his degree course.

In 1739 Walpole invited Gray to join him as his guest on the Grand Tour. They spent the next two years in France and Italy, but eventually quarrelled because Walpole thought Gray boring for spending his time in study and research, and Gray considered Walpole skittish for wanting to go out and enjoy himself.

Gray came back alone to England in 1741. Later that year his father died and his mother went to live with her sisters in Stoke Poges, Buckinghamshire. Gray returned to Peterhouse as a fellow-commoner. He was to remain at Cambridge for most of the rest of his life. "I am like a cabbage," he wrote. "Where I'm stuck I love to grow." At first, to please his mother, he studied to become a barrister, but after gaining a Bachelor of Civil Law degree, he lost all interest in a legal career and chose instead to spend his life among books.

The rift between Gray and Walpole was healed in 1745. Gray began to show his poems to Walpole who persuaded him to publish them. The "Elegy Written in a Country Churchyard" appeared in 1751. It went through four editions within two months of its publication and established his reputation.

Dorothy Gray died in 1753. On the headstone of her tomb in St Giles's churchyard at Stoke Poges her son described her as "the careful tender mother of many children, one of whom alone had the misfortune to survive her".

Gray moved to Pembroke Hall, Cambridge, in 1756. His library there is still preserved as The Gray Room and contains a copy of Benjamin Wilson's portrait of the poet in middle age.

On the death of Colley Cibber in 1757 Gray was offered the laureateship but refused it. He also refused an honorary doctorate from Aberdeen in 1765, but accepted the chair of modern history at Cambridge in 1768.

In 1769 Gray was introduced in London to Charles-Victor de Bonstetten, a handsome twenty-four year old Swiss who had come to England to improve his English. Gray was immediately attracted to the charming and high spirited young man and took him to Cambridge where he found him a room opposite Pembroke. He had fallen in love with Bonstetten and spent as much time as he could in his company. When after three months the time came for Bonstetten to return home Gray was broken-hearted. He wrote, "Alas! How do I every moment feel the truth of what I have somewhere read 'Ce n'est pas le voir que de s'en souvenir' ['Remembering him is not the same as seeing him'] and yet that remembrance is the only satisfaction I have left.

My life is now but a perpetual conversation with your shadow. The known sound of your voice still rings in my ears. There on the corner of the fender you are standing, or tinkling on the pianoforte, or stretch'd at length on the sofa."

Bonstetten invited him to spend a holiday in Switzerland during the following summer, but by then Gray was very ill and unable to make the journey. He died at Pembroke Hall of uraemia, resulting from a kidney infection, and was buried with his mother in the churchyard at Stoke Poges. A monument, with lines from the "Elegy" engraved on it, was erected near his tomb in 1799.

Addresses

★*39 Cornhill, EC3 – site* (now Union Discount premises). Gray was born here and later inherited the house from his father. It was destroyed by fire in 1748. A tablet bearing the words "The curfew tolls the knell of parting day" was placed on the wall of the present building in 1918. Below the tablet is a bronze medallion of Gray by F W Pomeroy.

★*Jermyn Street, SW1 – site*. From 1753, Gray took lodgings several times above the shop of a hosier named Roberts at the sign of the Three Squirrels.

★*Old Gloucester Street (formerly Gloucester Street), WC1 – site*. He had lodgings in a house here in 1759.

★*Russell Square, WC1* – between 1759–61 he took lodgings in a house which stood on the *site* of the Imperial Hotel.

★*Southampton Row, WC1* – he stayed in a house here in 1759 in order to visit the newly opened British Museum.

Works include

"Elegy Written in a Country Churchyard" (1751); his other most popular poems are "Ode on the Death of a Cat" and "Ode on a Distant Prospect of Eton College".

Portraits

Canvas by John Giles Eccardt (1747–48) – National Portrait Gallery. (It was painted at the request of Horace Walpole and shows Gray holding the manuscript of his "Ode on a Distant Prospect of Eton College".) Pencil drawing by J Basire after W Mason (c1771) – N.P.G. Plaster cast of bust (posthumous) by unknown sculptor – N.P.G. Print by W Doughty (1778) – N.P.G. (Archives) and British Museum. Print by J Chapman (1799) – British Museum.

Memorial

There is a memorial to Gray in Poets' Corner, Westminster Abbey. Designed to fit against the bottom of Milton's monument, it portrays the lyric muse. She sits pointing to the bust of Milton with one hand and in the other she holds a medallion portrait of Gray. (The medallion is by John Bacon.)

Memorabilia

Manuscript of "Elegy Written in a Country Churchyard" – British Museum. In St Michael's Church, Cornhill, EC3 (next door to Gray's birthplace), where Gray was baptised, there used to be on display a silver-topped walking-stick which once belonged to the poet. It was stolen a few years ago and has not yet been recovered.

Radclyffe Hall

(12 August 1880 – 7 October 1943)

Marguerite Radclyffe-Hall was born in Bournemouth, the daughter of Radclyffe Radclyffe-Hall, a wealthy playboy, and his wife, Mary Sager. As a child she was known as known as "Peter", but later she called herself "John", probably after her great-grandfather whom she strongly resembled and whose portrait she inherited. Her parents were divorced when she was three and she was brought up in London by her mother, stepfather and maternal grandmother. She seldom saw her father again.

She was educated at home by governesses and then studied for a year at King's College, London. When she was twenty-one she inherited her grandfather's fortune (her father having died in 1898) and was at last able to leave the family home which "had neither dignity nor repose, and moreover was deplorably lacking in beauty." She was never close to her mother whose callousness and emotional coldness is portrayed in the character of Lady Anna Gordon in *The Well of Loneliness.*

John moved into a house in Kensington. She also bought a house in the Malvern Hills and joined the local hunt. Between 1906 and 1915 she published five volumes of poetry, mostly about "that potent passion, that divine desire" which she felt for women. Several of her verses were set to music, some by Coleridge Taylor. Her most famous song was "The Blind Ploughman", with music by Coningsby Clarke.

The success of her poems brought John, in 1907, to the attention of Mabel Batten ("Ladye"), a social beauty and talented amateur soprano, who, it was rumoured, had had an affair with Edward VII before he became king. Ladye was fifty when she first met John, and was married with a grown-up daughter. They fell in love and, after Ladye's husband died, set up home together. Ladye was a Catholic convert and in 1912 John was also received into the Church. They then visited Rome and were granted an audience with the Pope.

In 1915 John fell in love with Ladye's cousin Una Troubridge (1887–1963), a sculptor who was married to an admiral and had a young daughter. Ladye died a year later and was laid to rest in the imposing catacomb vault that John had purchased in Highgate Cemetery. In 1917 John and Una began living together. Despite the fact that they were both Catholics, they turned to spiritualism. They attended seances in order to communicate with Ladye, and joined the Society for Psychical Research. In 1920 John brought a slander action against St George Fox-Pitt, a member of the Society, who had described her as "a grossly immoral woman" and accused her of causing the break-up of the Troubridges' marriage. John won the case and was awarded £500 damages.

In the 1920s John began writing novels, under the name "Radclyffe Hall". *Adam's Breed,* published in 1926, was the only novel, apart from E M Forster's *A Passage to India,* to be awarded both the Prix Femina and the James Tait Black Memorial Prize. Encouraged by the success of *Adam's Breed,* John wrote *The Well of Loneliness,* her pioneering and largely autobiographical "lesbian novel" which caused such a storm of hysterical homophobia. James Douglas, the editor of the *Sunday Express,* declared in a front-page article, "I would rather give a healthy boy or a healthy girl a phial of prussic acid than this novel. Poison kills the body, but moral poison kills the soul."

The book was banned in Britain, but John's publisher, Jonathan Cape, sent the typemoulds to Paris, where the Pegasus Press published it. Copies were sent all over the world – including Britain, where consignments were intercepted by the Customs, and Leonard Hill's bookshop in Great Russell Street was raided by the police. Hill was Pegasus's English distributor, and he and Cape were summonsed to show why the seized books should not be destroyed.

The defence solicitors tried to gather support for the book from leading intellectuals, and many, including Forster, Virginia Woolf and Laurence Housman, agreed to appear in court as defence witnesses. However, the magistrate disallowed evidence as to the book's merit. It was ruled an "obscene libel" and suppressed.

The Well of Loneliness continued to be a bestseller in Paris and many copies were smuggled across the Channel. As John had said after the trial, "The end is only the beginning." In America, where it had been judged not guilty of obscenity, its sales were enormous. It was translated into eleven languages and sold more than a million copies during its author's lifetime.

John wrote three more novels after *The Well* but never repeated her earlier success. She bought a house in Rye, and she and Una spent long holidays on the Continent, visiting old friends such as Naomi Jacob in Italy and Natalie Barney, Romaine Brooks and Colette in Paris. (Una was the first to translate Colette's work into English.) There was trouble when John became infatuated with a mercenary Russian nurse Evguenia Souline, but her relationship with Una survived and they stayed together to the end.

John died of cancer after a long painful illness. Her last work was a letter to Una which ended, "God keep you until we meet again. . . and believe in my love, which is much, much stronger than mere death." Her coffin was placed next to Ladye's in the vault at Highgate. On the coffin plate Una had engraved

". . .and if God choose
I shall but love thee better
after death",

a quotation from one of Elizabeth Browning's "Sonnets from the Portuguese". The same words are written, between the names Radclyffe Hall and Una, on the marble plaque which Una put up in the doorway to the vault.

When Una died twenty years later she was buried in the English Cemetery in Rome, despite her wish to be interred with John and Ladye. On her coffin was inscribed "Una Vincenzo Troubridge, the friend of Radclyffe Hall".

Addresses

★*14 Addison Road, W14* – she lived here 1890–1901.

★*Kensington Church Street, W8* – her first home of her own (1901–c1907) was in this street.

★*Carriage Road (formerly Albert Gate), SW1* – site of her home c1907–09.

★*7 Shelley Court, 56 (formerly 38–40) Tite Street, SW3* – she lived here 1909–11.

★*59 Cadogan Square, SW1* – her home 1911–15.

★*1 Swan Walk, SW3* – she lived here in 1916.

★*22 Cadogan Court, Draycott Avenue, SW3* – her home 1916–18.

★*7 Trevor Square, SW7* – her first London home with Una Troubridge 1920–21.

★*10 Sterling Street, SW7* – they lived here 1921–24.

★*37 Holland Street, W8* – their home 1924–29. (Most of *The Well of Loneliness* was written here.)

37 Holland Street, W8

★*Kensington Palace Mansions (now part of the Kensington Palace Hotel), De Vere Gardens, W8* – they stayed here in 1924 and again in 1928.

★*17 Talbot House, St Martin's Lane, WC2* – site of their home 1933–35.

★*502 Hood House, Dolphin Square, SW1* – their home in 1943. (Radclyffe Hall died here.)

Works include

Poetry: *Twixt Earth and Stars* (1906); *Songs of Three Counties, and Other Poems* (1913).

Novels: *The Forge* (1924); *The Unlit Lamp* (1924); *A Saturday Life* (1925); *Adam's Breed* (1926); *The Well of Loneliness* (1928); *The Master of the House* (1932); *Miss Ogilvy Finds Herself* (1934); *The Sixth Beatitude* (1936).

Portraits

Canvas by Charles Buchel (1918) – bequeathed by Una to National Portrait Gallery. Photograph of Radclyffe Hall in her Chinese silk smoking jacket – N.P.G. Photograph by Howard Coster (1932) – N.P.G.

Portrait on p. 94.

Fictional portraits

She appears as Lady Buck-and-Balk in *The Ladies Almanack* (1928) by Djuna Barnes, and as Hermina de Randan in *Extraordinary Women* (1928) by Compton Mackenzie.

Radclyffe Hall

John Gray

94

Lord John Hervey

Cicely Hamilton

95

Cicely Hamilton

(1872 – 6 December 1952)

Cicely Hamilton made it her life's work to prove that not only was spinsterhood, which she termed "single blessedness", a natural condition, but that the improvement of the position of women as a whole had been effected particularly through the efforts of women who chose to be single.

She was born Cicely Mary Hammill, but adopted the name of Hamilton when she began her stage career and retained it afterwards. She and her sister and brothers spent much of their early lives being "farmed out" while their mother accompanied their father, the commander of a Highland regiment, on army service abroad. The red-headed, freckle-faced Cicely's happiest times in her childhood were spent with her two unmarried aunts, Lucy and Amy, in Bournemouth.

Acting was an early interest with Cicely and was one of the few real enjoyments of her life at boarding school in Malvern. At the age of sixteen she was sent to a school in Bad Homburg for a couple of years, where her tuition fees were paid in part by her helping the other girls with English conversation.

Cicely's family had been impoverished for many years and when her father died in 1890 she and her sister and the older of her brothers had to start to earn their own living. After "struggling distastefully" for a few terms as a pupil-teacher at a school in the Midlands, Cicely decided that she was not cut out for a career in teaching. On the strength of a few pounds she had saved she ventured up to London and took a room in Chelsea, which she shared with her sister.

In order to support herself while she did the rounds of casting agencies and auditions she did German translating work, wrote short stories and verse for magazines and took a small reporting job. Finally, she got a character part in a touring production and entered on a life on the provincial stage which was to last over ten years. Melodramas were the stock-in-trade of the companies she toured with and she relished playing the role of the "heavy" in which she was usually cast, but the poor work conditions and the realisation that she was not really making a sound career for herself as an actress led her to leave the stage and resume writing for a living.

Her ambition was to write a good play and the sale of a one-act work, which was performed as a curtain-raiser in 1906, gave her encouragement. In between writing pot-boilers about the dastardly deeds of bandits and the improbable escapes of clean-cut detectives from fiendishly-laid traps, she wrote a full-length comedy, *Diana of Dobsons*. She precipitately sold the rights of the play for £100 when it could have earned her thousands in royalties, but the play's success opened new doors for her as a writer and, as a result of the commissions she received, "joy of joys, I could bid adieu to my weekly bandits and detectives." She was also able to take an extensive holiday trip abroad with her sister and indulge her fondness for cycling and walking tours.

It was at about this time that Cicely was drawn into the suffrage movement. "My revolt was feminist rather than suffragist," she wrote in her memoirs. "What I rebelled at chiefly was. . .the identification of success with marriage, of failure with spinsterhood, the artificial concentration of the hopes of girlhood on sexual attraction and maternity. . ." She was a member of the Women's Social and Political Union for a short while, but she disliked the militant suffragettes' emotionalism, their emphasis on conventional femininity and their leaders' autocratic ways, and so left it to join the Women's Freedom League, which she perceived as being more democratic. In the Women Writers' Suffrage League, which she helped to found, she was happiest, since her lesbianism and wicked sense of humour were appreciated by her fellow members, especially her friends Edith Craig and Christopher St John. (Cicely and Edith were also involved in the Actresses' Franchise League.)

The suffrage movement brought her back to the stage – "my first and most glamorous love" – through such plays as *A Pageant of Great Women,* which she wrote for the suffrage exhibition of 1910, and *How the Vote was Won,* about a general strike of women, written in collaboration with Christopher St John. Another essay in collaboration, which led to a valued friendship being formed, was writing the words for Ethel Smyth's *March of the Women.*

Cicely's first professional London engagement came about through Lillah McCarthy's seeing her perform in *A Pageant of Great Women* and recommending her for the role of

Mrs Knox in *Fanny's First Play* by Shaw.

During the First World War she served as an administrator in a Scottish Women's Hospitals unit in France. Eyebrows were raised at her substituting for the uniform she so disliked a French workman's blouse, trousers and boots. Later in the war she joined an entertainment group "Concerts at the Front".

After the war she continued her interest in feminist issues as a founding contributor to the influential journal *Time and Tide*. Her career as a freelance journalist subsidised the writing of a succession of plays and books, many of which were concerned with finding an explanation for the growth of "the aggressive instinct" and of what she termed "irresponsible democracy".

She was an active member of the Open Door Council, an organisation which strove to improve the economic and legal position of women. Voluntary motherhood was another cause which she championed vigorously in her later years, emphasising the need for improved facilities not only for contraception but also for abortion. "If I have a bee in my bonnet," she wrote, "that insect is birth-control."

Perhaps Cicely Hamilton's most important and longlasting contribution was her influential book *Marriage as a Trade* (1909), in which she very convincingly argued, with wit and ridicule, that romantic love is the means by which men secure the subjection of women to a secondary existence of economic and political dependency. She maintained that the single woman "is a witness. . .to the unpalatable fact that sexual intercourse is not for every woman an absolute necessity," and that the "spinster", far from being the pitiable "unchosen", was generally a woman who had chosen to be seen as independent of men, economically, psychologically and sexually.

Although her friends counted for a good deal in her life, Cicely preferred to live alone, with just her cats and her housekeeper for company.

44 Glebe Place, SW3

was Won (1909) – with Christopher St John; *The Pot and the Kettle* (?1910) – with Christopher St John; *A Pageant of Great Women* (1910); *Just to Get Married* (1911); *Jack and Jill and a Friend* (1911); *A Matter of Money* (1913); *The Brave and the Fair* (1920); *The Old Adam* (1925).

Books: *Marriage as a Trade* (1909; reprinted 1981); *Senlis* (1917); *William – an Englishman* (1919) – won the first Femina-Vie Heureuse Prize; *Theodore Savage* (1922; republished 1928 as *Lest Ye Die*); *The Old Vic* (1926) – with Lilian Baylis; *Fullstop* (1931); Series: *Modern Italy/Germanies/France/Russia/Austria/Ireland/Scotland/England/Sweden* (1931–39); *Lament for Democracy* (1940); *Holland Today* (1950).

Memoirs: *Life Errant* (1935).

Lyrics: She wrote the words for Ethel Smyth's composition "March of the Women" (1911).

Addresses

★*Lancaster Terrace (formerly 15 Sussex Gardens), W2* – Maitland Court stands on the *site* of her birthplace.

★*44 Glebe Place, SW3* – her home 1915–52. (She died here.)

Portraits

Photograph by Lena Connell – National Portrait Gallery. Photographs by Lena Connell and by unknown photographers – Fawcett Library. *Portrait on p. 95.*

Works include

Plays: *Diana of Dobsons* (1908); *How the Vote*

Memorabilia

Several autograph letters – Fawcett Library.

Jane Harrison

(9 September 1850 – 16 April 1928)

Jane Harrison described herself as being "a worshipper at the Temple of Learning". Of her life's work as a classical scholar researching the development of the Greek religion, she wrote: "It is the ritual which absorbs me, the darker and older shapes behind"; and it is largely under her influence that later scholars have come to recognise that the Olympian gods are relatively late and predominantly literary figures.

Jane Ellen Harrison was born at Cottingham, Yorkshire. Shortly after Jane's birth her mother died. One of the governesses to whom her father entrusted her education learned to read Latin, Greek, German and a little Hebrew with Jane; another, a strict Evangelical concerned chiefly with the children's religious education, became in 1855 her stepmother. Fortunately, Jane's father recognised her exceptional talent and intelligence, and he indulged her passion for education.

When she was seventeen Jane was sent to be "finished" at Cheltenham College for Ladies, under Dorothea Beale. Chiefly through determinedly "studying what *I like*", she obtained honours in the London University examination for women in 1870 and won a scholarship to Cambridge. Between 1874 and 1879 she read Classics at Newnham College. This was the turning-point of her life: her chosen career as a scholar would enable her to escape enforced domesticity and would satisfy her *"scientiae sacra fames"* (holy hunger for learning). She had by this time rejected the narrow religious views of her stepmother, and for most of her life she would describe herself as "a cheerful agnostic". In the Classical Tripos of 1879 she was placed at the head of the second class, the highest place taken hitherto by either of the new women's colleges. From then on she was often called "the cleverest woman in England".

It was perhaps inevitable that Jane, with her love of Ancient Greece, should adopt the tight-fitting olive-green serge dress of the Aesthetic vogue and, with her hair always coiled in a Grecian knot, retain this throughout her life as her "costume for all occasions".

Similarly, the epithets which attached themselves to this willowy, blonde woman with "laughter and delight filling her inner spirit" contained classical allusions; her favourite soubriquets were "Lady Themis" and "Potnia Keron" – "The Lady of the Sprites".

Jane moved to London in 1879 to study archaeology at the British Museum. For a time she lectured on Greek art and in 1882 she published her first book, *Myths of the Odyssey in Art and Literature*. During her three trips to Greece, her studies of Dörpfeld's topographcial views of Athens, and the writing of two works on the mythology and monuments of that city, she discovered that Greek religion and its origins was her main interest.

She served as Vice-President of the Hellenic Society from 1889 to 1896, in which year she was made a corresponding member of the influential Berlin Classical Archaeological Institute.

In 1898 she returned to Newnham College and accepted the offer of the college's first Research Fellowship and a position as resident lecturer in classical archaeology. With F M Cornford and Gilbert Murray she furthered a new movement in classical studies, turning from the criticism of texts to studies informed by the disciplines of philosophy, archaeology and anthropology. She was sometimes criticised for being almost too "resonant" – her favourite description of the mind that absorbs from every source – but this was, in fact, one of her greatest qualities as a scholar and as a teacher.

Jane's infectious enthusiasm for her subject and her wit and charm won her many young friends. One of her brightest pupils, the writer Hope Mirrlees (1887–1978), became her closest friend and, from the First World War until Jane's death, her constant companion. In her *Reminiscences* Jane paid tribute to the love and friendship of Hope: "I admit, Fate has been very kind to me. In my old age she has sent me a ghostly daughter dearer than any child of the flesh. . ."

The war caused Jane, as she said, "to fly from Greece and seek sanctuary in other languages and civilisations. . . bringing with them no bitter tang of remembrance." In 1915 she and Hope went to Paris to study Russian, on which she lectured after her return to Newnham College in 1917. According to one of her friends, "learning languages was the only game she found worth playing." Spanish, Swedish, Persian and Hebrew were the other languages which she studied in her later years.

Jane retired from lecturing in 1922 and left Cambridge in order "to see things more freely and more widely". She and Hope settled in "a tiny mousetrap of a house" in Bloomsbury.

"Learning and friendship," Jane wrote, "are the crowning glories of my life." She and Hope included among their friends Virginia and Leonard Woolf (who described Jane as being "one of the most civilised persons I have ever known"); Dorothy Bussy, who thought Hope, of whom she was fond, "a curious young woman with a passionate and complicated inner life"; and Lady Ottoline Morrell.

Jane declared that old age was a good and pleasant thing and that "life does not cease when you are old: it only suffers a rich change. You go on falling in love – only you fall so gently." Having played her part in a life of learning, she was "more than content to sit down and watch". She constantly asserted that Hope kept her young, and she never tired of sitting and watching Hope demonstrating the latest dance steps, trying on her collection of dangling pendant earrings (which Virginia Woolf thought so vulgar), painting her eyelids with kohl, or playing with their dogs.

Address

★ *11 Mecklenburgh Street, WC1* – the building numbered 34 Mecklenburgh Square stands on the *site* of the "tiny mousetrap of a house" where Jane lived with Hope from 1926 until her death.

Works include

Prolegomena to the Study of Greek Religion (1903); *Themis: A Study in the Social Origins of Greek Religion* (1912); *Epilegomena to the Study of Greek Religion* (1921); *Reminiscences of a Student's Life* (1925).

Translations (with Hope Mirrlees): *The Book of the Bear* (1926) – a series of translations from the Russian; *Life of the Arch-Priest Avvakum, by himself* (1926) – a translation of the classic 17th century Russian novel.

Portrait

Pencil drawing by Theo van Rysselberghe (1925) – National Portrait Gallery.

Fictional portrait

J– H– in *A Room of One's Own* (1928) by Virginia Woolf is Jane Harrison.

Lord John Hervey

(15 October 1696 – 5 August 1743)

John Hervey's effeminacy led his contemporaries to conclude that the world was peopled with "men, women and Herveys". Historians remember him for his political pamphlets and his cool, cynical account of the morals and manners of the court of George II in his *Memoirs*. For students of literature he is the man satirised by Pope as "Lord Fanny" and "Sporus", ". . .this Bug with gilded wings/ This painted Child of Dirt, that stinks and sings. . ."

He was born at Ickworth, Suffolk, the eldest son of the 1st Earl of Bristol, and was educated at Westminster School and Clare Hall, Cambridge.

In 1716, a year after graduating from Cambridge, Hervey made the Grand Tour of Europe. On his return to England he spent some time at the family home in "the perpetual pursuit of poetry", and then began visiting the court of the Prince and Princess at Richmond. His marriage, in 1720, to Mary ("Molly") Lepell was politically useful, as his wife was a maid of honour to Princess (later Queen) Caroline.

Hervey was elected Member of Parliament for Bury St Edmunds in 1725 and, although he was not a politician of any great originality, he was, being an influential favourite of Queen Caroline, a most effective aide to the Prime Minister, Sir Robert Walpole. He became the chief intermediary between Walpole and the Queen, upon whose confidence the Prime Minister depended to rule the less politically astute George II. (Hervey had been a follower of Sir William Pulteney, Walpole's rival within the Whig party, but changed his allegiance when George II adopted Walpole as his Minister.)

His services in keeping the Queen amused and entertained were rewarded by George II's increasing his salary by £1,000; and in 1730 Walpole showed his gratitude for the support which Hervey gave him in his many excellent pamphlets and speeches for the Ministry by securing his appointment as a Privy Councillor and as Vice-Chamberlain of the Royal Household.

The grand passion of Hervey's life was Stephen Fox (1704–76), a good-looking and wealthy Tory Member of Parliament. Hervey began visiting Fox at his estate at Redlinch, in Somerset, and they spent two months together in Bath. He addressed Fox as "Thou dearest youth, who taught me first to know / What pleasures from a real friendship flow. . ."

Throughout his life Hervey suffered from ill health. (He was an epileptic and, at least once, contracted a venereal disease, but his father ascribed the poor state of his health to Hervey's use of "that detestable and poisonous plant, tea".) Fox suggested that they should go abroad, for the sake of Hervey's health. According to Hervey, Fox offered "to go with me to any part of the world, and for as long as I please". They left England early in 1728 and spent eighteen months in Italy. During Hervey's bouts of illness there Fox nursed him day and night.

Hervey and Fox were both delicate, slightly-built men. Fox, however, was more the country squire in behaviour and dress, and felt that, compared with his flamboyantly attired, intelligent and witty courtier friend, he probably seemed dull and lacking in charm. Hervey reassured Fox, saying that he preferred him "rusty [sc. rustic] than anybody polished". (For his part, Hervey was described by the Duchess of Marlborough as having "a painted face and not a tooth in his head".)

His appointment to the Royal Household required Hervey to spend much of his time at Windsor. "I can't live without you," he wrote to Fox. "Choice, taste, habit, prejudice, inclination, reason – everything that either does or ought to influence one's thoughts or one's actions makes mine centre in and depend upon you." Fox visited Hervey often at Windsor, usually on his way home to Somerset. After one of their meetings Hervey wrote, "The tears came into my eyes a hundred times between Windsor and London, with reflecting we were now to be divided for a longer time than ever we had been asunder before since our first acquaintance." He wrote to Fox, after another of his visits, "You have left some such remembrancers behind you that I assure you . . . you are not in least danger of being forgotten. The favours I have received at your Honour's hands are of such a nature that they are written . . . in such lasting characters upon every limb that 'tis impossible for me to look on a leg or an arm without having my memory refreshed."

Hervey's wife, the mother of his eight children, remained on good terms with him throughout his relationship with Fox, whom she liked and depended upon for news of her husband, and, apparently, she raised no objection to Hervey's setting up a home for Fox near his quarters at St James's Palace. ("I have made it impossible for me to live without you," wrote Hervey to Fox.)

This setting up of a joint home by the friends, however, further outraged Pulteney, who believed Hervey to have been the author of a pamphlet in which he was attacked. He wrote, "There is a certain unnatural reigning vice, indecent and almost shocking to mention." After an exchange of pamphlets, in 1731, Hervey and Pulteney fought a duel, in which they both sustained injuries.

In 1733 Hervey succeeded as Baron Hervey and entered the House of Lords, where he was one of the most able advocates of Walpole's policies. He became Lord Privy Seal in 1740 and, before being dismissed from his office after the fall of Walpole's administration in 1742, he arranged for Fox to be appointed Joint Secretary of the Treasury and to receive a peerage. (He had helped Fox in his marriage plans in 1736 and had given him the house near Green Park which was their home.)

Count Francesco Algarotti (1712–64), who was visiting England to do research for a book on Newton's philosophy, became Fox's successor in Hervey's love. To Algarotti, the "Swan of Padua", Hervey wrote, "If you can stay or if you go, do not forget me, mon cher: I shall never forget you all my life."

Hervey spent the remaining months of his life completing his *Memoirs*, exchanging letters and gossip with his old friend Lady Mary Wortley Montagu, and proving himself an active member of the opposition in the House of Lords, where he had retained his seat. He died at his family home at Ickworth and is buried there.

Addresses

★*31 Old Burlington Street, (formerly Great Burlington Street), W1* – Hervey held the lease of the house from 1725–30 and then assigned it to Stephen Fox, who lived there until his death in 1776. In December 1731 Hervey wrote to Fox, concerning the redecoration of the house, "It is quite finished and looks the smuggest, sprucest, cheerfulest thing I ever saw. Nothing can improve it but a piece of moveable goods, which I expect home with more impatience than I can tell you."

★*(6 St James's Square, SW1* – contrary to information given in several guides to London, the house which stood on this site was owned by John Hervey, Treasurer of the

31 Old Burlington Street, W1

Household to Queen Catherine of Braganza, in 1677, and not by John Hervey, Baron Hervey of Ickworth, who was born nineteen years after this date.)

Works include

Memoirs (which appeared as *Memoirs of the Reign of George the Second* in 1884; complete work in 3 volumes edited by R Sedgwick, 1931, revised edition, 1952).

Poems, letters and pamphlets.

Portrait

Canvas, full length, by studio of J B van Loo (c1740–41) – National Portrait Gallery.

Portrait on p. 95.

Fictional portraits

He is portrayed as Lord Fanny in Alexander Pope's *Miscellanies* (1727–28) and *The Dunciad* (1728), and as Sporus in Pope's *Epistle to Dr Arbuthnot* (1735).

Memorabilia

Autograph letters from Hervey to Stephen Fox – British Museum.

Harriet Hosmer

(9 October 1830 – 21 February 1908)

Harriet Goodhue Hosmer, the most famous woman sculptor of her day, was renowned also for her genius for friendship. Henry James wrote of her that she "was, above all, a character, strong, fresh and interesting, destined, whatever statues she made, to make friends that were better still even than these at their best."

She was born at Watertown, Massachusetts. Her mother, brother and sisters died while she was a child, and to strengthen Harriet her father, a physician, instituted a rigorous physical training programme for her. She became expert in skating, rowing, riding and shooting. Strong-willed and boisterous, the young "Hatty" was regarded by her neighbours and teachers as a pest and a terror.

At the age of fifteen she was sent to Mrs Sedgwick's school at Lenox in the Berkshires. There she won the friendship of her schoolmates as well as that of several older women, notably Fanny Kemble and the novelist, Catherine Maria Sedgwick. Encouraged by Fanny Kemble to do something more with her knack at clay modelling, she decided upon making sculpture her profession.

She set up a studio at home and studied drawing and modelling. As the study of anatomy was then thought an improper subject for a woman, she enlisted the help of Wayman Crow, the father of a schoolfriend, to arrange for a friend of his who taught at the medical school in St Louis to give her private lessons. (Wayman Crow later became a close friend and patron.) Finishing her studies, she took a steamboat trip, on her own, down the Mississippi. During this holiday she visited some Indians and smoked a peace pipe with them, and, on a dare, climbed a tall bluff overlooking the river. (This bluff was later given the name Mount Hosmer.)

In 1852 she was introduced to Charlotte Cushman, who had returned to her home town of Boston on a professional engagement, and Charlotte's companion, Matilda Hays. The actress supported the aspiring sculptor in her ambition of going to Rome to study, and helped her gain Dr Hosmer's consent to this.

By the end of 1852 Harriet had travelled to Rome, convinced the eminent English sculptor John Gibson that she had a passionate vocation for sculpture, and had been accepted as his only pupil and given a workroom in his studio.

The relationship which Harriet formed with Charlotte Cushman was long-lasting, and for five years she had a small apartment in the house in Rome in which Charlotte and her lover Emma Stebbins resided. The three women lived as a family, as it were, surrounded by their many friends. Sarah Jane Clarke, an American journalist whose pseudonym was "Grace Greenwood", was a particular friend of Harriet's at this time; in later years Harriet's love for Louisa Stewart-Mackenzie (Lady Ashburton) would be more than partly reciprocated. Her other friends included Elizabeth and Robert Browning, the "Clasped Hands" of whom she modelled in 1853, Anna Jameson, Frances Power Cobbe and her lover Mary Lloyd, and Frederick Leighton, who called her "the queerest, best natured little chap possible".

With the strong character and frankness which complemented her great charm, Harriet was looked on as a phenomenon of feminine independence and of unimpeachable integrity. For work, and often for leisure activities, she adopted a masculine style of dress of jacket, shirt, cravat and Zouave trousers. The forage caps and velvet berets which topped her boyish face and short curly hair earned her the nicknames "Capellina" and "Berettina".

Advanced in some measure through the association with Gibson, Harriet's reputation as a sculptor grew quickly. Her full-length marble figures such as "Oenone", the "Beatrice Cenci" and "Zenobia" were highly acclaimed, and she won the accolade for being the leader of Rome's so-called "white marmorean flock". However, it was the "fun" sculpture of Puck which brought her popular success and the beginnings of a reasonable income (particularly after the purchase of a replica of this figure by the Prince of Wales). She became financially independent in 1862, upon inheriting her father's moderate fortune. That same year she exhibited in London; two years later she exhibited in the United States.

The classical allusions in her work and her mythological subjects captured the sentiment of the age. Civic authorities commissioned works from her, and her statues and busts and her designs for fountains and gates were in great demand with Continental royalty and the British aristocracy, many of whom became both friends and patrons. (She wrote that she regarded her many decorations from European royalties as "souvenirs of friends rather than as decorations".)

She began spending every summer in Britain, visiting her friends at their castles and stately homes and executing commissioned works. In her later years much of her time was spent in England, with only occasional visits to Rome.

After 1880 Harriet's output of sculpture lessened. Her last great work was a statue of Queen Isabella, commissioned by the city of San Francisco and unveiled in 1894. She returned to the United States in about 1900 and settled in Watertown, her birthplace. There she resumed one of the favourite pursuits of her youth: inventing labour-saving gadgets for the home and machinery for the sculptor's studio. A more ambitious project, to which she devoted much time and money, was a device for effecting perpetual motion.

She died (of influenza) satisfied that she had realised most of her ambitions and had proved Fanny Kemble wrong in her prediction, made to Wayman Crow, that "Hatty's peculiarities will stand in the way of her success with people of society and the world."

Address

★*Kent House, Knightsbridge, SW1* – site of the home of Lady Ashburton. Harriet's lengthiest sojourns here were during 1867, 1873 and 1876, but she spent at least a night here during each of her visits to England. (The house stood opposite what are now the Knightsbridge Barracks.)

Works include

Bronze cast of Elizabeth Barrett Browning's right hand clasping that of her husband, Robert Browning (1853) – National Portrait Gallery.

Publications: *Harriet Hosmer: Letters and Memories* (1912) – edited by Cornelia Crow Carr.

Portraits

Photographs, engravings and lithographs – National Portrait Gallery (Archives).

Fictional portrait

She is included as one of "the loyal subjects of Her Majesty" in *The Court and Camp of Queen Marian* (attributed to Mary Boyle; published by Emily Faithfull c1868).

A E Housman

(26 March 1859 – 30 April 1936)

Alfred Edward Housman, the poet and classical scholar, was born at Catshill, near Bromsgrove, Worcestershire. He was the eldest brother of Laurence Housman, the artist and dramatist, and of Clemence Housman, the writer and wood-engraver.

While studying at St John's College, Oxford, Housman fell in love with a fellow student, Moses Jackson, who became the inspiration for many of his poems.

He failed his finals through lack of study of those parts of the syllabus which did not interest him, and was reduced, in 1882, to accepting a low-paid job as a clerk in the Patent Office in London. For three years he shared lodgings with Moses Jackson and Moses's younger brother Adalbert, but when it became clear to him that his feelings for Moses would never be reciprocated he moved out and took rooms on his own. In 1887 Moses married and went to live in India.

Housman had not written verse since his schooldays, but he now began to write poems about his lost love and about the countryside of his Worcestershire childhood. He also began to apply himself to his classical studies, and spent his evenings in the Reading Room at the British Museum.

After Moses's departure Housman became more closely involved with Adalbert Jackson. Little is known about the nature of their relationship, but when Laurence Housman was an old man he told a biographer that his brother and Adalbert had been physically attracted to each other.

In 1892 Housman was appointed a professor of Latin at University College, London. In the same year Adalbert died after contracting typhoid. Housman's grief and sense of loss is evident in the poems he wrote at this time.

His reputation as a classical scholar was already established when, in 1896, Housman published, at his own expense, *A Shropshire Lad,* a series of nostalgic poems mainly set in a half-imaginary Shropshire, and often addressed to or spoken by a farm boy or a soldier.

The inspiration for the poems came partly from his one-sided love affair with Moses Jackson and the death of Adalbert, and partly from the trial and imprisonment of Oscar Wilde which took place in the year that *A Shropshire Lad* was written. He was also affected by reports of the suicide of a young homosexual naval cadet at Woolwich.

Although his poems were not an immediate success, sales steadily mounted and they became very popular during the First World War. However, as the critic James Agate pointed out many years later, "The popularity of the most widely read modern English poet is based on a complete misunderstanding of what his poems are about."

Oscar Wilde was in prison when *A Shropshire Lad* first appeared, but Robert Ross memorised some of the poems and recited them to him when he visited him. After Wilde's release Housman sent him a copy of the poems, and shortly afterwards Wilde began writing the *Ballad of Reading Gaol.* It is possible that Wilde, whose sufferings had inspired Housman, was in turn inspired by *A Shropshire Lad* to write his greatest poem.

In 1900 Housman went on holiday to Venice, where he befriended a twenty-three year old gondolier called Andrea. Thereafter Housman visited Venice regularly for several years, and when Andrea became ill and unable to work, he provided him with a generous allowance. After Andrea's death his relatives pestered Housman to continue sending money, but he refused to have anything more to do with them.

Housman also made frequent visits to Paris where he indulged his gastronomic and sexual tastes. He made coded notes in a document found after his death which refer to a number of male prostitutes and the prices he paid for their services.

Between 1903 and 1930 he produced five volumes of his editions of the works of the Latin poet Manilius. In 1911 he was elected a Fellow of Trinity College, Cambridge. He still corresponded with Moses Jackson, whose impending death from cancer in 1922 inspired Housman's *Last Poems* which met with huge acclaim.

He lived in Trinity until his death, an aloof and rather formidable figure, though a highly respected lecturer.

Addresses

★*82 Talbot Road, W2 – site* of the house in which he had lodgings (1883–85) with Moses and Adalbert Jackson.

★*39 Northumberland Place, W2* – he lived here 1885–86.

★*17 North Road, N6*   his home 1886 1905. He wrote *A Shropshire Lad* here. (Blue *plaque* – 1969.)

Works include

A Shropshire Lad (1896); *Last Poems* (1922); *More Poems* (1936).

He also published, between 1903 and 1930, a five-volume edition of the works of the Latin poet Manilius. The first volume was dedicated to Moses Jackson.

Portraits

Chalk drawing by Sir William Rothenstein (1906)   National Portrait Gallery. Pencil drawing by Francis Dodd (1926) – N.P.G. Medallions by Theodore Spicer-Simson (c1922) – N.P.G.

Memorabila

Holograph poems – British Museum.

Alexander von Humboldt

(14 September 1769 – 6 May 1859)

Baron Friedrich Heinrich Alexander von Humboldt, scientist, explorer and geographer, was born in Berlin, the second son of a Prussian army officer. While studying law at Göttingen University he met Georg Forster, the naturalist who had accompanied Captain Cook on his second world voyage. Forster encouraged Humboldt's ardent desire, held from earliest youth, "to explore distant lands".

In 1792 Humboldt entered the Prussian Mining Service. After a year he became an Inspector of Mines and worked hard to improve conditions for the miners. He designed a safety lamp and rescue apparatus, drafted plans for a pension scheme, and set up evening classes for the miners, funded from his own pocket.

During this time Humboldt fell passionately in love with a young army officer, Reinhard von Haeften. When Haeften eventually married, Humboldt wrote him a letter filled with pain and indignation breaking off their relationship.

After his mother's death in 1797 (his father had died in 1779) Humboldt became financially independent and began planning a "great journey beyond Europe". "Even as a child," he wrote, "the sight of exotic trees, foreign maps, and descriptions of tropic zones, had been able to move me to tears. The yearning of my childhood was indeed a longing for a homeland for my soul." With his friend Aimé Bonpland (1773–1858) he went to Madrid where he was presented to the King and obtained permission to travel in Spanish America.

Humboldt and Bonpland sailed from Corunna in June 1799 and six weeks later landed at Cumana, in what is now Venezuela. Journeying on foot and by packhorse and canoe, they followed the course of the Orinoco River through uncharted jungle. They discovered the Casiquaire, the unique natural canal connecting the Orinoco with the Amazon, and set a new mountaineering altitude record with their ascent of Chimborazo – nearly 20,000 feet. As they went they sketched,

measured and recorded what they saw, and collected some 60,000 plant specimens, 6,300 of which were at that time unknown in Europe. Humboldt made maps and amassed information in the fields of magnetism, meteorology, geology, mineralogy, zoology and ethnography. But he believed that it was not enough merely to discover or collect or classify: science must serve philosophy. "Nature to me was no mere objective phenomenon, but a mirror image of the spirit of man."

In 1804 the two friends travelled to the United States. They were invited to lunch with President Jefferson and reported on their 6,000 mile journey, which has justly been called the scientific discovery of America.

They returned to Europe in August 1804 and received a heroes' welcome in Paris, Humboldt's spiritual home. He remained there for over twenty years, writing his detailed accounts of the expedition. This mammoth work of thirty-four volumes, covering a wide range of subjects, brought him enormous prestige. "Humboldt," said his friend Simon Bolivar, "has done more good for America than all her conquerors."

Lack of money forced Humboldt in 1827 to return to Berlin, where he was appointed Court Chamberlain. Two years later he led an expedition through central Asia and Siberia. In 1830 he went back to Paris on a diplomatic mission.

Besides his extensive literary, scientific and court activities, Humboldt also worked tirelessly for humanitarian causes. He was responsible for anti-slavery legislation in Prussia, and spoke out against anti-semitism and racism.

He had a lasting relationship with the French scientists Joseph Gay-Lussac and François Arago, the latter being the great love of his life, and to many young men, who regarded themselves as "his children", he gave help and financial support.

Humboldt spent his last years working on his masterwork, *Cosmos,* in which he described and illustrated all that was known about the Earth and the universe. Although he was famous, and revered as the grand old man of European science, and had honours showered upon him, he was, towards the end of his life, desperately poor. His travels had been costly and he earned little from his writings.

He died in Berlin while working on the fifth volume of *Cosmos.*

A. Krausse sc.

Address

★*17 Portland Place, W1* – he stayed here in 1817 and 1818. (It was the home of his brother Wilhelm, the Prussian Ambassador.)

Works include

The Voyages of Humboldt and Bonpland (34 vols) (1805–34); *Views of Nature* (1808); *Personal Narrative of Travels to the Equinoctial Regions* (1814); *Cosmos* (5 vols) (1845–62).

Portraits

Engravings and prints – National Portrait Gallery (Archives).

Memorials

Over 2,000 places, mountains, rivers, ocean currents (and even a crater on the moon) are named after him. He gave a qualitative explanation for the amplification of sound at night, and this became known as the "Humboldt Effect".

George Ives

(1867 – 4 June 1950)

George Cecil Ives was born in Germany, the illegitimate son of an English army officer and a Spanish baroness. He was brought up by his grandmother, partly in the south of France and partly at the family home at Bentworth in Hampshire.

While an undergraduate at Magdalene College, Cambridge, Ives began his lifelong practice of pasting newspaper cuttings into scrapbooks. The thousands of cuttings, which eventually filled forty-five scrapbooks, cover a wide range of topics, including crime and punishment (he was an active campaigner for prison reform and for the rehabilitation of released prisoners), transvestism, and everything to do with homosexuality.

He was particularly obsessed by the injustice and oppression suffered by homosexuals, whom he believed to be a superior, high-born species. In 1897 he founded a secret homosexual society which he called the Order of Chaeronea. Its name derived from the battle of Chaeronea in 338 BC, when the Sacred Band of Thebans, a highly trained force of three hundred young men bound together by ties of friendship and love, held their position and were slaughtered by the cavalry of Philip of Macedonia.

The Order was run on masonic lines, with its own regalia and ceremonial and a complicated system of codes and passwords. Among its members were Laurence Housman, Charles Kains Jackson, Samuel Ellworth Cottam, Montague Summers and John Gambril Nicholson. C R Ashbee and A E Housman are also believed to have been members.

Ives was a great admirer of Edward Carpenter, and he visited him at Millthorpe in 1897. They became friends and thereafter corresponded regularly. Carpenter called on Ives several times in London.

Ives was twenty-five when he first met Oscar Wilde, whom he described as "extravagant and unreal" and worshipped as a "Superman". Wilde was attracted by Ives's handsome boyish looks. He persuaded him to shave off his moustache so that he might look more hellenic, and once kissed him passionately at the Travellers' Club. In 1894 Ives had a brief affair with Lord Alfred Douglas. He later regretted the involvement because of Douglas's disgraceful behaviour towards Wilde.

In 1914 Ives joined, or perhaps co-founded, the British Society of Sex Psychology, and delivered a series of lectures on the Graeco-Roman view of youth and on the "Plight of the Adolescent". Several members of the Society belonged also to the Order of Chaeronea and he soon recruited many more.

As he grew older Ives developed a passion for melons, and filled his house with them. When the war ended he refused to believe that hostilities had ceased, and to the end of his life he carried a gas mask in a cardboard box slung over his shoulder. He was also afraid of sleeping alone, and would go to great lengths to ensure that he had at least one bedfellow. Whenever it was necessary for him to visit his family he would arrange to stay in a hotel so that he could keep the company he desired.

Throughout his long life Ives had many lovers. He called them his "children", took care of them, gave them money and bought them houses. Often he lived with more than one young man at a time, and some of them stayed with him for many years. When he was old and dying, his "children" looked after him.

Addresses

★*7 Park Road, NW1* – his grandmother's London home. He lived here with her until 1894, and again (after her death) between 1897–98.

★*E4 The Albany, Piccadilly, W1* – he lived here 1894–97.

★*93 Park Road, NW1* – *site* of his home 1899–1905.

★*196 Adelaide Road, NW3* – *site* of his home 1906–50.

Works include

Poetry: *A Book of Chains* (1897); *Eros' Throne* (1900).

Non-fiction: *A History of Penal Methods* (1914); *The Graeco-Roman View of Youth* (1926); *Obstacles to Human Progress* (1926); *Man Bites Man*, a selection from his scrapbooks, edited by Paul Sieveking (1980).

Naomi Jacob

(1 July 1884 – 27 August 1964)

Naomi Ellington Jacob, or "Mickie" as she preferred to be called, was born in Ripon, Yorkshire. Her parents separated when she was a child. She saw very little of her father, and when her mother emigrated to the United States she was left, at the age of fifteen, to fend for herself.

She was educated at Middlesbrough High School, and for a time was a teacher in a Church of England school. Then she became the secretary and travelling companion of a music-hall artiste, Marguerite Broadfoote.

At a time when she was feeling lonely and depressed Mickie got married. She and her husband stayed together for only a few weeks. Mickie rarely mentioned the episode in later years, except to say, "That was one of the disastrous mistakes you only make once in your life."

Through most of the First World War Mickie worked as a canteen supervisor in a munitions factory in Willesden. She fell in love with Henrietta Simione ("Simmy"), a barmaid at her local pub. Within a few days of their meeting Simmy had moved into Mickie's flat, given up her job behind the bar, and joined Mickie at the factory, where she found work as a machine operator.

After the war Mickie drifted in and out of several unsatisfying jobs. She was found to be suffering from tuberculosis and had to spend six months in a sanatorium in Kent.

On her return to London she decided to try her luck on the stage. She went along to an audition and, despite her lack of acting experience or training, she was given a small part in a new West End play called Scandal. Her success in Scandal led to her being offered other roles. She appeared with Noel Coward in his play The Young Idea and played a drunken old woman in Edgar Wallace's The Ringer.

When she was taken ill and had to go into a nursing home for treatment Mickie realised that it could mean the end of her career as an actress. "Well that settles it for Jacob," she said. "She's got to become an author and the sooner she makes a real start the better." For several years she had been writing in her spare time and she had a cupboard full of half-finished manuscripts.

Her first novel, Jacob Ussher, was published in 1926. It was well received by the critics and sold well. From now on she published on average two books every year.

Mickie was advised by her doctors to spend the winter months out of England. In 1930 she went to Italy and bought a villa, which she called "Casa Mickie", at Sirmione on the shores of Lake Garda. Her books were beginning to earn her sufficient money for her to enjoy a standard of living she had never known before.

Soon she became a well-known figure in Sirmione, with her closely cropped black curly hair, collar and tie and perfectly tailored suits. Her lover, Sadie Robinson, spent several months of the year with her at "Casa Mickie" and the rest of the year in England with her husband and child.

Mickie's mother, newly returned from America, came to visit. So did Simmy and many other friends including Radclyffe Hall, who wrote of Mickie, "She smokes all day and sometimes drinks a great deal of red wine but never gets drunk. She is funny – a really remarkable mimic, and tells very coarse stories."

In 1941 Mickie returned to the London stage, playing the mother of a troupe of acrobats in Margery Sharp's comedy The Nutmeg Tree and the bawdy nurse in Love for Love by Congreve. For the remainder of the war she worked as a welfare officer on tour with ENSA.

When the war ended Mickie went back to live in Italy. Every spring she visited England to meet old friends and to broadcast on "Woman's Hour".

She died at Casa Mickie shortly after her eightieth birthday, and was buried in the little cemetery in Sirmione.

Addresses

★*Chapel Street, NW1* – she lived here c1909–c1914. (*Site.*)

★*126 Harrow Road, W2* – she and Simmy lived here c1918–c1930. (*Site.*)

★*29 Alma Square, NW8* – she lived here in 1930.

★*49 Grosvenor Square, W1 (formerly the Sesame Club).* She stayed here on her annual visits to London c1931–64.

Works include

Jacob Ussher (1926); *Rock and Sand* (1929); *Young Emmanuel* (1932); *Four Generations* (1934); *The Lenient God* (1937); *This Porcelain Clay* (1939); *They Left the Land* (1940).

She also wrote several books of reminiscences – the "Me" books.

Portrait

Photograph (unknown photographer) – National Portrait Gallery (Archives).

Memorabilia

Several autograph letters – Fawcett Library.

Anna Jameson

(19 May 1794 – 17 March 1860)

Anna Jameson is sometimes referred to as "the mother of art criticism". Her works helped create and reflect the taste of the Victorian era, in both Britain and the United States. She also deserves a place in the history of the women's movement in England.

She was born in Dublin, the eldest of five daughters of D Brownell Murphy, a painter of miniatures. The family came to England at the end of the 1790s, and lived for a time in Hanwell and then in the vicinity of Pall Mall.

At the age of ten, having received only a basic education herself, Anna took on the task of educating her sisters. She began her fifteen-year career as a governess when she was sixteen years old. A tour of the Continent, in the early 1820s, accompanying the family for whom she worked, provided her with a taste for travel and for the sights and art treasures of Europe. It also served as inspiration and material for her first book, *Diary of an Ennuyé* (1826), which was a popular success, with a chiefly female readership.

Anna was a short, plump woman with red hair. She was proud of her light, soft voice, her small, white hands, and her skill as a guitarist. Aware of her reputation for garrulousness, she nicknamed herself "Lady Blarney".

She married Robert Jameson, a barrister, when she was thirty. This marriage, which was unhappy from the start (and which, according to Anna's mother, was never consummated), was probably entered into to satisfy convention and deflect attention from their sexuality. Furthermore, single-person status would have hampered the careers of both partners. Robert Jameson held several posts overseas before his appointment as Vice-Chancellor of Upper Canada. Anna did not accompany him, but remained in London and set about establishing herself as a serious writer.

In 1833 she went to Germany, where she met Ottilie von Goethe, daughter-in-law of the poet. An association with the name of Goethe may have provided the initial interest for Anna, but before long she was in love with Ottilie.

Ottilie's reckless love affairs with men provided Anna with ample opportunity for "bossing", as she termed her well-known enthusiasm for looking after, whilst attempting to organise the lives of, those she loved. They also provided her with passionate experiences by proxy, since she was probably too conventional to enter into any kind of "illicit" relationship herself.

Anna was, nevertheless, very assertive in her friendships with women: her persistence in courting the friendship of Fanny Kemble caused the actress much embarrassment and Fanny's mother to observe that her "invitations were so frequent and importunate as to threaten the rules of decorum".

In 1836 she joined her husband in Canada at his request. There her direct manner and independence shocked her provincial neighbours, but her daring and courage in the canoeing and exploring trips which she undertook gained her the admiration of the Indians, whom she visited with a view to writing about them. (She later told friends that these Indians had named her "The Woman of Bright Foam").

She returned to London in 1838 with Robert Jameson's agreement to a formal separation. Another positive consequence of the trip was the publication of *Winter Studies and Summer Rambles in Canada* later that year.

Although she sometimes used marital unhappiness as a means of getting sympathy, Anna assured her closest friends that their friendship and the satisfaction of having a successful literary career afforded her more fulfilment than she imagined married life could.

Among her many friends were Elizabeth Barrett and Robert Browning (whom she and her niece, Gerardine, accompanied on the Paris-to-Pisa stage of their elopement), Sarah Austin (a translator of Goethe), Caroline Kindersley, Catherine Maria Sedgwick, Jane Welsh Carlyle, and especially, Lady Noel Byron. (The loss of Lady Byron's friendship was one of the most painful blows of Anna's life.)

She also made the acquaintance of other brilliant and independent women, such as Harriet St Leger, Joanna Baillie, Elizabeth Blackwell and Geraldine Jewsbury.

In 1841 Anna began work on the series of publications on the history, appreciation and interpretation of art, for which she is now chiefly remembered: several essays on art criticism and her major work, *Sacred and Legendary Art*. She visited Italy and Germany several times to obtain material for these works and to visit Ottilie von Goethe. (A competent engraver, Anna provided the illustrations for these and other of her publications.)

From the beginning of her career Anna had made pleas in her work for reforms and opportunities for women. As she gained confidence and security from her position as a popular and respected writer, her cautious and oblique treatment of the issue of women's rights gave way to forthright and passionate lectures. Her championing of the cause in her lectures *Sisters of Charity* (1855) and *The Community of Labour* (1856) caused a sensation in London.

Anna's most direct influence on the "rights of women" movement came in her later years through the encouragement she gave to the group of young women whom she called her "adopted nieces". They included Adelaide Procter, Barbara Bodichon and Emily Faithfull, and they used her rooms in Bruton Street as their stopping place. It was at Anna's suggestion that *The English Woman's Journal* and the Society for the Promotion of Employment for Women (of which she was a founder member) were established.

She died at her sister's home in Ealing, where she had gone to recover from a severe cold which she had caught when returning to her rooms in Conduit Street from the British Museum. She is buried in Kensal Green Cemetery.

volumes, 1832) – essays on female characters in Shakespeare's plays, dedicated to Fanny Kemble; *Winter Studies and Summer Rambles in Canada* (1838); *Companion to the Public Picture Galleries of London* (1842); *Memoirs and Essays on Art, Literature and Social Morals* (1846); *Sacred and Legendary Art* (4 volumes, 1848–60; completed after Anna Jameson's death by Lady Eastlake).

Portraits

Marble bust by John Gibson, R.A. (1862) – National Portrait Gallery. Photograph by D O Hill & R Adamson – N.P.G. Print by H Adlard (1878) – N.P.G. Print by R J Lane – N.P.G. Lithograph by H P Briggs – N.P.G. (Archives). Engraving from a miniature by her father Thomas Brownell Murphy – N.P.G. (Archives) and Victoria and Albert Museum.

Memorabilia

Autograph letter (c1841) – Fawcett Library.

Addresses

★*Uxbridge Road, Hanwell* – (her family stayed in a lodging-house here c1803 (*site*).

★*Chenies Street, WC1* – she and her husband lived in a house in this street c1825–29.

★*Cavendish Place (formerly 7 Mortimer Street), W1* – she stayed here with her sister and brother-in-law c1826.

★*51 Wimpole Street, W1* – the home of Caroline Kindersley where she stayed c1844.

★*Bruton Street, W1* – she had lodgings in a house in this street 1851–54.

★*57 Conduit Street, W1* – site of the house in which she had lodgings 1854–60.

Works include

Diary of an Ennuyé (1826); *Loves of the Poets* (1829); *Celebrated Female Sovereigns* (2 volumes, 1831); *Characteristics of Women* (2

Geraldine Jewsbury

(22 August 1812 –
23 September 1880)

The novels of Geraldine Jewsbury have not aged well. Although they contain some fine passages of gentle satire, highly imaginative recreations of 18th-century society, descriptions of working-class life in the north of England, and fascinating digressions into, for example, the rights of women, their high content of conventional melodrama is off-putting to most modern readers. Geraldine herself was, above all, a personality, a woman of strong passions and great aspirations. Thomas Carlyle said of her that she spent her life "seeking passionately for some Paradise to be gained by battle", and Lillian Faderman has described her as being a New Woman before the age of the New Woman had dawned.

Geraldine Endsor Jewsbury was born at Measham, Derbyshire. After her mother's death she was reared and educated by her sister Maria (afterwards Mrs Fletcher), who was known in her time as a writer and was a friend of the Wordsworths. When Maria married (in 1832) Geraldine took charge of the Jewsbury household; after the death of her father she acted as housekeeper for her brother until he too married in 1853.

She spent forty years of her life in Manchester, where her father worked as a cotton manufacturer, merchant and insurance agent. Proud of her housekeeping skills, she was nevertheless grateful for the outlet which writing gave her and for the company of her many friends, who were frequent visitors to the Jewsburys' succession of homes. In 1841 she met Thomas Carlyle and his wife Jane Welsh Carlyle (1801–66), and soon they were visiting her in Manchester and she them in London. (To Jane's annoyance Geraldine, whom she thought resembled "a little boy in petticoats", always "brought a good stock of cigarettos with her.") In London she attended "genteel swarries", at which she delighted the company with her faux-naïf enquiries, addressed to the hostesses, on "divers intimate matters" in a loud and memorably vibrant voice. She also visited Paris in 1848 to experience the excitement of the revolution.

She particularly enjoyed the company of women writers. The German-Jewish novelist and feminist Fanny Lewald, whom she met in 1850, she regarded as her most kindred spirit. Eliza Ashurst, a translator of George Sand's stories, was one of the many women with whom she swore everlasting friendship; another, also a translator of George Sand, was Matilda Hays, who became the lover and travelling-companion of Charlotte Cushman. Her own writing was generally well received, although some readers and reviewers expressed shock at her "indelicacy" and commented on how, in her career, she had come forward "in a right daring and in some respects a masculine spirit". As well as writing novels she worked for thirty years (from 1849 onwards) as a reviewer for the *Athenaeum,* and wrote a little for Charles Dickens's *Household Words* and for the *Westminster Review*. She also translated for Giuseppe Mazzini many of the articles which he published in English magazines. It was, however, in the thousands of letters she wrote that she expressed her concerns best. For many years she wrote fervently affectionate letters to Charlotte Cushman, whom she had met on the actress's provincial tour of 1846 and who became a visitor to her home, and she would write to Jane Welsh Carlyle virtually every day, even after she had moved to London (in 1857) at Jane's request, to be near her.

The "whirlwinds of emotion" that Geraldine was always being carried away on caused her friend much heartache, but as she often assured Jane, her eternal friendships with other women and her occasional heterosexual relationships were insignificant compared with her love for her: "You are of infinitely more worth and importance in my eyes. . .you come nearer to me." Early on in their relationship she had written, "I feel to love you more and more every day, and you will laugh, but I feel towards you much more like a lover than a female friend," and, "I love you more than anything else in the world. . .It may do you no good now, but it may be a comfort some time. It will always be there for you."

The love between Geraldine and Jane was reinforced by their striving to attain a state of womanhood denied them by Victorian society. That the world would be radically altered by the efforts of women of the intellectual calibre of herself and Jane, Geraldine was certain. She wrote of her vision in a letter to Jane in 1849: "I believe we are touching on better days, when women will have a genuine, normal life of their own to lead. There, perhaps, will not be so many marriages, and women will be taught not to feel their destiny manqué if they remain single. They will be able to be friends and companions in a way that they cannot be now. . .We are indications of a development of womanhood which is as yet not recognised . . . There are women to come after us, who will approach nearer the fulness of the measure of the stature of a woman's nature." She maintained also that the love and encouragement which she and Jane provided for each other would sustain them while they awaited the coming of this new age.

For twenty-five years their love continued, although the relationship was often stormy. "It is beyond your power to vex or estrange me permanently," Geraldine wrote. "As long as you are in this world the tie exists with a strength that has been proved." When Jane died it was to Geraldine, about whom he had so often been condescending, that Thomas Carlyle turned for sympathy, recognising that her grief was akin to his own.

In her distress over Jane's death Geraldine could no longer summon up the energy or interest for writing novels, although she continued to do a little writing for literary periodicals. She moved to Sevenoaks, Kent, where she lived quietly, like one of the many wise and beneficent spinsters in her novels. Her friends' children remembered her as a kind and humorous woman who wore enormous hats with plumes, black-tinted spectacles (for her eyesight was failing) and earrings in the shape of parrots which dangled as she talked.

The last months of her life were spent in a private hospital in Paddington, where she died of cancer. One of her last acts was to destroy Jane's letters to her, as her friend had instructed.

Geraldine had been a great favourite of the salon hostess and woman of letters Sydney Owenson, Lady Morgan, and had helped to edit her memoirs. She is buried in Lady Morgan's vault, near the Fulham Gate, in Brompton Cemetery.

Addresses

★*Charlotte Street, W1* – she stayed here for several months in 1830 at the home of the Misses Darby, whose boarding school near Tamworth she had attended.

★*3 Oakley Street, SW3* – she had lodgings here from 1857 until 1860.

★*The Rectory, 56 Old Church Street, SW3* – the home of the Kingsleys, where Geraldine stayed for a time in 1860 when she was between homes.

★*43 Markham Square, SW3* – she had lodgings here from 1860 until c1867.

Works include

Novels: *Zoë: The History of Two Lives* (1845); *The Half-Sisters* (1848) – dedicated to Jane Welsh Carlyle (whose husband forbade her to read it); *Marian Withers* (1851); *Constance Herbert* (1855); *The Sorrows of Gentility* (1856); *Right or Wrong* (1859).

Books for Children: *The History of an Adopted Child* (1852); *Angelo, or The Pine Forest in the Alps* (1855).

She also wrote many articles on social subjects. These include: "Social Barbarisms: Hiring Servants"; "The Lower Orders" (dealing with workers' education); and "The Civilisation of the Lower Orders".

Portrait

Daguerrotype (1845) – Carlyle's House, 24 Cheyne Row, SW3.

Memorabilia

A collection of letters exchanged between her and Jane Welsh Carlyle – Carlyle's House.

Sophia Jex-Blake

(21 January 1840 – 7 January 1912)

Sophia Jex-Blake, one of the first women doctors and campaigner for the rights of women to qualify in and practise medicine in Britain, was born into a wealthy landowning family at Hastings. A bold, rebellious child, her unruliness confounded her deeply religious and respectable parents. An early clash with educational authority led to her expulsion from one of the various boarding schools to which she was sent.

Youthful high spirits gave way to the often ungovernable passionate outbursts of the adult Sophia. Although she grew more and more resolute in adversity she never lost her sense of the ridiculous; her laugh was deep and generous and her dark eyes flashed almost as often with glee as they did with fury. She was a tall and heavily-built woman with a purposeful stride. The vehemence with which she expressed an opinion or argued her case caused many of her more "polite" young friends to wince and, later, some of her supporters to fear she would alienate those they most needed to win over.

Sophia's great intelligence and her love for women were, like her "wildness", evident at an early age. She managed, after much argument, to obtain her parents' permission to live in London and attend lectures – at that time regarded as a most unladylike activity – at Queen's College. She became, within a year, mathematics tutor there and, although her father insisted that for a woman the honour of that position was enough, accepted a salary.

Sophia had written, as a teenager, "I believe I love women too much ever to love a man." Whilst at Queen's College she had a deep and passionate friendship with another strong-minded young woman, Octavia Hill, who was later a pioneer in housing reform and a co-founder of the National Trust. She lived with her for a year, until Octavia's mother, who believed Sophia to have too "vivid" a personality and questionable influence over her daughter, demanded that the friendship be broken and that Octavia order Sophia to leave the Hill home. Sophia grieved over this for the rest of her life.

After leaving Queen's College in 1861 Sophia took teaching posts in Germany and America. She became an energetic educational reformer with a strong interest in feminism.

During a visit to America in 1865 to investigate advances in female education there Sophia met, and became a life long friend of, Lucy Sewall, an early follower of Dr Elizabeth Blackwell, who had opened a dispensary for women and children in Boston. Living with Lucy Sewall and studying her work, Sophia became convinced of the need for women doctors. With the help of Elizabeth Blackwell she began studying medicine in New York. However, her father died soon afterwards and she was summoned home.

On her return to England Sophia set about writing and lobbying to force the authorities to allow women to qualify and practise as doctors in Britain. Early the following year she applied to attend classes at the medical school of the University of Edinburgh, which she and her friends had decided was the most likely school to accede to their requests. She and the small group of women who had followed her example were finally allowed to attend lectures, although separately from the men students. The women gained the support of only one or two of the professors and they experienced all kinds of difficulties. On not being permitted to complete their studies and take a degree, Sophia, with other of the women students, brought an action against the university. The action was practically gained, but on appeal the decision was reversed in 1873. Costs of £1,000 were awarded against Sophia and her supporters. Even at the women's graduation (without full medical degrees) the following year they were harassed: many of the male students shouted abuse at them and sheep were let loose in Students' Hall.

Sophia returned to London in 1874 and took a house in Bloomsbury where she founded the London School of Medicine for Women. An enthusiastic early member of staff was Dr Elizabeth Garrett Anderson, who greatly helped Sophia in her efforts to obtain the Royal Free Hospital's agreement (gained in 1877) to accept students from the new school for clinical work for their degrees. (Parliament passed an Enabling Act in 1876 allowing universities to examine women students for medical degrees, and in 1878 London University admitted women to all degrees.)

Sophia, however, had had to qualify abroad. She gained her MD from the University of Berne and the Licentiate of the Irish College of Physicians, Dublin, in 1877 and so her name finally appeared on the Register of the General Medical Council.

She returned to Edinburgh in 1878 where she began to practise medicine and opened the Dispensary for Women and Children, and the Cottage Hospital in 1885. The following year she founded the Edinburgh School of Medicine for Women which the University of Edinburgh recognised for graduation in 1894.

Sophia's friend, lover and supporter in all her later struggles was Ursula Du Pré, with whom she lived for many years in Edinburgh.

The recognition and position her achievements merited were repeatedly denied her because others could not cope with her uncompromising manner nor the vociferous, "unladylike" way in which she fought for women in medicine.

On her retirement from practice in 1899 Sophia settled in her native Sussex. She died in Rotherfield in 1912 and in her will left what little property she had to Octavia Hill.

Addresses

★14 Nottingham Place, W1 – she lived here with Octavia Hill and Octavia's mother and sisters, 1861.

★Handel Street, (formerly 30 Henrietta Street), WC1 – site of the "perfect, small, two-storeyed Georgian house" where Sophia founded the London School of Medicine for Women in 1874. The school later became affiliated to the University of London. It was enlarged and extended and neighbouring houses were acquired and incorporated, and so the address of the London (Royal Free) School of Medicine became 8 Hunter Street, WC1.

★32 Bernard Street, WC1– site of her home 1874–c1877.

Works include

American Schools and Colleges (1866); Medical Women (1872) – a history of early women doctors; Puerperal Fever – graduation thesis; Care of Infants (1844).

Journalism: Various articles in Fortnightly Review in 1875, and in Nineteenth Century in 1887 and 1894.

Portrait

Canvas by Samuel Laurence (1865) – Royal Society of Medicine.

Memorabilia

Autograph letter (1886) – Fawcett Library.

Earl Kitchener of Khartoum

(24 June 1850 – 5 June 1916)

The achievements of Horatio Herbert Kitchener through his long and illustrious career as a soldier and statesman are without parallel in modern British history.

His most famous campaign was the relief of Khartoum after the murder of General Gordon in 1885, followed by the defeat of the Khalifa at Omdurman in 1898. He was later Commander-in-Chief in South Africa during the Boer War and in India. In Egypt, as British Agent, in the face of considerable opposition from local politicians and pashas, he set about improving the living conditions of the poor, or fellahin, by providing better housing, setting up clinics and improving sanitary conditions. In 1914 he was appointed non-political Secretary for War, with the task of raising a vast army of volunteers. His was the stern staring face behind the outstretched index finger in the famous poster saying "Your Country Needs You".

Kitchener himself had chosen a military career to please his father, a retired army officer, and entered the Royal Military Academy at Woolwich in 1868. As a cadet he was shy, serious and hard-working. He felt ill at ease with the other young men who were mostly from public schools. (Kitchener had been eduated at home by tutors until he went to a boarding school in Switzerland at the age of fourteen.) A lack of interest in sports also set him apart and as a result he was not popular and gained the reputation of being aloof.

Later in life, however, he gathered about him a small group of younger men who were known as "Kitchener's Band of Boys" and after he became a general his staff were given the same name. Kitchener himself called them "a happy family of boys". Queen Victoria commented, "They say he dislikes women but I can only say he was very nice to me." He made it an absolute rule that his officers were single men, and he took great care in personally interviewing all candidates for positions on his staff. Thus he managed to bring under his command a closely knit group of unusually young colonels totally dedicated to their leader.

Kitchener's preference for attractive young men on his staff caused a great deal of comment and speculation. A Reuters correspondent declared, "He drinks and has the other failing acquired by most Egyptian Officers, a taste for buggery."

In 1904 Kitchener met Captain Oswald Fitzgerald (1875–1916) of the 18th Bengal Lancers who became his aide-de-camp and later his military secretary. A mutual friend observed, "Never was there a stronger or more loyal bond than that which these two men had for one another." They were inseparable and lived together openly for the rest of their lives, arousing even more interest among Kitchener's detractors, as did his passion for collecting porcelain and his liking for flower arranging.

In June 1916 Kitchener, accompanied by Fitzgerald, set off on HMS *Hampshire* on a goodwill mission to Russia. A few hours out of Scapa Flow, and at the height of a fierce storm, the ship struck a mine off Marwick Head on the Orkney coast. Attempts were made to launch the lifeboats but these were dashed against the sides of the ship. Kitchener was last seen standing on the quarterdeck talking calmly to Fitzgerald. Fifteen minutes after the explosion the *Hampshire* suddenly pitched forward and sank. There were only twelve survivors. Fitzgerald's body was washed ashore but Kitchener was never seen again.

When the news of the disaster was announced there were those who refused to accept that their great hero was dead. Some, including his sister, believed that he had been taken aboard an enemy submarine and was being held prisoner in Germany. A service in his memory, attended by the King and Queen, members of parliament and other national leaders, was held at St Paul's Cathedral.

Addresses

★*44 Phillimore Gardens, W8* – he lived here c1875–76.

★*Queen Anne's Gate, SW1* – he lived in a house here in 1885.

★*17 Belgrave Square, SW1* – the home of his friend Pandeli Ralli MP. Kitchener stayed here several times when on leave in London before 1914.

★*2 Carlton Gardens, SW1* – he lived here with Fitzgerald 1914–15, and launched his mammoth recruitment campaign here. (*Blue plaque* erected 1924.)

★*York House, St James's Palace, SW1* – George V offered him York House for the rest of the war. Kitchener and Fitzgerald moved here in March 1915.

Portraits

Pastel by C M Horsfall (1899) – National Portrait Gallery. Watercolour by Sir Leslie Ward (1899) – N.P.G. Canvas by Sir Hubert von Herkomer and Frederick Goodall (1890) – N.P.G. Chalk and wash by unknown artist (undated) – N.P.G. Chrome lithograph by W Nicholson (1902) – Victoria and Albert Museum. Political cartoon by E L Sambourne (1880s) – V & A Museum. Poster "Your Country Needs You" and various photographs of Kitchener – Imperial War Museum.

Statues and memorials

Statue of Kitchener in field-marshal's uniform and riding boots by John Tweed. Erected on south side of Horseguards Parade, at the back of 10 Downing Street in 1926.

Small stone bust by unknown artist (1902) in first floor pediment of 73 Knightsbridge, SW1.

All Souls Chapel, St Paul's Cathedral, was converted into a memorial chapel to Kitchener in 1925. The white marble effigy, the statues of St Michael and St George and the altar with a pieta were all sculpted by Sir W Reid Dick.

Memorial cross, erected in 1916, in the churchyard of St Helen's Church, Bishopgate, EC2.

Memorabilia

Several relics, including manuscript memoranda and his scarlet tunic and hat – Imperial War Museum.

Edward Lear

(12 May 1812 – 29 January 1888)

Edward Lear, the twentieth of the twenty-one children of Jeremiah and Ann Lear, was born in London. When he was four years old he was entrusted to the care of his sister Ann, to ease the burden on their mother. (Ann never married but devoted herself to the upbringing of her brother, becoming his tutor, confidante and nurse.) He could be teased and jollied by Ann out of the bouts of depression from which he suffered from early childhood, and which he called "the Morbids"; when he had attacks of epilepsy, however, he would withdraw from her (and from all those whom he loved later), feeling deeply ashamed of his "Demon", probably because of the association in those days of epilepsy with masturbation and sexual incontinence. Throughout his life he suffered also from asthma, bronchitis and poor eyesight.

Lear's talent for drawing and painting was nurtured by his sister, and at the age of fifteen he began to earn his living by selling sketches, doing anatomical studies for medical students, and teaching drawing. He worked for a time as a draughtsman for the Zoological Society, and was commissioned to illustrate a book on parrots. This work brought him to the attention of Lord Stanley (later Earl of Derby), who was looking for an artist to illustrate a book he planned on his private menagerie at Knowsley, the Derby estate near Liverpool.

Between 1832 and 1837 Lear stayed often at Knowsley Hall, where he charmed the aristocratic company with his witty conversation and his piano improvisations, and, with his special talent for producing nonsense rhymes, absurd drawings and outrageous recipes, he delighted the Earl's grandchildren. (All his life he was happiest in the role of "Adopty Duncle".) When his health suddenly deteriorated in 1837 a subscription was raised for him by the Earl to send him to Rome where he could recover his health and study landscape painting (which he had taken up the previous year).

In Rome, where he remained for ten years, returning only occasionally to London, he supported himself by giving drawing lessons and by selling paintings to his patrons, the friends of Lord Derby. There, in 1845, he met twenty-two year old Chichester Fortesque (the future Lord Carlingford, Lord Privy Seal and President of the Council), with whom he formed the first of his many intimate friendships. They were to remain friends until Lear's death, but when Fortesque married, Lear observed, "Every marriage of people I care about rather seems to leave one on the bleak shore alone."

Lear established himself as a nonsense poet in 1846 when he published, under the pseudonym "Derry down Derry", a collection of his limericks and illustrations, *A Book of Nonsense* (which went into thirty editions in his lifetime). In the same year he gave drawing lessons to Queen Victoria at Osborne House and at Buckingham Palace. In 1848, in Malta, he met Franklin Lushington, a young barrister and the brother of the Government Secretary at Malta, and toured southern Greece with him. Lear developed an intense passion for Lushington, and although many of the happiest periods in his life were those spent with him, the fact that his passion was never reciprocated during their lifelong friendship was a constant torment to him.

On his return to London Lear spent a year studying painting at the Royal Academy Schools. He later studied under Holman Hunt, with whom he formed a close friendship.

When, in 1855, Lushington was appointed to the Supreme Court of Justice in the Ionian Islands, Lear accompanied him to Corfu. He established a home for himself there and, when his pictures began to sell on the island, he took on a servant, Giorgio Kokali. (Kokali stayed with Lear for twenty-seven years and was his constant companion on all his travels, as was Lear's marmalade cat, Foss.)

The expanded edition of *A Book of Nonsense*, brought out in 1861 under Lear's own name, had an enthusiastic reception. Lear had always hoped that it would be his "landskip" work, his topographic landscape paintings, which would bring him fame, but the book's success was gratifying nonetheless, and he began producing more nonsense verse with illustrations which were collected in three volumes during the 1870s.

During the two decades following his arrival in Corfu, Lear travelled incessantly throughout the Middle East and the Mediterranean countries. He spent some summers painting in England and wintered in Corfu or Italy. For a time he made his home in Rome, then in Cannes (where he enjoyed the company of John Addington Symonds, for whose youngest daughter, Janet, he composed "The Owl and the Pussycat"). Finally he settled in San Remo and there built the Casa Emily, named after Emily Tennyson, wife of the Poet Laureate, who replaced his sister Ann (who died in 1861) as his closest woman friend and confidante. For many years Lear worked on line drawings and colour illustrations which would, he hoped, complement Tennyson's poems, which he much admired, but the project remained incomplete at his death.

The year-long trip which he made to India and Ceylon (1873–74) as the guest of his friend Lord Northbrook was physically debilitating, and "the Morbids" grew in intensity and frequency after his return to San Remo. In 1880 he paid his last visit to England. He stayed at Lushington's home in Norfolk Square, where he had an exhibition of his works.

Soon after his return to San Remo he moved into his new home, Villa Tennyson, where he was visited by Fortesque and by Lushington. He contracted a severe case of bronchitis in 1886 and his health deteriorated rapidly after the death of his beloved cat, Foss, the following year. His failing eyesight and his epilepsy, together with the frustrations of friendships with men who never returned his love beyond warm affection, increased Lear's sense of isolation. (An attitude of growing despair marks the writings of his later years, and the loneliness of the Dong with the Luminous Nose and of the Yonghy-Bonghy-Bò is Lear's own.)

Attended by his servant, Giuseppe Orsini, Lear died peacefully at the Villa Tennyson. His last words were instructions to Orsini to give his thanks to his friends, especially Fortesque, Lushington and Lord Northbrook, for the good they had always done him.

Addresses

★*Bowman's Lodge, Bowman's Mews, N7* – *site* of Lear's birthplace. He lived here until 1822. (*Plaque.*)

★*151 Gray's Inn Road (formerly 38 Upper North Place), WC1* – he and his sister moved here in 1828.

★*124 Albany Street, NW1* – *site* of the home he shared with his sister in 1831.

★*61 Albany Street, NW1* – *site* of their home 1831–35.

★*Southampton Row, WC1* – they moved to a house here in 1835.

★*27 Duke Street, W1* – he stayed here in 1845 and worked here on *A Book of Nonsense*.

★*17 Stratford Place, W1* – *site* of the house in which he had a studio in 1850.

★*30 Seymour Street, W1* – he had rooms here 1857–58. (*Blue plaque*, 1960.)

Works include

Books: *A Book of Nonsense* (1846; new and enlarged edition 1861); *Nonsense Songs, Stories, Botany and Alphabets* (1871); *More Nonsense Pictures, Rhymes, Botany etc* (1872); *Laughable Lyrics, A Fourth Book of Nonsense Poems &c* (1877); *The Complete Nonsense of Edward Lear* edited by Holbrook Jackson (1947); *Lear in the Original* edited by Herman W Liebert (1975); *Views in Rome and its Environs* (1841); *Journals of a Landscape Painter in Greece and Albania, &c* (1851).

Letters: *Letters of Edward Lear* edited by Lady Strachey (1907); *Later Letters of Edward Lear* edited by Lady Strachey (1911).

Paintings, etc: There are large collections of Lear's oil paintings, watercolours, drawings and lithographs in both the Tate Gallery and the Victoria & Albert Museum.

Portraits

Silhouette (c1830) – National Portrait Gallery. Pencil drawing by Wilhelm Nicholai Marstrand (1840) – N.P.G. Pen and ink self-portrait (1862–63) – N.P.G.

Portrait on p. 122.

Fictional portraits

Many of the characters in Lear's limericks and nonsense verses (and accompanying sketches) are self-portraits.

Memorabilia

Letter with sketch from Lear to Evelyn Baring (1st Earl of Cromer), a close friend – National Portrait Gallery.

Edward Lear

'Athlete Struggling With a Python' (Lord Frederick Leighton)

Leighton House (Lord Frederick Leighton)

'Vernon Lee'
(Violet Paget)

(14 October 1856 –
13 February 1935)

Violet Paget, who under the pseudonym "Vernon Lee" wrote novels and essays on aesthetics, was born in France to British parents. Her family travelled around Europe throughout her childhood before settling in Florence. Her half-brother Eugene Lee Hamilton, also a writer, was her closest friend when she was young and she chose her pseudonym as a mark of her affection for him.

When she was fourteen Violet visited the meeting place of the Arcadian Academy in Rome and began researching its history. This led to the writing of her first book, *Studies of the Eighteenth Century in Italy*, which was published in 1880. She was the first British writer to deal fully with this neglected era of Italian art and thought, and her book was highly praised for its scholarship.

In 1878 Violet fell in love with Annie Meyer, an Englishwoman living in Florence. Their relationship ended after two years, and shortly after the parting Annie died. To the end of her life Violet kept a photograph of Annie over her bed.

Violet paid her first visit to England in 1881. With her tailored clothes and short hair she became a conspicuous figure in London's artistic circles. She soon acquired a reputation as a brilliant conversationalist and came to know many prominent artists and writers, such as Rossetti, Wilde and Pater. In her novel *Miss Brown* she satirised the Aesthetic Movement with which they were associated.

While she was in London Violet stayed at the home of her friend Mary Robinson. They had met during the previous year when Mary had gone to Florence on holiday. In 1887, when Mary became engaged to be married, Violet suffered a nervous and physical breakdown.

She was nursed back to health by a new friend, Clementina Anstruther Thomson, a Commissioner in the Girl Guides, who was known as "Kit". Violet described her as a "handsome creature . . . She is a picturesque personality, paints very well, dresses crâne and rather fast, drives tandem and plays polo . . . talks slang like a schoolboy."

For ten years Kit spent the winter months in Florence with Violet. Most of her life was devoted to the care of others and when her friend Christine Head became ill Kit decided to stay in England to look after her.

Violet had made Kit her heir and was heartbroken when she decided to remain with Christine. They kept in touch by letter and saw each other occasionally, but Violet had wanted a more committed relationship, and the realisation that Kit was happier elsewhere caused her great suffering.

After Kit's death in 1921 Violet gathered together some of her writings and published them in *Art and Man* as a tribute to their friendship.

Violet published over forty books. Her novels and short stories were not very successful in their time and are little read today. Her best writing was in the field of aesthetic and intellectual commentary. She also wrote bitter attacks on what she regarded as the greatest evils – the inequality of women in society, vivisection, nationalism and war.

As she grew older Violet became deaf and resorted to an ear-trumpet which she used only when she herself was speaking. She received an honorary degree of Doctor of Literature from Durham University in 1924, and in 1934 saw an Italian version of her play *Ariadne in Mantua* (which had been dedicated to her friend Ethel Smyth) performed in Florence.

She died at Il Palmerino, the Florentine villa which had been her home for many years. Her ashes were placed in the grave of her half-brother Eugene, in Allori Cemetery, in Florence.

Addresses

★*84 Gower Street, WC1 – site*. She stayed here in 1881 and in 1882 at the home of Mary Robinson.

★*13 Pembroke Square, W8* – she stayed here in 1883 at the home of her friend Bella Duffy.

★*12 Earls Terrace, W8* – (the home of Walter Pater). She stayed here several times before Pater's death in 1886.

Works include

Aesthetics and criticism: *Studies of the Eighteenth Century in Italy* (1880); *Renaissance Fancies and Studies* (1895); *Beauty and Ugliness* (with Clementina Anstruther Thomson) (1912).

Sociology: *Gospels of Anarchy* (1908); *Satan the Waster* (1920).

Fiction: *Miss Brown* (1884); *Hauntings* (1892); *Penelope Brandling* (1903).

Drama: *Ariadne in Mantua* (1903).

Portrait

Oil by John Singer Sargent (1881) – Tate Gallery.

Lord Frederick Leighton

(3 December 1830 – 25 January 1896)

The "Great Olympian" of Victorian art, Frederick Leighton, was born in Scarborough, the son of a wealthy doctor. His talent for drawing and painting was recognised early, and after a spell at University College School he was sent, at the age of twelve, to study at the Academy of Florence. From there he went to Frankfurt where he became a pupil at the Stadel Institute and was greatly influenced by the work of Edward Johann Steinle.

When he was seventeen Leighton set out on a study tour of Europe before settling in Rome. There he was taken up by a rich patroness, Mrs Sartoris, sister of the actress Fanny Kemble, who claimed him as the brightest adornment of her salon. She encouraged his taste for picturesque clothes and his passion for music. His perfect profile and charming (if perhaps a little ingratiating) manner brought him many admirers. He possessed a good tenor voice and often sang at Mrs Sartoris's musical soirées. George Du Maurier was present at one of these gatherings, and described Leighton as being "quite spoilt – one of the world's little darlings, who won't make themselves agreeable to anything under a duchess".

Leighton's early sketches and paintings were eagerly sought after by the English communities in Rome and Florence. The Prince of Wales visited his studio in Rome, as did Thackeray, who prophesied that the young artist would one day become President of the Royal Academy.

In 1855 Leighton's enormous painting "Cimabue's Celebrated Madonna is carried in procession through the streets of Florence" was exhibited at the Royal Academy. Ruskin considered it "a very important and very beautiful picture". It was a precursor of the cult of aestheticism, of beauty for its own sake in the absence of moral preoccupations. When Queen Victoria bought it for £600 to hang in Buckingham Palace, Leighton's future was assured.

It was widely known that Leighton was homosexual, but by exercising discretion in England and spending his winters in the more enlightened climate of Egypt and North Africa he avoided censure and scandal. He also disguised his feelings in his paintings, which is why they so often lack passion and vitality. On the other hand, his two bronzes "Athlete Struggling with a Python" and "The Sluggard" have a sensual and vigorous quality rarely found in his canvases.

He lavished money and gifts on many young protégés. They, like his male models, were chosen for their good looks. Among them was John Hanson Walker. Leighton met him in Bath in 1858, and in 1861 painted two pictures of him which he called "The Johnnies".

In 1860 Leighton took a studio in London and in 1866 he moved into the house in Holland Park Road designed for him by his friend George Aitchison at a cost of £4,500. The gorgeously rich and colourful interior of the house, contrasting with the rather austere but imposing exterior, seems to reflect its owner's private and public personae. Leighton was happy in his sanctuary. There were concerts and parties, to which Rossetti and Simeon Solomon came, as did Vernon Lee who thought the Arab Hall (based on a Moslem palace) "quite the eighth wonder of the world". Here Leighton painted guardsmen while "sacrificing himself to the muses".

His fame and success continued to grow and honours were heaped upon him. He was knighted in 1878 and created a baronet in 1886. In 1878 he was elected President of the Royal Academy, an office he held until his death. During Leighton's presidency the Academy reached heights of influence and prosperity never since equalled.

In addition to his work for the Royal Academy Leighton organised a number of exhibitions and served on the committees of several museums and art galleries. He commissioned and set up many public statues and memorials, including Alfred Stevens's Wellington Memorial. Also during this period he painted most of his great masterpieces.

The constant pressure of work affected his health. He was found to be suffering from a heart disease and, forced to give up many of his duties, he took a long holiday in Algiers.

In January 1896 it was announced that Leighton had been given a peerage (the first painter to be so honoured), with the title of Baron Leighton of Stretton. Although in great pain, he went to the Academy to receive the congratulations of his fellow artists. On the following day he died, his last words being, "Give my love to the Royal Academy."

Addresses

★*2 Orme Square, W2* – he lived here 1860–66.

★*Leighton House, 12 Holland Park Road, W14* – he lived here 1866–96. (The house is open to the public, admission free, Monday to Saturday, and contains a fine selection of paintings by Leighton and his circle.)

Works

Works in the Tate Gallery, National Portrait Gallery, Leighton House, Victoria and Albert Museum and Guildhall Art Gallery. The bronze "Athlete Struggling with a Python" is in the garden at Leighton House.

Portraits

Pencil self-portrait (c1848–50) – National Portrait Gallery. Canvas by G F Watts (1881) – N.P.G. Miniature by Rosa Carter (1896) – N.P.G. Pencil and watercolours of Leighton and his family, by Edward Foster – N.P.G. (Archives). Leighton is the central figure in H Jamyn Brooks's canvas "Private View of the Old Masters Exhibition at the R.A. Burlington House" (1889) – N.P.G. Various prints from photographs – N.P.G. Watercolour – Leighton is one of the group in "Conversazione at the R.A., 1891" by G Greville Manton – N.P.G. Pen & ink – as one of the group in "Hanging Committee, R.A., 1892" by Reginald Cleaver – N.P.G. Pencil self-portrait (c1848) – N.P.G. Pencil drawing – with Clifford Lloyd at the Parnell Commission, by S P Hall (1889) – N.P.G. Plaster and bronze casts of bust by Thomas Brock (c1901) – N.P.G. Various caricatures – N.P.G., Royal Academy, and Victoria & Albert Museum. Drawing – with others at the Parnell Commission, by Frederick Pegram (1889) – V & A Museum. Watercolour "The Man from Hymettus, Mr Frederick Leighton" by Sir Max Beerbohm (1916) – Tate Gallery. Pencil and chalk drawing by Edward von Steinle (c1852) – British Museum. Drawing by Rudolph Lehmann (1889) – B.M. Prints by A Legros (c1880) and J Brown (c1881) – B.M. Bust by Thomas Brock (1892) – Leighton House.

Photos of Leighton House and 'Athlete Struggling with a Python' on p. 123.

Fictional portraits

The character of Gaston Phoebus in Disraeli's novel *Lothair* (1870) is based on that of Leighton, with his love of youth and his interest in Greece and Greek principles. In his short story "The Private Life" (1892) Henry James caricatured him as "Lord Mellifont", an artist whose "reputation was a kind of gilded obelisk, as if he had been buried beneath it". He appears also as Kioski in Adelaide Sartoris's *roman à clef, A Week in a French Country House* (1867).

Statues and memorials

Stone statue by Sidney Boyes (1909) – south front of V & A Museum. Memorial (recumbent bronze effigy by Thomas Brock, c1901), unveiled in 1902, in St Paul's Cathedral. Leighton is buried in the crypt.

Memorabilia

Leighton's notebooks – Royal Academy. Among the streets named after him is Leighton Road, Enfield.

Matthew Gregory 'Monk' Lewis

(9 July 1775 – 14 May 1818)

Remembered chiefly for his Gothic novel *The Monk*, from which his nickname was derived, Matthew Gregory Lewis was born in London into a wealthy and powerful family. His father was the Deputy Secretary of War and owner of large estates in Jamaica. His mother, a celebrated beauty, was the daughter of the Master of the Rolls.

Lewis was educated at Westminster and at Christ Church, Oxford. Since his father wanted him to take up a diplomatic career he became, at the age of nineteen, an attaché to the British Embassy at The Hague. There, in the space of ten weeks, he wrote *Ambrosio, or The Monk*, a lurid account of scandalous goings-on in monasteries and in the prisons of the Inquisition.

The novel was widely read and widely condemned, and the Attorney-General moved for an injunction against its sale, on the grounds that it was indecent and irreligious. The prosecution was dropped when Lewis agreed to remove the most objectionable passages from the second edition.

At the age of twenty the "immoral Monk Lewis" was famous and was received in the highest society. He went on to write many more works of fiction, verse and drama which were popular in his lifetime. Some of them he set to music. Sir Walter Scott, who acknowledged the influence which Lewis's writing had on his own, described him as "a man of very diminutive though well-made figure, with singular eyes, projecting like those of some insect. He looked like a schoolboy all his life, and retained many of the qualities of a precocious and ill-educated schoolboy."

For six years, from 1796, Lewis was the Member of Parliament for Hindon, Wiltshire. In 1802 a widow, Mrs Kelly, applied to him for help in claiming a sum of money which she believed was owed to her father. He visited her home and met her young son William, to whom he was immediately attracted. As his friend Byron noted, "He was fond of the society of younger men than himself . . . I remember Mrs Hope once asking who was Lewis's male love this season."

Lewis paid for William's schooling and got him a job in the War Office. Unfortunately William became a heavy drinker, was unreliable, and used Lewis's name to obtain credit from tradespeople. On more than one occasion Lewis had to pay for his release from jail. He carried on supporting his young friend, however, and when he died he left him an allowance of the then generous sum of £2 a week for life.

Lewis's writings and utterances continued to excite controversy. The nobility admired his work, but he was denounced by the Church when he recommended that certain passages of the Bible should be kept from the young. His opulent lifestyle and "laxity of morals" offended even the most unlikely people. Byron came away from a dinner party which Lewis had given at his Albany chambers, saying, "I never will dine with a middle-aged man who fills up his table with young ensigns, and has looking-glass panels to his bookcases."

When Lewis's father died in 1812 he left all his property to his son. In 1815 Lewis set sail for Jamaica to investigate the condition of his five hundred slaves. Immediately upon his return he went to visit Byron at Geneva. There he drew up a codicil to his will, witnessed by Byron, Shelley and Polidori, which stated that no slave was to be sold and that any future owner of the property must spend three months in Jamaica every third year, in order to make sure that the slaves were being "properly treated".

At the end of 1817 Lewis again sailed to the West Indies, on board the *Sir Godfrey Webster*. This time he took with him his piano, on which he entertained the passengers and crew through even the roughest seas. He was given a rapturous welcome by the slaves. As he came ashore he shook each one by the hand and thereafter spent all of his time in their company, sharing his meals with them and joining in their singing and dancing. Such unheard-of behaviour caused consternation among his white companions.

After a three-months stay in Jamaica, Lewis boarded the *Sir Godfrey Webster* for his return voyage to England. Almost immediately he was struck down by yellow fever, and ten days later, after writing some final instructions on his servant's hat, he died.

In order to protect the other passengers from contagion the captain ordered a burial at sea. Lewis's body was placed in an improvised coffin which was wrapped in a sheet with some weights and dropped overboard. There then occurred something which might have

been written in one of Lewis's Gothic tales. After the plunge into the ocean the weights slipped out and the coffin reappeared on the surface. With the loosened sheet acting as a sail it drifted slowly off on the wind towards Jamaica until it was lost to sight.

Addresses

★*9 Devonshire Place, W1* – his childhood home.

★*Nassau Road, SW13* – site of Lewis's cottage which stood near the junction with Church Road. He lived here 1801–09.

★*1k, The Albany, Piccadilly, W1* – he lived here 1809–18.

Works include

Novels: *Ambrosio, or The Monk* (1795); *The Bravo of Venice* (1804); *Feudal Tyrants* (1806).

Drama: *The Castle Spectre* (1796); *Adelmorn the Outlaw* (1800).

Journal: *The Journal of a West India Proprietor* (1834).

Portraits

Oil by H W Pickersgill (1809) – National Portrait Gallery. Miniature by G L Saunders (c1790–1800) – N.P.G. Prints by W Ridley (1796) and J Hollis (1834) – British Museum.

Memorabilia

His letters – Victoria & Albert Museum. His will and a codicil to his will – Public Records Office.

Christopher Marlowe

(6 February 1564 – 30 May 1593)

Christopher Marlowe was born in Canterbury, the son of a shoemaker. He was educated at the King's School near his home until he was fifteen, when he was awarded a scholarship to Corpus Christi College, Cambridge.

While at Cambridge Marlowe met the poet Thomas Watson who was visiting the university. They became close friends and made plans to live together in London when Marlowe had finished his studies.

Under the conditions of his scholarship Marlowe was obliged to take holy orders before gaining his degree. He was, however, singularly unsuited for clerical life. Instead of studying theology he spent his time translating Ovid and writing a play *The Tragedy of Dido, Queen of Carthage*, based on Virgil's *Aeneid*. Although an immature work, the play contains some wonderful lines. In the opening scene Ganymede sits on Jupiter's knee and states his price:

> I would have a jewel for mine ear,
> And a brooch to put in my hat,
> And then I'll hug with you an hundred times.

Watson introduced Marlowe to Sir Francis Walsingham, the powerful Secretary of State, who operated a network of spies throughout Europe. Their objective was to thwart the armada which Philip of Spain was preparing for the invasion of England, and to gather information against the imprisoned Mary, Queen of Scots. Marlowe offered his services to Walsingham, partly for the money and adventure, but also because it gave him a powerful protector who could overrule the university authorities and order them to grant him his Master's degree without his having to take holy orders. Marlowe was sent to Rheims where he spied on the Catholic seminary and sent back information about the priests and students who were planning to return secretly to England. He was paid well for his efforts and gained his degree.

While still at Cambridge Marlowe met (through his involvement with the spy service) Sir Francis Walsingham's nephew, Thomas,

who was then about seventeen years old. Thomas became his patron, closest friend and probably his lover. He had a country house, Scadbury, near Chislehurst in Kent, and Marlowe stayed there many times.

Marlowe came to London in 1587 and began writing in earnest. His plays became enormously popular and established him as the leading English dramatist of his day.

In September 1589 Marlowe was involved in a sword fight with a certain William Bradley. When Watson tried to separate them Bradley turned on him, saying, "Art thou now come? Then I will have a bout with thee." Marlowe stood aside and Bradley lunged at Watson, wounding him and driving him into a ditch. Watson, unable to escape, thrust his sword through Bradley's heart. Marlowe and Watson were arrested for murder and thrown into Newgate Prison. After thirteen days Marlowe was released, but Watson had to wait five months for his freedom. He never recovered from his prison ordeal and died soon afterwards.

Marlowe shared a room, in 1591, with the playwright Thomas Kyd. They were employed to write plays by the patron of a company of players. When the plague broke out in London in the following year, Marlowe went to Scadbury to stay with Thomas Walsingham. While he was away a number of anti-immigrant placards were hung on the city walls. Kyd was suspected of being involved and his room was searched by the authorities. When they discovered some papers containing "vile heretical conceits denying the deity of Jesus Christ our Saviour", Kyd was arrested, taken to Bridewell Prison, and tortured. He denied having written the pages and insisted that they were in fact the work of Marlowe and had been shuffled with his own manuscripts by mistake. It was Marlowe's habit, said Kyd, to "jest at the divine scriptures" and to "jibe at prayers". Furthermore, "he would report St John to be our Saviour Christ's Alexis. That is, that Christ did love him with an extraordinary love." Marlowe was arrested and brought before the Privy Council. Statements were made against him that "almost into every company he cometh he persuades men to atheism" and that he believed that "all they that love not tobacco and boys were fools." Marlowe was ordered to attend the Privy Council every day until Kyd's case had been heard. This meant that he could not return to Scadbury.

Ten days after his first appearance before the Privy Council, Marlowe was invited by Ingram Frizer, Thomas Walsingham's business manager, to dine with him at Eleanor Bull's tavern at Deptford. Two government spies, Robert Poley and Nicholas Skeres, were also present. After they had eaten, Marlowe lay down on a couch behind the others who sat with their backs to him. They had probably been drinking heavily and an argument broke out about the payment of the bill. Marlowe, in a fury, drew Frizer's dagger which he was wearing at his back, and cut him twice on the head. Frizer struggled to his feet and tried to get back his dagger. In the scuffle that followed Frizer stabbed Marlowe above his right eye, killing him instantly.

This was the version of events heard by the jury at the inquest held two days later. But questions remain: was Marlowe lured to Deptford and murdered because of his spying activities? There may have been fears that he knew too much and might, if sentenced to torture by the Privy Council, implicate others in acts of treachery or treason. Or was Frizer, who had worked for Thomas Walsingham for several years, jealous or resentful of Marlowe's relationship with his employer and eager to be rid of him? Anyway, all three men were pardoned. Because of the plague, Marlowe's body was buried immediately after the inquest, in an unmarked grave.

man (1598); *The Complete Plays and Poems of Christopher Marlowe*, edited by E D Pendry (1976).

Fictional portrait

The fight in *Romeo and Juliet* among Mercutio, Tybalt and Romeo may have been based on that of Marlowe, Bradley and Watson, and the character of Mercutio may be a portrait of Marlowe: impulsive, hot-tempered and passionate.

Memorial

Brass tablet (1919) – St Nicholas's Church, Creek Road, SE8 (at the junction of Stowage and Deptford Green). Marlowe is buried in the churchyard.

Memorabilia

The 1598 edition of *Edward the Second* – British Museum. Burial register, which reads "1st June 1593, Christopher Marlowe slain by Francis Frizer" – St Nicholas's Church.

Addresses

★*Norton Folgate, E1 – site*. Marlowe lived within this vicinity from 1587 until 1593.

★*Worship Street (formerly Hog Lane), EC2 – site*. Here Marlowe and Watson fought with Bradley.

Works

Plays: *Dido, Queen of Carthage* (c1586; published 1594) – possibly written with Thomas Nashe; *The Massacre at Paris* (1593); *Tamburlaine the Great* (1587); *Doctor Faustus* (1593); *The Rich Jew of Malta* (c1590); *Edward the Second* (c1592; published 1593) – the first English play to deal openly with homosexuality, it tells of the King's love for the French Knight, Piers Gaveston, and of the lovers' deaths at the hands of their enemies.

Verse: *Epigrams and Elegies of Ovid*, with John Davies (c1595); *Lucan's First Book, translated line for line* (1600); *Hero and Leander*, begun by Marlowe and completed by Chap-

Sir Edward Marsh

(18 November 1872 –
13 January 1953)

Edward Howard Marsh, the founder and editor of *Georgian Poetry*, was the central figure of a group including most of the notable British poets and painters of the early 20th century. He did more than anyone else, from 1911 to 1922, to further the cause of modern poetry.

He was born in London, the son of Frederick Howard Marsh, an eminent surgeon and Master of Downing College, Cambridge, and Jane Perceval Marsh, the founder of the Alexandra Hospital for Children with Hip Disease and granddaughter of Spencer Perceval, the Prime Minister who was assassinated in 1812 in the lobby of the House of Commons.

Marsh was educated at Westminster and Trinity College, Cambridge. He then entered the civil service and in 1906 became private secretary to Winston Churchill, a post he held for twenty-three years.

Through his friendship with the painter Neville Lytton, Marsh developed an interest in art and began to collect paintings, beginning with classical English masters. With the help of Robert Ross he acquired the Horne Collection of drawings which made him one of the most important private collectors in the country. His purchase in 1911 of a painting by Duncan Grant (from Ross's Carfax Gallery) led to his interest in contemporary British painting. He became a patron to several struggling young artists such as Mark Gertler, Paul Nash and Stanley Spencer, and began collecting their work.

At the same time his flat in Raymond Buildings became a meeting-place for poets as well as painters. Marsh enjoyed being a benefactor. He was generous with his time and money and worked tirelessly to promote the work of his young protégés.

When he first met Rupert Brooke at Cambridge in 1906 Marsh was reluctant to read his poems because "I liked him so much that I should have hated not to like his work." The publication of Brooke's *Poems* in 1911 convinced Marsh that he was a first-rate poet. It was Brooke who, during a stay at Raymond Buildings in 1912, gave him the idea which led to his compiling an anthology of modern verse under the title *Georgian Poetry*.

Harold Monro published the first volume in December 1912. Over the next decade five further volumes appeared. Among the original "Georgians" were Brooke, Monro, Flecker, de la Mare and D H Lawrence. They were followed in 1917 by a group of war poets including Sassoon, Graves and Robert Nichols.

By establishing a royalty system instead of outright payment Marsh was able to benefit the contributors over several years. In addition, he made gifts to those who were suffering hardship, from what he called his "murder money" – his share of the compensation granted to the Perceval family in 1812.

Marsh's love for Rupert Brooke was the high point of his life, and he never entirely recovered from the poet's death in the Aegean in 1915. He wrote to Mrs Brooke on the evening that news of her son's death reached England: "Most things in my life depended on him for a great part of their interest and worth. It is your glory to be his mother – and mine to be his friend – The loss to the future cannot be guessed." And to Brooke's friend Denis Browne, soon to die in battle, he wrote: "I feel that my whole plan of life has broken down." In 1918 he wrote a memoir of Brooke as an introduction to the *Collected Poems*.

For many years Marsh was a regular theatre-goer with a penchant for musical comedy, and was a familiar figure at West End first nights. He was tall, fair haired and stately, wore a monocle and was always elegantly dressed. "Even when the theatre is half empty," said James Agate, "every actor feels he has a full house if Eddie's in front." In December 1915 he went to see Lily Elsie in *Mavourneen* at His Majesty's Theatre. During the interval he was introduced to twenty-two year old Ivor Novello, who had recently written the popular song "Keep the Home Fires Burning".

In many ways the glamorous young actor and composer took Brooke's place in Marsh's affections. Marsh began the custom, which lasted almost unbroken for the next twenty years, of walking to Whitehall in the mornings so that he could call at Novello's flat on the way. Through the early years of their friendship Novello shared his flat above the Strand Theatre with his parents. Marsh had a piano installed at Raymond Buildings so that Novello could compose or practise away from the distractions caused by the interminable comings and goings of his mother's music pupils. Over the years Marsh shared every

36 Bruton Street, W1

vicissitude of Novello's career and watched his young protégé become one of the greatest stars of the British theatre.

When he retired from the civil service in 1937 Marsh was given a knighthood. In his retirement he translated the odes of Horace, produced a volume of verse translations from the French and translated Eugene Fromentin's novel *Dominique*. His eightieth birthday was celebrated by numerous tributes in the press and by a gathering of his many friends. He died two months later.

Addresses

★*38 Guilford Street, WC1 – site*. Birthplace.

★*36 Bruton Street, W1* – he lived here 1874–86.

★*30 Bruton Street, W1* – he lived here 1887–99.

★*3 Gray's Inn Place, WC1* – he lived here 1899–1903.

★*5 Raymond Buildings, WC1* – his home from 1903 to 1940. (See also E.M. Forster.)

★*86 Walton Street, SW3* – his home from 1946 to 1953. (Died here.)

Works include

Translations: *The Fables of Jean de la Fontaine* (1933); *The Odes of Horace* (1941); *Minima* (1947); *Dominique* (1948).

Memoirs and reminiscences: *Rupert Brooke* (1918); *A Number of People* (1938).

Lyrics: Under the name Edward Moore he wrote the words to Ivor Novello's song "The Land of Might Have Been" (1924).

Portraits

Canvas by Sir Oswald Birley (1949) – National Portrait Gallery. Photographs by Howard Coster and Karl Pollak – N.P.G.

Fictional portraits

He appears as Freddy Mush in H G Wells's *Men Like Gods* (1923), and as Mattie Dean in *Triple Fugue* (1924) by Osbert Sitwell.

133

Constance Maynard

(19 February 1849 – 26 March 1935)

Constance Louisa Maynard was one of the pioneers in the higher education of women in Britain, and it was to her that the existence of Westfield College, University of London, is mainly due.

She was born in Highbury into a strict Evangelical upper-middle class family. After she came home from boarding school at the age of fifteen, she filled her time with projects, such as painting, teaching Sunday School, reading, and studying theology, Greek and history, and she took turns with her sisters in nursing their invalid mother. Although she was ostensibly a "dutiful daughter", Constance resented the lack of privacy at home and her mother's intrusions (she had stopped Constance's correspondence with a special friend at school), the restrictions placed on her movements (her father would not permit her to leave Oakfield, the family estate in Kent, unescorted), and her mother's continual "pat, pat, patting down of all ambition". In her unpublished autobiography, Constance later wrote that she and her sisters had been confined "like eagles in a hen house".

In 1872 Constance entered Girton College, then only three years old and still in its temporary quarters at Hitchin, Hertfordshire. She was overjoyed (and rather surprised) at her father's giving her permission to go to Girton for a year, and, later, his agreeing to her remaining at the college for three years. At Girton she was happy "in the glorious conviction that at last, *at last*, we were afloat on a stream that had a real destination, even though we hardly knew what that destination was," and it was during her first year there that she conceived the idea which led to the founding of Westfield College, with the aim of uniting "true religion and sound learning". She formed also a passionate attachment to an older student at Girton, Louisa Lumsden (1840–1915), who called Constance her "wife".

Constance became, in 1875, the first Girtonian to take the Moral Sciences Tripos. She then joined Louisa in Scotland, where Louisa had been appointed the first headmistress of the girls' school which later became St Leonard's School, St Andrews. While teaching at the school Constance fell deeply in love with a succession of her students, but her main relationship was her "marriage" with Louisa. "Work, friends, pleasure, everything shared", she wrote, "& then the long clasp of living love that needs no explanation".

During this period she received, and turned down, an offer of marriage from a Scots minister. In her autobiography she wrote, "As I put on my cloak and went off to School I used to hug myself & think, 'Now I know what love is!' & anything Dr Robertson offered seemed timid & colourless in comparison." Louisa gave Constance the emotional reassurance she desired and loved her passionately "with such a force that was almost terrible. It was as if I had waked a sleeping lion," but their relationship foundered as a result of their irreconcilable religious differences. The devout Constance, who always saw her relationships in religious terms, observed of the agnostic Louisa, "If this noble heart submitted to Christ, I think I should never wander more." Relations between the two women became strained, and this situation and Constance's realisation that classroom teaching was not her forte led to her leaving St Leonard's School.

On her return to London Constance enrolled at the Slade School of Art, where she spent two years. Early in 1882 a friend recommended her to a wealthy religious woman, Miss Dudin Brown, who was thinking of founding a women's college. Constance swiftly won the confidence of Miss Brown and that of another devout and wealthy woman, and gained the financial means to open Westfield College in 1882.

As the first head of Westfield College, a position she held for thirty-one years, Constance was known as "The Mistress", a title borrowed from Girton. In 1883 she persuaded Anne Richardson, a young student at Newnham College, to transfer to the new college in Hampstead. Frances Ralph Gray, Anne's close friend whom she brought with her, was hired to teach classics. The triangular emotional relationship which grew up between Constance, Anne and Ralph was for a time a supportive one, but apparently Constance's excessive demands on Ralph, to whom she was more strongly attracted, for emotional support and intimacy, drove Ralph from her and alienated Anne's affection (but not her loyalty). In 1886 Ralph moved out of the college to live on her own. She returned, however, five years later and attempted to effect a reconciliation, but Constance would not renew the relationship, even though she felt "like an iron-bound bud that has lost the spring, and now no rain and no sunshine can open it". A few years later she fell in love with a young student, whom she described as her "white bud" whom she was privileged to open into "passion pure in snowy bloom".

In 1888 Constance had adopted a six year old girl whom she called "Effie". She found it difficult to cope with Effie's rebellious nature and her refusal to heed her advice and take "moral instruction", and, although each genuinely loved the other, relations between herself and her adopted daughter were, by Constance's own account, invariably awkward and dispiriting.

During her career Constance's religious outlook had broadened considerably and so she was not too greatly disappointed that, as Westfield College had grown and taken its place as an integral part of the reconstructed University of London, her goal of "the teaching of religion in intellect" had become to a degree subsumed under the wider aims of higher education for women.

After her retirement in 1913 she maintained contact with many of her former students and colleagues by letter and through their occasional visits to The Sundial, her cottage in Gerrard's Cross, Buckinghamshire, where she lived alone, but for her housekeeper. (Effie had died of tuberculosis in her early thirties.)

Constance had a great love of writing. She wrote reminiscences of the early years of Girton and Westfield, occasional verse and pamphlets and books on religious and social matters, and contributed from time to time to religious and literary journals. In her old age she decided that writing is "the real centre of life", and in a letter written a few years before her death she stated, "I *do* so want to do a little good through my writing before I go hence."

★*(formerly Kidderpore Hall) Kidderpore Avenue, NW3* – the college moved into its new premises here in April 1891. Constance lived here until her retirement in 1913.

★*Grosvenor Hill, SW19* – she stayed here for a few months (1919–20) with the widow of her brother Harry.

Works include

An Alpine Meadow (1903); *The Moral Equivalent of War* (1905); *Between College Terms* (1910); *Watching the War: thoughts for the people* (1914–15); *The Kingdom of Heaven is like . . .* (1924); *We Women: A Golden Hope* (1924); *The Perfect Law of Liberty, etc* (1925); *Then Shall We Know* (1927); *The Birth of Conscience* (1928); *The Threefold Revelation* (1928).

Portrait

Pastel by F A de Biden Footner (1923) – Westfield College, Kidderpore Avenue, NW3. Numerous photographs – Westfield College (Archives).

Memorial

The modern wing of Westfield College was named after her.

Memorabilia

Her unpublished notebooks/diaries and autobiography, as well as other archive material – Westfield College.

Addresses

★*Highbury Park, N5 – The Chestnuts* stands on the site of Park Terrace where Constance was born. In 1853 the Maynards moved from here to the country and settled at "Oakfield", Hawkhurst, in Kent – sometimes given as her birthplace.

★*4, 6, 8, 10 Maresfield Gardens, NW3* – the first home of Westfield College (1882–91). Constance "lived in" here.

Charlotte Mew

(15 November 1869 –
24 March 1928)

Champions and admirers of Charlotte Mew's poetry were many during her lifetime, but until recently her work has been neglected. To Virginia Woolf she was "very good and interesting and unlike anyone else" and "the greatest living poetess", and Thomas Hardy declared that she was "far and away the best living woman poet – who will be read when others are forgotten".

Charlotte Mary Mew was born in Blooms-bury. Her father was a reasonably successful architect whose wife nevertheless felt that she had married beneath herself. There were seven children, three of whom died in infancy. A brother and sister suffered from schizophrenia and were confined to private hospitals for most of their lives. The fear that she too might become mentally ill haunted Charlotte all her life.

She was educated at Gower Street School (run by Lucy Harrison), attended lectures at University College and read extensively in the British Museum Reading Room. Through her sister, Anne, who became a painter, she made a number of friends who were involved in, or interested in, art and literature.

Charlotte began writing feature articles, short stories and poems in the 1890s. Throughout her life her writing was done in moments stolen from her routine of house-work, voluntary social work (which young women of her class were expected to do), and nursing first her widowed mother, a chronic invalid with no identifiable illness, and, later, Anne, who died of cancer.

Her first published story, "Passed", appeared in the second number of *The Yellow Book* in 1894. Subsequent work appeared in such journals as *The Englishwoman, The Nation, The Egoist* and *Temple Bar.*

Charlotte conceived a passion for Ella D'Arcy, a fellow contributor to *The Yellow Book*, and during 1902 she spent several months in Paris trying to help Ella over her depression at having been deserted, penniless, by her lover. Ella, however, wanted neither her comforting nor her love.

The few literary contacts Charlotte had were made chiefly through Mrs Dawson Scott ("Sappho"), a patron of writers, who took her up, the novelist May Sinclair, and Sidney Cockerel, director of the Fitzwilliam Museum at Cambridge. Cockerel introduced Charlotte to Thomas Hardy, and May Sinclair, through her acquaintance with the editors of literary journals, introduced Charlotte's work to them. Ezra Pound, of *The Egoist*, was particu-larly enthusiastic about her poetry.

Alida Monro, who became a good friend to Charlotte and her sister Anne, recalled at their first meeting how "electrified" she had been by Charlotte's poem "The Farmer's Bride", which she had read in *The Nation* a few years earlier. She arranged for this poem to be included, with "The Changeling", in a reading at The Poetry Bookshop in November 1915, and recommended Charlotte's poetry to her husband, Harold. A collection of seventeen of Charlotte's poems, *The Farmer's Bride*, was published under the Poetry Bookshop imprint in 1916.

In her analysis of Charlotte's life and writ-ings, Alida Monro wrote of "the warring pair within her". The timid dutiful daughter was in constant struggle with the witty bohemian who smoked, swore, and danced the cancan in her knickers. Her impulse to reveal all about herself clashed with a need for mystification; her passionate, unfulfilled yearning for the love of other women was denied by her determined avoidance of commitment and intimacy.

All three of Charlotte's great loves were unrequited. Her passion for Lucy Harrison was so strong that, upon hearing that this teacher was to leave the school, the young Charlotte, according to a classmate, "in a wild state of grief began to bang her head against the wall". (Lucy Harrison, in fact, later fell in love with her successor as head of the school, Amy Greener, and they lived together for thirty years.) Ella D'Arcy's spurning of her love left Charlotte feeling humiliated and foolish; and her three-year long close friendship with May Sinclair was terminated by the novelist in 1916, as a result of Char-lotte's uncharacteristic confession of her desire for her and, according to May Sinclair, her attempt at forcibly making love to her. (She rejected Charlotte's advances with the insult-ing advice, "My good woman, you are simply wasting your perfectly good passion.")

A legacy from an aunt had improved Char-lotte and Anne's financial situation slightly, and Anne took a studio and resumed her painting (which she had been forced to give up for more lucrative furniture restoring work).

Charlotte, who was devoted to Anne and regarded her more as a friend than as a sister, used occasionally to entertain her friends at Anne's studio, where she felt more at ease than she did at home.

Her work continued to gain admirers; among them were the Poet Laureate Robert Bridges, Hugh Walpole and Siegfried Sassoon (who championed her work in England and in Germany); and in 1923 she was awarded a Civil List pension of £75 a year. The following two years were the happiest in Charlotte's life: her reputation was growing and she was making new and interesting friends.

When Anne became seriously ill in 1926 Charlotte terminated the lease of their house (their mother had died a few years earlier) and moved into Anne's studio to nurse her. Anne died in June 1927, and Charlotte was inconsolable. She began suffering from the delusion that Anne had not died of cancer, but had been poisoned by the black specks (soot) in the studio, where Charlotte continued to live. In February 1928 she began receiving treatment for neurasthenia at a nursing home in Beaumont Street, where she committed suicide a month later by drinking Lysol, a strong disinfectant. Her last words were, "Don't keep me, let me go."

Charlotte was buried in the same grave as Anne, in Fortune Green Cemetery, Hampstead. A line from Dante's *Purgatorio* is inscribed on the headstone: "Cast down the seed of weeping, and attend."

Portraits

Pen and wash drawing by Dorothy Hawksley (1926) – National Portrait Gallery. Photograph (from an article in *The Bookman*) – N.P.G. (Archives).

Addresses

★*30 Doughty Street, WC1* – birthplace. Her family lived here until 1888.

★*9 Gordon Street, WC1* – her family's home 1888–1922. (*Site.*)

★*86 Delancey Street, NW1* – *site* of the house in which Charlotte, Anne and their mother lived 1922–26.

★*6 Hogarth Studios, 64 Charlotte Street, W1* – Anne's studio, where she and Charlotte lived from 1926 until their deaths.

Works

The Farmer's Bride (1916); *The Rambling Sailor* (1929); *Collected Poems* (1953); *Charlotte Mew: Collected Poems & Prose*, edited with an introduction by Val Warner (1981).

(Her play "The China Bowl" was broadcast by the BBC in 1953).

John Minton

(25 December 1917 – 20 January 1957)

John Francis Minton was born at Great Shelford, near Cambridge. When he was twelve years old his father, a solicitor who belonged to the family famous for its china, died and the family was left in greatly reduced circumstances. He and his younger brother lived with their mother and her taxi-driver lover, and spent their school holidays at the home of their wealthy grandmother. "Johnnie" was his grandmother's particular favourite: he accompanied her on several trips abroad and she took responsibility for his education and social grooming. (Minton was a romanticiser and even his closest friends were sometimes taken in by his fanciful versions of his family background, which included a father who had gone to Australia when Minton was a child and had never been heard of again, and a malformed brother living in Kent.)

At St John's Wood School of Art, which he attended between 1935 and 1938, Minton met Michael Ayrton whose infectious enthusiasm for the Parisian neo-romantics led to their going to France to study and paint. He and Ayrton shared a studio in Paris; later they shared an exhibition at the Leicester Galleries and, in the same year (1942), they collaborated on designing the costumes and decor for Gielgud's production of *Macbeth*.

Minton hated serving in the Pioneer Corps, which he entered in 1941 rather than become a conscientious objector, and he was released two years later after declaring his homosexuality and, apparently, threatening to rape his fellow soldiers. Although it achieved the end he sought, Minton's statement of his sexuality was not merely an outrageous, selfish tactic. He was openly homosexual and was to show great courage in defending homosexuality in the conformist climate of Britain in the 1950s: his letter to *The Listener* (which J R Ackerley ensured was published) was most outspoken; and, on the occasion of the publication of a biography of Oscar Wilde, he wrote to the *New Statesman* listing the many great artists of the past who were also homosexual, which horrified and outraged the art establishment. As remarkable as Minton's courage was his

generosity. He did not make much money from the sale of his pictures, but became well-off through the inheritance of a fairly large sum. His friends and poorer students (and not only those to whom he was sexually attracted) benefited from his gifts of cash and his purchase of their more expensive paintings.

After obtaining his release from war service Minton taught illustration at the Camberwell School of Art. During these three years he shared the studio of his friends Robert Colquhoun and Robert MacBryde in Kensington. He left this studio to share a house with Keith Vaughan, who was a fellow teacher at Camberwell and was later acclaimed as a great painter of the male nude.

Minton's mature style as a painter was formed in the mid-1940s. The rich colour he employed, his superb graphic skills and the compound of urban romanticism and rural intricacy in his works, found a ready response in the austerity of the years immediately following the war. Minton quickly became recognised as one of the leading figures of the group of young artists known as the neo-romantics, and a generation of British art school students imitated his style of drawing and adopted his topographic mannerisms.

During the heady decade or so of his success Minton's output was prodigious and his activities manifold: he continued teaching (at the Central School of Arts and Crafts and at the Royal College of Art); did illustrations for books and periodicals, as well as posters for the Ealing film studios; worked on designs for the stage, for the Chelsea Arts Ball, for wallpapers; and produced many paintings reflecting his travels in the West Indies, Spain, Corsica and North Africa, as well as dozens of fine drawings and paintings of his friends. (These portraits and self-portraits and his sketches and watercolours of the Kent countryside near Shoreham are the most highly regarded of his works.)

However, he was discontented with the scope of his work and dismissive of his achievements. He became increasingly dissatisfied with his painting and began to question his creative powers. The trend towards abstraction in the 1950s depressed him intensely and he responded by turning in his work to the treatment of academic subjects in modern (but still naturalistic) terms, using brighter colours and larger canvases than before.

His many friends recognised that beneath the outward signs of a carefree, even reckless, existence Minton was deeply committed to his work and that at heart he was a melancholy, depressive man, for all his exuberance, outrageous wit and incessant clowning. Alcohol became a major problem for him and he suffered a broken nose in a drunken row. Coupled with his loss of confidence in himself as an artist and the fear that art as he knew it had no future, was his growing despair of finding, in the succession of young men who passed through his studio and home, the ideal companion. (Invariably, those to whom he was sexually attracted were heterosexual.)

In 1956 he gave up his teaching post at the Royal College of Art and went to Spain to try to find his way again in his painting and to sort out his life. He produced some fine work during this period, but was dissatisfied with it and returned to England frustrated and depressed. After a long, frenzied bout of drinking he committed suicide by taking an overdose of drugs.

He was described, rather glibly, in an English newspaper article after his death as being the James Dean of painting – his last big picture was "The Death of James Dean".

Minton bequeathed money in a trust fund to the Royal College of Art to be given to help young artists who displayed a special talent in drawing.

9 Apollo Place, SW10

Addresses

★*77 Bedford Gardens, W8* – he shared a studio here with Robert Colquhoun and Robert MacBryde (1943–46).

★*37 Hamilton Terrace, NW8* – he shared the house with Keith Vaughan 1946–c1954.

★*5 Shaftesbury Villas, Allen St, W8* – he lived here in 1954.

★*9 Apollo Place, SW10* – he lived here c1955–57. (Died here.)

Works include

Drawing "A soldier writing a letter home" (c1943) – Imperial War Museum. Drawing "A Town Destroyed, Poplar" (1943) – Imperial War Museum. Drawing "Sunflowers" (1945) – Victoria & Albert Museum. Canvas "Street and Railway Bridge" (1946) – Tate Gallery. Drawing "Corte, Corsica" (1947) – Tate Gallery. Canvas "Portuguese Cannon, Mazagan, Morocco" (1953) – Tate Gallery. Canvas "Composition: The Death of James Dean" (1957) – Tate Gallery.

Books illustrated: *The Snail that Climbed the Eiffel Tower* (1947) by Odo Cross. *The Wanderer* (trans. 1947) by Alain-Fournier. *Time was Away* (1948) by Alan Ross. *A Book of Mediterranean Food* (1950) and *French Country Cooking* (1951) by Elizabeth David. *Leaves of Gold* (1951) by George M Whiley. Also, illustrations for *Radio Times.*

Portraits

Self-portrait (c1953) – National Portrait Gallery. He is one of the figures in Rodrigo Moynihan's canvas "Portrait Group" (1951) – Tate Gallery. *Portrait on p. 146.*

Memorabilia

Designs for book covers, posters, etc. – Victoria & Albert Museum. Designs for stage costumes and scenery, etc. – Theatre Museum.

Harold Monro

(14 March 1879 – 16 March 1932)

Monro lived to make poetry popular. A Fabian Socialist, he felt he could assist in the social and cultural development of the British people by nurturing the renaissance of poetry: new poetry for the people of the New Age. Although he was a poet in his own right he is remembered chiefly as the proprietor of The Poetry Bookshop, editor of several influential poetry journals and publisher of new poets and, especially, of the five volumes of *Georgian Poetry*.

Harold Edward Monro was born in St Gilles, near Brussels, and was educated at Radley and Caius College, Cambridge. Failure at the various occupations he tried and disappointment in his first marriage led to his going abroad. He joined a colony of expatriate British writers in Florence, which included Edward Carpenter and Vernon Lee. In 1908 his romantic idealism led him to begin training himself to join the Samurai.

On his return to England in 1911 from his European travels, he devoted himself to "doing something about poetry". A reasonable income derived from his family's private mental hospital enabled him to acquire and edit his own magazine, *Poetry Review* (later *Poetry and Drama*). When Rupert Brooke and Edward Marsh resolved to bring to the attention of the public "the voice of the new poets", through a volume of representative poems, Monro's commitment to popularising poetry and his knowledge of publishing made him a natural choice as publisher of *Georgian Poetry*, the first volume of which appeared in 1912.

Later that year Monro established The Poetry Bookshop in Bloomsbury, with the aim of stocking "all the poetry in print by every living English poet" and enabling the public to experience poetry more directly through hearing it spoken by the poets themselves. The Poetry Bookshop, which Monro described as a "depot for poetry", provided a meeting-place for poets and those interested in poetry, lodgings for such poets as Wilfred Owen, Robert Frost and Wilfred Gibson in rooms above the shop, and, of course, the famous poetry readings. (At one of these

readings Amy Lowell bellowed from the back row that she couldn't hear a word of what Rupert Brooke was reading.)

Most of the writers whom Monro encouraged and published would probably have agreed with Conrad Aiken's description of him as being "stubborn, crotchety, perverse and difficult", but few would have denied that Monro, with his diffident smile, "stiff soldierly little bows" and the appearance of a conventional businessman, was a true and generous friend of poetry and its practitioners.

In 1913 Monro met Alida Klementaski who shared his love of poetry and the belief in its ability to "evolve a higher human life". She came to work at the Bookshop. A close and lasting friendship grew up between them and they later married (in 1920, Monro's first marriage having been dissolved in 1916), but Monro could never bring himself to tell her that he was homosexual. (Many of the Bookshop regulars, however, knew this. Wilfred Owen told Siegfried Sassoon that he and Monro "exchanged some delicious winks" when copies of Robert Graves's *Fairies and Fusiliers* were delivered to the Bookshop.) Alida was, apparently, bemused by his explanation of it being possible to love one person for their mind and another for their body and his admission that he was doing her "a great sad wrong". Nevertheless, she was aware that Monro had been deeply fond of, and desperately missed, the young men "Basil", who was killed at the Front, and "Jim", who sent him poetic descriptions of life in the trenches along with requests for poetry. She recounted, with either equanimity or naivety, to a friend how, after Monro's disappearance at the start of their honeymoon he came to bed and said to her, "Come here, boy."

While Monro was away during the war (after initial training he was discharged as "unfit for General Service"), during his frequent unexplained absences and, from 1922, his withdrawals for treatment for his alcoholism, Alida valiantly managed the Bookshop and as much of its publishing work as she was able.

The Poetry Bookshop was never a success in financial terms, despite its renown and the impact of its associated publishing enterprises, and often came close to bankruptcy. When the lease expired in 1928 the Bookshop moved to smaller premises nearby.

At about this time what Monro called his "period of horror" began. Whereas previously he could be drawn into chatting with dry humour to customers, discussing poetry and

recommending books, visitors to the Bookshop now found him depressed and withdrawn, or drunkenly railing against his lack of success as a poet and complaining about his financial state and the disillusionment the lack of fidelity in his young lovers had caused him.

During his final painful illness he wrote some of his best poems: strong and precise accounts of melancholy, physical pain and erotic despair. (His earlier poems are generally regarded as being palely Georgian, interestingly executed but trivial in their themes.)

"If it is possible to imagine a world without poetry," Monro had once said, "I for one should not wish to be an inhabitant of it." To the instructions that his ashes be scattered at the foot of a young oak tree, he added, "This romantic notion should on no account be taken seriously unless it proves practicable."

Addresses

★*93 Chancery Lane, WC2* – *Poetry Review* office 1911–12.

★*South Square, Gray's Inn, Gray's Inn Road, WC1* – he had chambers here c1912.

★*Cecil House, 34–35 Boswell Street (formerly 35 Devonshire Street), WC1* – site of The Poetry Bookshop 1912–26. (See also *Wilfred Owen*.)

★*38 Great Russell Street, WC1* – premises, shared with the publisher Kegan Paul, of The Poetry Bookshop 1926–35. (Monro's office-cum-bedroom was used for some of the early poetry readings here.)

Works include

Poems (1906); *Evolution of the Soul* (1907); *Chronicle of a Pilgrimage* (1909); *Before Dawn* (1911); *Children of Love* (1914); *Strange Meetings* (1917); *Some Contemporary Poets* (1920); *One Day Awake (Morality)* (1922); *Collected Poems* (1933) – with a critical introduction by T S Eliot. Edited *Twentieth Century Poetry* (1929) and published, in volumes and in his "Chapbooks", the work of many new and established poets.

Portrait

Ink and chalk drawing by Jacob Kramer (1923) – National Portrait Gallery.

Fictional portrait

Arnault in Conrad Aiken's *Ushant* (1952) is Harold Monro.

Cardinal Newman

(21 February 1801 – 11 August 1890)

John Henry Newman was the eldest of six children of a London banker. They were not a particularly religious family, though his mother did read to the children from the scriptures. It was while he was at Ealing School in 1816 that Newman had his first deep spiritual experience, or what he called his "Great change of thought". He was strongly influenced by his schoolmaster, the Rev. Walter Mayers, who was for Newman "the human means of the beginning of divine faith".

In 1817 he went up to Trinity College, Oxford, intending, after he had taken his degree, to become a barrister. He was shy and studious, awkward in the company of his more boisterous contemporaries, and took little part in the social side of university life, spending much of his free time in his rooms, studying or playing his violin. His tutors expected him to do well in his final examinations, but he had a breakdown brought about by overwork and did badly. However, a year later, in 1822, he succeeded in passing an examination for a fellowship at Oriel College.

Newman was ordained deacon in the Church of England in 1824, and in 1828 he became Vicar of St Mary the Virgin, the university church. Whilst travelling in Europe he was taken ill in Sicily, and wrote, "I must act as if I were to die, but I think God has work for me yet." Back in England Newman joined with his fellow dons Keble and Hurrell Froude in forming what became known as the Oxford Movement, which called for reforms in the Church of England and a return to its Catholic roots.

It was at about this time that he first met Ambrose St John (1815–75), then an undergraduate of Christ Church College, who became his most devoted friend. Newman resigned as vicar of the university church and from his Oriel fellowship after his *Tract 90*, which attempted to reconcile the Anglican thirty-nine articles with Catholic doctrine, caused a storm of protest both from his church and from his university.

In 1845 Newman and Ambrose were re-ceived into the Catholic Church and a few months later they set out for Rome. They were ordained priests together and joined the oratorian order of St Philip Neri, a congregation of secular priests. On their return to England Newman founded, in Birmingham, the first English Oratory, while some of his companions went to open the London Oratory under Frederick Faber.

In response to a written attack on him by Charles Kingsley, who questioned his integrity and claimed that he had abandoned his national identity when he left the Church of England, Newman wrote his most famous book, *Apologia Pro Vita Sua*, in which he examines his life and his conversion to Roman Catholicism. It was written in just seven weeks, with Newman "constantly in tears and constantly crying out with distress", and contains many beautiful and revealing passages as well as a tribute to Ambrose. It was enthusiastically received, not only by Catholics, and hailed as a classic.

When Ambrose died in 1875 the distraught Newman was inconsolable. He flung himself onto the deathbed and remained with his friend all night. For the rest of his life he grieved for Ambrose and could never more hear his name without, as the Bishop of Birmingham noticed, "weeping and becoming speechless for the time".

Newman was made a Cardinal in 1879, by Pope Leo XIII. He had always been a controversial figure, castigated when an Anglican for being too close to the doctrines of Rome, yet accused as a Catholic of being a free thinker and a dangerous influence. In 1864 the previous Pope's secretary had written of Newman, "Poor man, by living almost ever since he has been a Catholic surrounded by a set of inferior men who idolise him, I do not think he has ever acquired the Catholic instincts." So with the cardinalate he found acceptance at last; "The cloud is lifted from me," he exclaimed when he heard the news.

He died at the Oratory in Birmingham. His dying words were, "It's true these have been years of strife, but after all there's the Cardinal's hat." In accordance with Newman's own instructions he was buried in the same grave as his dear friend Ambrose St John, in the graveyard adjoining the country house of the Oratory Fathers at Rednal Hill. On their memorial stone is written "Ex umbris et imaginibus in veritatem" – "From shadow and images into truth".

Addresses

★*80 Old Broad Street, EC2* – *site* (*plaque* on Stock Exchange wall near visitors gallery) – Newman was born in a house near this spot.

★*Grey Court, Ham Street, Ham, Richmond* (GLC *plaque*, c1981) – Newman lived here until 1807. He wrote, "When, at school, I dreamed of heaven, the scene was Ham."

★*17 Southampton Place, (formerly Southampton Street) WC1* – (*plaque* placed by Duke of Bedford in 1908). There is a tradition that Newman and Disraeli played together as children in the gardens of Bloomsbury Square.

★*24–25 King William Street, EC4* – *site* of first London Oratory, founded 31 May 1849. (Charing Cross Hospital was built on the site.)

★*Brompton Oratory, Brompton Road, SW3* – a temporary church was built on the site in 1854; the present church opened in 1884.

Works include

Poetry: "Lead Kindly Light" (1833); "The Pillar of the Cloud" (1833); "The Dream of Gerontius" (1865) – which was later to become the text of Elgar's oratorio.

Tracts: *Tracts for the Times* (1833–41) – not all by Newman.

Essay: *The Development of Christian Doctrine* (1845).

Autobiography: *Apologia Pro Vita Sua* (1864).

Statue

Just outside Brompton Oratory there is a marble statue of him holding a cardinal's hat in his hand. It is by Leon-Joseph Chavalliaud (1896) and was erected by public subscription.

Photo on p. 146.

Portraits

Canvas by Emmeline Deane (1889) – National Portrait Gallery. Chalk by G Richmond (1844) – N.P.G. Plaster cast of bust by Thomas Woolner (1866) – N.P.G. Photographs by Barraud (1888) and H J Whitlock (undated) – N.P.G. Several cartes by McLean & Haes; R W Thrupp; and H J Whitlock – N.P.G. Print by W Humphreys (1844) – N.P.G. Caricatures by "Spy" (1877) and by unknown artist (1850) – N.P.G. Prints by R Woodman (c1845), J A Vinter (1850) and S Cousins (1880) – N.P.G. and British Museum. Caricature of Newman as Vicar of St Mary's, by J R Green (undated) – N.P.G. and British Museum. Caricature by Richard Doyle (undated) – British Museum.

Memorabilia

The manuscript of "The Dream of Gerontius" – British Museum. Autograph letter (early, undated) to Arthur Hugh Clough – Fawcett Library.

Ivor Novello

(15 January 1893 – 6 March 1951)

"I want glamour with a capital G. I want great crystal chandeliers, and satin trains fourteen foot long, and footmen in velvet liveries. I want grace, dignity, curtsies and royal salutes."

Ivor Novello realised his dream in the series of lavish and spectacular musical romances which made him not only King of Ruritania, but also King of the British Theatre.

David Ivor Davies was born in Cardiff. His father, David Davies, was a tax collector, and his mother, Clara Novello Davies, a singing teacher. He had a fine soprano voice and won a scholarship to Magdalen College Choir School. While still a schoolboy he began writing songs, under the name of Ivor Novello. Some of them were published and became popular, and he was called "the Welsh Prodigy".

Soon after Ivor left school the family moved to London, where his mother was much in demand as a singing coach. Sometimes musical or theatrical celebrities would come to tea, and Ivor would be introduced to them by his proud mother as "my composer son". He was very good-looking, with raven black hair and big brown eyes, and his natural warmth and charm won him many friends.

In 1914 Ivor wrote "Keep the Home Fires Burning", which became one of the most popular songs of the British Army. It earned him £15,000 in royalties and made him famous. As a result he was asked to write music for several West End productions, including *Theodore and Co* which ran for eighteen months at the Gaiety Theatre.

One day in 1916, during a break in rehearsals, Ivor met a twenty-one year old actor, Bobby Andrews. They became friends and lovers, remained inseparable for thirty-five years, and appeared together in many of Ivor's plays and musicals. After the war they went on holiday together to New York. Halfway across the Atlantic on their way home, Ivor received a cable offering him a starring role in a film *The Call of the Blood*. The director of the film had never met Ivor, but a photograph of the famous profile convinced him that he would be ideal for the part of a young Sicilian.

The film was a success and Ivor became a star overnight. He was hailed as "the New Valentino" and "the British Adonis" and went on to make twenty more silent films. Later, in talking pictures, Ivor's beautiful speaking voice added to his success.

In 1924, in collaboration with the actress Constance Collier, Ivor wrote his first play, *The Rat*, in which he also starred under his own management. It played to packed houses and was made into a successful film, with Ivor repeating his stage role.

His flat above the Strand Theatre became a magnet for theatre people. Everyone came to his parties. They began at midnight with supper ordered from the Savoy. Sometimes Ivor would engage an orchestra. The Dolly Sisters danced, Mrs Patrick Campbell recited, and once Paul Robeson sat on the floor and sang spirituals. Noel Coward, Gertrude Lawrence, Jack Buchanan and Sir Edward Marsh were regular guests.

Over lunch one day, H M Tennent, the impresario, mentioned that he was having difficulty finding a show to follow the 1934–35 pantomime at Drury Lane. Ivor offered to write a musical play and outlined the plot of *Glamorous Night*. Tennent was enthusiastic and even agreed to Ivor's request for a forty-piece orchestra and a cast of a hundred and twenty, plus complete control of production.

Glamorous Night was the first of Ivor's famous Drury Lane shows, in which he also starred. With their mixture of operetta, musical comedy and melodrama, they filled the theatre for many years.

When the outbreak of war closed Drury Lane he went on tour for eighteen months with *The Dancing Years*, which later ran for over two years at the Adelphi Theatre.

In 1944 Ivor was summonsed for misuse of petrol coupons. Despite his plea that he needed the petrol to enable him to drive from the theatre to Redroofs, his country house near Maidenhead, he was sent to prison for a month. The sentence was so severe that it was widely supposed that he was either being made an example of, or being punished for another kind of "offence".

After Ivor's release from Wormwood Scrubs he and Bobby went with an ENSA company to entertain the troops in France and Belgium. Ivor played his latest song, "We'll Gather Lilacs", which became so popular with the troops that he decided to put it into his next show.

Perchance to Dream opened in April 1945. As the curtain rose on the opening night Ivor turned to Bobby and said, "With luck this will be our victory production." It was another huge success and played to full houses for over a thousand performances.

The last show in which Ivor appeared was *King's Rhapsody*, his greatest commercial success. He left the cast at Christmas 1950 and went with Bobby on a long holiday to Jamaica, where he had recently bought a house. On his return he attended the first night of his last show, *Gay's the Word*, and although he was unwell, rejoined the cast of *King's Rhapsody*.

A week later, while having supper in his flat after the show, he collapsed. In the early hours of the morning he died of a coronary thrombosis. The fact that Bobby was with Ivor at the end was not mentioned in the newspaper reports of his death.

Thousands lined the streets for Ivor's funeral at Golders Green Crematorium. The service was broadcast live, and that evening at the BBC's Aeolian Hall a recording was played back for his close friends and relatives.

Addresses

★*55 New Bond Street, W1* – Ivor and his parents lived here from 1910 to 1913.

★*11 Aldwych, WC2* – Ivor's home from 1913 until 1951. He died here. (Blue *plaque* unveiled in 1973 by Olive Gilbert who appeared in all his musical plays.)

Photo of 11 Aldwych on p. 147.

Works include

Musical plays: *Glamorous Night* (1935); *Careless Rapture* (1936); *Crest of the Wave* (1937); *The Dancing Years* (1939); *Arc de Triomphe* (1943); *Perchance to Dream* (1945); *King's Rhapsody* (1949); *Gay's the Word* (1950).

Plays: *The Rat* (1924); *The Truth Game* (1928); *I Lived With You* (1932).

Song: "Keep the Home Fires Burning" (1914).

Portraits

Photograph by Angus McBean (c1947) – National Portrait Gallery. Photographs by Cecil Beaton, Foulsham & Banfield, Sasha, Claude Harris, and Paul Tanqueray – N.P.G. (Archives). Bust by Clemence Dane (unveiled 1952) – Grand Circle rotunda, Theatre Royal, Drury Lane, WC2.

Memorials

Bust at Golders Green Crematorium, unveiled by Sir Edward Marsh in 1952. Nearby, in the memorial garden, a lilac tree, recalling Novello's famous song, was planted to his memory. Memorial tablet – St Paul's Church, Covent Garden, WC2.

Memorabilia

Playbills, programmes, photographs, etc. – Theatre Museum.

Cardinal Newman

John Minton

146

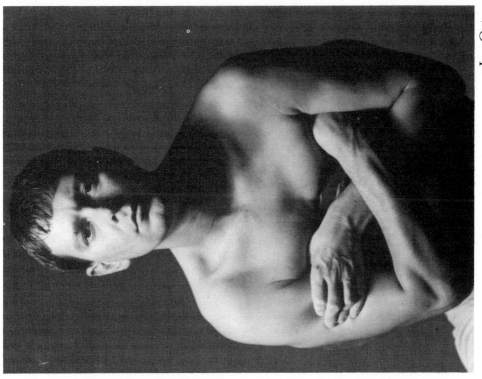

Joe Orton

11 Aldwych, flat above Strand Theatre (Ivor Novello)

Joe Orton

(1 January 1933 – 9 August 1967)

Joe Orton, creator of some of the wildest, funniest and most savage plays seen on the modern stage, was born John Kingsley Orton in Leicester. He was the eldest child of William Orton, a gardener, and his wife, Elsie, a machinist in a factory. After failing his eleven-plus examination, he was sent by his mother to what she thought was a "good school", but which was primarily a secretarial college. Not surprisingly, Orton did not receive there the liberal education his mother had hoped for as a means of his "bettering himself": he learned Pitman's shorthand, but little else.

He was sacked from most of the jobs he had between the ages of sixteen and eighteen, chiefly because he was not interested in them. What he was interested in was the theatre, which offered a glamorous escape from the drabness and squalor of the housing estate where he lived. Deciding to become an actor, Orton joined an amateur theatre group and took elocution lessons to get rid of his slight lisp and strong Leicester accent.

In May 1951 he came to London, having won a scholarship to the Royal Academy of Dramatic Art. At RADA he met Kenneth Halliwell (1926–67), became his lover, and shortly afterwards moved into Halliwell's flat in West Hampstead. Halliwell took responsibility for filling in the large gaps in Orton's education, and introduced him to the works of his favourite writers, especially Aristophanes, Euripides, Firbank and Wilde.

Acting had been Orton's ambition, but he joined Halliwell in his literary efforts when, after RADA, neither got any significant stage work. Together they wrote a series of unpublishable novels, which included "The Mechanical Womb", "The Last Days of Sodom" and "The Boy Hairdresser".

They also created a character, Mrs Edna Welthorpe, in whose name they wrote spoof letters of complaint about tinned pie fillings and outraged decency, and requests for the hire of a Baptist church hall for performances, by the Phallus Players, of "The Pansy" – "a play which pleads for greater tolerance on the subject of homosexuality".

It was not their writing, but a much more elaborate prank, which brought them the public attention they desperately wanted. It also brought them each a jail sentence. Since 1959 Orton had been stealing library books, the illustrations from which were used to make surrealistic collages to decorate the walls of the bedsitter in Islington into which they had moved. Together they also doctored dozens of stolen books, which they replaced on the library shelves. They then hung around waiting to observe readers' reactions to the blurbs they had expertly inserted into the dust-jackets of the books and the incongruous pictures and captions which they had pasted over the originals: a photograph of an old man in bathing trunks, his body covered in tattoos, graced the cover of a biography of John Betjeman; a female nude, the cover of a book of etiquette; and a gorilla peered out from the petals of a rose on the *Collins Guide to Roses*.

Orton and Halliwell were arrested in 1962 and charged with "wilfully damaging" 83 books and with removing 1,653 plates and illustrations from books stolen from the Islington and Hampstead public libraries. Although neither had any previous convictions they were both sentenced to six months imprisonment and made to pay damages. Orton contended that he and Halliwell were so severely treated "because we were queers".

Imprisonment was a deeply humiliating experience for Halliwell, and he twice tried to commit suicide. For Orton, however, it crystallised his vague awareness of there being "something rotten somewhere" and brought detachment to his writing. The rather precious Firbankian pastiches were to be replaced by aggressive comic attacks on the hypocrisy of British society, its obsession with law and order, and the middle-class proprieties of sexual morality. "Laughter is a serious business," Orton wrote, "and comedy is a weapon more dangerous than tragedy, which is why tyrants treat it with caution."

Within a year of his release from prison the BBC had accepted a radio version of his play *Ruffian on the Stair*. His next play, *Entertaining Mr Sloane*, produced at the New Arts Theatre in 1964, outraged many of the West End's traditional theatre-goers. The redoubtable Mrs Edna Welthorpe was promptly resurrected to fan the flames of the resulting controversy in the press.

Orton's work progressed from the comedy of manners of *Entertaining Mr Sloane* through the violent, anarchic comedy of *The Erpingham Camp* and *Loot* to the manic farce of *What the Butler Saw*, his posthumously produced masterpiece. Sex and death were the two principal subjects in his work; along the way the police, the church, psychiatry and suburban gentility were dealt painful blows.

By 1967 Orton had seen *Loot* become a hit in a remounted production directed by Charles Marowitz; received a commission from The Beatles to write a film script for them; and gleefully noted that the term "Ortonesque" had entered the English vocabulary as a shorthand means of describing macabre outrageousness.

In private Orton acknowledged the assistance he received from Halliwell in tightening up dialogue, editing, and coming up with titles for the plays, but Halliwell wanted a greater share in Orton's success as well as recognition for his own work. Orton remained loyal to his friend and made excuses for his evidently increasing insecurity and his neuroses, but their professional paths had separated: Halliwell was still working on unsaleable literary pastiche and collage, while Orton's plays were not only being produced but were winning awards and bringing their author the heady mixture of adulation and public outrage that he craved.

In the early hours of 9 August 1967 Halliwell beat Orton to death with a hammer and then killed himself with a drug overdose. The reasons for his actions could be found in Orton's diary, he explained in a suicide note. The diary contained Orton's musings on his success and detailed accounts of his frequent sexual liaisons.

At Orton's secular funeral service at Golders Green Crematorium a recording of his favourite song, The Beatles's "A Day in the Life", was played. Permission was given, by Orton's brother, for Orton and Halliwell's ashes to be scattered together – on one condition: that nobody heard about it in Leicester.

Works include

Plays: *The Ruffian on the Stair* (broadcast 1964; produced 1966); *Entertaining Mr Sloane* (produced 1964); *Loot* (produced 1965); *The Erpingham Camp* (televised 1966; produced 1967); *The Good and Faithful Servant* (first produced on television 1967); *Funeral Games* (televised 1968); *What the Butler Saw* (produced 1969); (*Joe Orton: The Complete Plays* with an introduction by John Lahr, 1976).

Filmscript: *Up Against It* (commissioned by The Beatles in 1967, but unproduced; stage adaptation produced 1985).

Novel: *Head to Toe* (original title "The Vision of Gombold Proval") – (completed in 1961; published 1971).

Portraits

Photographs by Lewis Morley (c1963) – National Portrait Gallery.

Portrait on p. 147.

Memorabilia

The collection of books, etc. doctored by Orton and Halliwell may be seen, by prior arrangement, at the Islington Central Library.

Addresses

★*31 Gower Street, WC1* – Orton had lodgings in the basement (May–June 1951).

★*161 West End Lane, NW6* – Halliwell owned a flat in this house. They lived here 1951–59.

★*25 Noel Road, N1* – their bedsitter (top floor) where they lived from 1959–67. They died here. (*Plaque* erected 1985.)

Wilfred Owen

(18 March 1893 – 4 November 1918)

In what has become one of the most famous literary manifestos, the Preface for the volume of poems he envisaged (only five of his poems were published in his lifetime), Wilfred Owen wrote: "Above all I am not concerned with poetry. My subject is war, and the pity of war. The Poetry is in the pity . . . All the poet can do is to warn. That is why true poets must be truthful."

Wilfred Edward Salter Owen was born in Oswestry and grew up in Birkenhead and Shrewsbury. An early interest in poetry and religion was encouraged by his mother, a devout evangelical Anglican. His father was disappointed that Wilfred seemed likely to enter the church rather than follow a trade.

When Owen failed to win a scholarship to London University he accepted an unpaid post as lay assistant to the Vicar of Dunsden, Oxfordshire, in 1912. He received little of the promised tuition at Dunsden which he had hoped would enable him to make a successful second attempt at winning a scholarship, and although he enjoyed his parish work, his encounters with what he called "pulpit professionals" and the tension he felt between conventional church teachings and homoerotic humanism led to his rejection of orthodox belief. He was forced to recognise that his career was to be in neither the church nor the academic world.

In 1913 he took a poorly paid job teaching English in Bordeaux, which led to a private tutoring job in the Pyrenees. There he met the poet Laurent Tailhade who encouraged him to continue with the poetry he had begun writing again.

Indecision about whether or not to join up and the supposed dangers of the Channel crossing in wartime delayed his return to England until September 1915. In London he enlisted in the Artists' Rifles in October of that year and met Harold Monro, at whose Poetry Bookshop he became a regular browser. (He later took lodgings there and had "the time of my life" when Monro came up to his room to discuss Owen's manuscripts of poems and told him that he was "very struck" with them.)

Seven months after being commissioned in the Manchester Regiment, Owen was sent to France, and early in January 1917 he joined the 2nd Manchesters on the Somme near Beaumont Hamel. There one of his first tasks was to hold a dugout in No-Man's-Land (an ordeal described in his poems "The Sentry" and "Exposure").

Having suffered concussion after a fall into a cellar, he spent a fortnight in a Casualty Clearing Station. He was involved in heavy fighting all through April 1917, and at the beginning of May he was diagnosed as suffering from neurasthenia (shell-shock) and evacuated to England. (He had been thrown into the air by the blast from a shell and had spent several days, sheltering from gunfire, in a trench in which a fellow officer's remains lay scattered around him.)

At the end of June he was admitted to Craiglockhart War Hospital, Edinburgh. His meeting there with Siegfried Sassoon, in August, provided Owen with the "literary shock" that generated the writing of the series of poems for which he has become famous. It was also the start of the deepest friendship and love he ever had.

Sassoon recognised Owen's talent and shared his disillusionment with the later course of the war. (In the Somme battles between July and November 1917 both sides suffered over one million casualties, with no significant gains.) With gentle, but pertinent, criticism he helped Owen, who was considerably influenced by his poetry, to realise his own poetic powers. Both contributed poems to *The Hydra*, the hospital magazine which Owen edited.

Owen's attitude towards Sassoon was virtually one of hero-worship and, by readily accepting the homoerotic element in Owen's poetry, Sassoon helped the younger poet to feel more at ease about his sexuality. It is certain that their strongly homoerotic and comradely identification with the young men they knew and led into battle, as much as their great technical skills, made Owen and Sassoon the most eloquent poets of the new mood of the war.

Robert Graves, who first met Owen at Craiglockhart while visiting Sassoon, claimed to have recognised early in their association Owen's achievements as a poet and his homosexuality. Of Owen, whom he described in *Goodbye To All That* as "a quiet round-faced little man" and later dismissed as being "an idealistic homosexual with a religious background", he wrote to Edward Marsh, "I have a new poet for you, just discovered . . . the real thing . . ."

Owen was discharged from hospital at the end of October 1917, and spent some of his three weeks' leave in London, where, bearing a letter of introduction from Sassoon, he visited Robert Ross. Through Ross he met H G Wells, Arnold Bennett, Charles Scott Moncrieff and (the following year) Osbert Sitwell. "I go out of this year a Poet . . . I am a poet's poet. I am started . . ." he wrote to his mother.

He was promoted to full lieutenant in December 1917, and spent the next few months doing light duties in Yorkshire, writing, spending his leaves in London and seeing five of his poems appear in *The Nation* and *The Bookman*.

When Sassoon was sent home wounded in July 1918, Owen felt it his duty to take his friend's place at the Front to testify, through his poems, on behalf of the men there. He crossed to France in September not expecting to return. In October he was awarded the Military Cross "for conspicuous gallantry and devotion to duty" and a few weeks later, just seven days before the war ended, he was killed leading his men across the Sambre Canal.

"What more is there to say that you will not better understand unsaid – your W.E.O.," he wrote in his last letter to Sassoon. Many years later Sassoon wrote, "W's death was an unhealed wound, & the ache of it has been with me ever since. I wanted *him* back – not his poems."

Addresses

★*38 Worple Road, SW19* – Owen stayed here while sitting the London Matriculation Examination in 1911.

★*(Les Lilas) 54 Tavistock Square, WC1* – he had lodgings here October–November 1915. (*Site*. Now part of Tavistock Hotel.)

★*Cecil House, 34–35 Boswell Street (formerly 35 Devonshire Street), WC1* – site of The Poetry Bookshop's first premises. There was a room here for Owen's use during his London leaves (end 1915 and February–March 1916). He also took a room over a coffee shop which stood opposite, having been forced out of his room at the Bookshop by the arrival of Robert Frost and his family. (See also *Harold Monro*.)

★*40 Half Moon Street, W1* – in May 1918 he stayed in the flat over *Robert Ross's* (where he met Osbert Sitwell). (See also *Ronald Firbank*.)

Works

Poetry: Siegfried Sassoon and Edith Sitwell edited the first collection of Owen's poems in 1920. Since then his poems have been published in various collections and included in many anthologies. One of the most recent editions is *The Poems of Wilfred Owen*, edited by Jon Stallworthy (Hogarth Press, 1985).

Letters: *Wilfred Owen: Collected Letters*, edited by Harold Owen and John Bell (1967).

Portraits

Photograph by John Gunston – National Portrait Gallery. Photographs – Imperial War Museum (Archives).

Memorabilia

Most of Owen's autograph poems are in the British Museum.

Glyn Philpot

(5 October 1884 – 16 December 1937)

During his lifetime Glyn Philpot was one of the most famous and respected painters of portraits and figure compositions. After years of neglect following his death there are signs of a renewed interest in his work, especially in the wake of the major exhibition at the National Portrait Gallery in 1984 to mark the centenary of his birth.

Glyn Warren Philpot was the youngest of the four children of John Philpot, a chartered surveyor, and Jessie Carpenter Philpot. His mother died when he was seven, and five years later John Philpot married his first wife's half-sister, Julia. The children were very fond of their stepmother and they were a close-knit family.

Through ill-health Philpot lost a lot of his schooling and was mainly educated at home, where his talent for drawing was noticed and encouraged. When he was fifteen he became a student at the Lambeth School of Art. The school's most distinguished ex-pupils were Ricketts and Shannon, and Philpot was greatly influenced by their work.

In 1903 Philpot visited France for the first time. In Rouen he painted "The Elevation of the Host" which a year later was exhibited at the Royal Academy. On his return to London he borrowed a friend's studio and put on his first one-man show. As a result he received his first commission – a portrait of a child – for which he was paid £5.

He became a Catholic in 1905. His Baptist family strongly disapproved of his conversion and he lived away from home for a couple of months until their anger abated.

In 1906 Philpot moved into his first studio. His work began to be noticed and exhibited. By the time he was twenty-four he had achieved a reputation as an accomplished portraitist and was receiving enthusiastic reviews for paintings such as "The Stage Box" (1909) and the elegant and restrained portrait of Mrs Emile Mond (1910).

Philpot first met Ricketts and Shannon in 1911 and through them, Robert Ross, who became a close friend and helped him to obtain several important commissions. An evening at the opera in 1913 led to Philpot's chance meeting with an American millionaire, Robert Allerton, who invited him to visit his mansion near Chicago. He duly set sail on the *Lusitania*. Little is known about Philpot's relationship with Allerton, but in a letter to his sister Daisy, he insisted that Allerton was "not just a silly infatuation". He painted his host's portrait "The Man in Black" (1913) and sculpted a pair of enormous male figures for his garden.

Philpot's closest relationship was with Vivian Forbes (1891–1937), whom he met in 1913. Forbes wanted to be an artist and Philpot taught him personally and arranged for him to study at the Chelsea Polytechnic and later in France. In 1920 Forbes had a painting "Nature, Man and Poetry" accepted by the Royal Academy, and thereafter his pictures were regularly exhibited.

In 1917 Robert Ross introduced Philpot to Siegfried Sassoon who was convalescing after being wounded in France. Philpot painted his portrait and they became friends. They went to fancy-dress parties together. Philpot dressed as a Middle Eastern woman or, as Sassoon related in *Siegfried's Journey* (1945), as "an Elizabethan Spaniard in black velvet. His face powdered dead white, white spur straps on long black boots, and long green gem-rings on his fingers."

Sassoon in turn introduced Philpot to Wilfred Owen's younger brother, Harold, who had come to London to study art. Philpot found him a place at the Byam Shaw School, took an interest in his work, and made sure that he was never short of money. In 1922 Owen helped Philpot with the painting "Altarpiece of the Sacred Heart" which was given to Father John Gray and André Raffalovich for their church in Edinburgh.

In 1923 Philpot was elected to the Royal Academy, the youngest member at that time. But he was becoming dissatisfied with his public role as establishment portrait painter, and set about widening his range and finding new modes of expression.

He took a studio in Paris in 1931 and over the next year produced some of his most individual and powerful works. He met a young German, Karl Heinz Müller, and went with him to Berlin, where he was introduced to the life of the city's underworld which he celebrated in "Lokal Berlin" (1932). Müller was the inspiration for some of Philpot's most intensely felt pictures; he had lost the ends of two of the fingers of his left hand, which identifies him in the paintings "St Sebastian" (1931) and "Fugue" (1932).

When Philpot's "modern" paintings were

put on show the British public were shocked and bewildered by his change of style, and his portrait commissions ceased almost overnight. He eventually had to sell his country house and give up his studio in Paris, but undaunted he continued to experiment and to widen his repertoire. Some of the strongest paintings of his last years are of his black model, Henry Thomas: "Balthazar" (1929) and "Negro Sitting – Backview" (1937); and of the young Norwegian, Jan Erland: "The Badminton Player" and "Man with a Gun" (1933–34). These pictures and the subtle, unassertive later portraits, including one of Vivian Forbes, won him a new circle of admirers.

Philpot died of a heart attack while working in his studio. A requiem mass was sung at Westminster Cathedral and he was buried at St Peter's Old Church in Petersham. The day after the funeral Vivian Forbes committed suicide. A privately printed memorial volume to Forbes includes some explicit love poems addressed by him to Philpot.

Addresses

★*Este Road (formerly 31 Grove Road), SW11* – site of Philpot's birthplace and childhood home.

★*14a Cheyne Row, SW3* – his first studio, 1906–09.

★*52 Glebe Place, SW3* – his home 1909–10.

★*Tower House, 46 (formerly 28) Tite Street, SW3* – his home 1910–18.

★*33 Tite Street, SW3* –his studio 1918–23.

★*5 Park Row, SW1* – site of his home 1919–23. (Bowater House, Knightsbridge, stands on the site of the whole of Park Row.)

★*Lansdowne House, Lansdowne Road, W11* – his home and studio with Forbes, 1923–35. (Blue *plaque*.) (See also *Ricketts & Shannon*.)

★*1 Marlborough Gate House, cnr Elms Mews and Bayswater Road, W2* – his home 1935–37. (Died here.)

Works include

Paintings: "The Man in Black" (Robert Allerton) (1913) – Tate Gallery. "A Young Breton" (1917) – Tate Gallery. "Italian Soldier, No. 2" (1923) – Courtauld Institute Galleries. "Richard I leaving England for the Crusade" (1927) (together with "Sir Thomas More and Cardinal Wolsey" by Vivian Forbes) – St Stephen's Hall, Westminster.

Drawings: "Study of Standing Male Nude" (c1904–10) – Victoria & Albert Museum. "Two Figures" (c1919) – Victoria & Albert Museum. Composition study for "The Coast of Britain" (No. 23) (1919–20) – Courtauld Institute Galleries. Studies for "A Street Accident" (No. 38) (1925) – Courtauld Institute Galleries. "Three Figures" (c1919–21) – Tate Gallery. "Study of Seated Negro" (c1934) – British Museum. Study for "Acrobats Waiting to Rehearse" (No. 62) (1935) – British Museum. Figure study for "André Eglevsky" (No. 70) (1937) – British Museum.

Sculpture: "Oedipus Replying to the Sphinx" (1930–31) – Tate Gallery.

Portraits

Canvas self-portrait (1908) – National Portrait Gallery. Canvas by Oswald Birley (1920) – N.P.G. Photograph by F J Gutman (1937) – N.P.G. (Archives).

Memorabilia

Fifteen drawings from his sketchbook – British Museum.

William Pitt (the Younger)

(28 May 1759 – 23 January 1806)

Britain's youngest Prime Minister, "the pilot that weathered the storm", was born at Hayes Place, near Bromley in Kent. He was the second son of the Prime Minister William Pitt (the Elder), later Earl of Chatham, and Hester Grenville Pitt.

He was a delicate child and was educated at home until at the age of fourteen he went to Pembroke Hall, Cambridge. While he was there he became ill. The family doctor diagnosed gout and prescribed as treatment a daily bottle of port wine. Pitt made a complete recovery but developed the taste for alcohol which later proved fatal.

There was a coldness in Pitt's manner which set him apart. Yet in the company of a few carefully chosen friends his conversation could be "abounding in playful wit and quick repartee". In appearance, he was tall and slim with narrow shoulders, a long neck and a sharp nose.

Pitt entered Parliament at the age of twenty-two. In his maiden speech he supported Edmund Burke's call for economic reform in public administration. In a voice that was "rich and striking, full of melody and force", he outlined the objectives of peace, retrenchment and reform which remained the principal aims of his political career.

By distancing himself from the various warring factions in Parliament Pitt earned the respect of the small group of uncommitted members. He did not enjoy formal social gatherings, preferring instead to relax in the company of a few young men who were "very nice in their admissions" and "seemed to be impressed with an awe of him, at times it appeared, like boys with their master."

In December 1783 the shaky coalition government of Fox and North collapsed and George II asked Pitt to form a new administration. There were shouts of derision in the House of Commons when the announcement of his appointment was made. He was just twenty-four years old, with little experience in politics and none whatsoever in government. Yet despite his youth he was confident and composed, and the longer he remained in office the stronger he became as the most able and ambitious members gave him their support.

Pitt came to power at a time when the government's prestige had been seriously damaged, both at home and abroad, by the loss of the American colonies. He was initially more concerned with domestic reforms and the restoration of the economy than with Britain's standing in Europe. He ignored the French Revolution, considering it to be an internal dispute which need not concern Britain, and he refused demands for intervention. He concentrated rather on seeking the reform of Parliament and of the national economy, and he gave his wholehearted support to Wilberforce's campaign for the abolition of the slave trade.

In 1784 Richard Brinsley Sheridan caused uproar in the House of Commons by referring to Pitt as the King's minion and comparing him with James I's Buckingham. The jibe was later taken up by Macaulay who wrote that Pitt's influence over George III equalled that of Robert Carr and Buckingham over James I. Scurrilous verses and lampoons appeared, drawing attention to Pitt's relationship with Tom Steele, a young man with whom he spent a number of holidays in Brighton. Pitt's preference for exclusively male company was well known and was the subject of much gossip. The Prime Minister who "loved wine but not a woman" furthered the careers of many of his young friends and Tom Steele was given the job of Secretary to the Treasury.

By now Pitt was drinking heavily and suffering from painful attacks of gout. His friend Henry Addington noticed that "Mr Pitt liked a glass of wine very well, and a bottle still better."

In 1800 the Act of Union with Ireland was passed, which Pitt hoped would allow Catholics to be admitted to Parliament. However, George III opposed the plan and Pitt resigned after seventeen years as Prime Minister.

He spent most of his time while out of office at Walmer Castle in Kent. His niece Lady Hester Stanhope acted as his housekeeper. "There are generally three or four men staying in the house," she noted. "Military and naval characters are constantly welcome here; women are not, I suppose, because they do not form any part of our society."

Pitt returned to office in 1803. The war with France was not going well for Britain and its allies, despite Nelson's victory at Trafalgar. When news reached England of Napoleon's crushing defeat of the allied forces at Austerlitz, Pitt was reported as saying, "Roll up that map. It will not be wanted these ten years."

He was prematurely aged by overwork and illness. His hair was almost white and his face bore the signs of disease and drink. He retired to his house in Putney, where he died of kidney failure on the twenty-fifth anniversary of the day on which he had first taken his seat in Parliament. According to his niece his last words were, "Oh my country; how I love my country." Others heard him say, "I think I could eat one of Bellamy's veal pies."

He was laid in state in the Painted Chamber of Westminster Hall before being taken in procession to the Abbey where he was buried in the family vault beside his parents.

Addresses

★*Stone Buildings, Lincolns Inn, WC2* – Pitt lived here in 1779.

★*47 (formerly 6) Berkeley Square, W1* – the home of Pitt's brother, John, 2nd Earl of Chatham. Pitt lived here c1780.

★*10 Downing Street, SW1* – from 1782–1800 Pitt's home as Chancellor of the Exchequer and then as Prime Minister.

★*12 Park Place, SW1* – *site* of the house in which Pitt lived c1801.

★*120 Baker Street (formerly 14 York Place), W1*. Lady Hester Stanhope kept house for him here. He lived here 1803–04. (*Plaque*.)

★*Bowling Green Close, Putney Heath, SW15* – *site* of Bowling Green House, where Pitt lived from 1804 until his death in 1806.

Portraits

Canvas by George Romney (c1783) – Tate Gallery. Canvas by (Studio of) John Hoppner (c1806–07) – Tate Gallery. "The Spiritual form of Pitt Guiding Behemoth" by William Blake (c1805) – Tate Gallery. Watercolour by James Gillray (c1789) – National Portrait Gallery. Canvas "Pitt Addressing the House of Commons" by Karl Anton Hinkel (1793) – N.P.G. Canvas by John Hoppner (1805) – N.P.G. Marble bust by J Nollekens (1808) – N.P.G. Marble bust by D A Olivieri, after Nollekens (undated) – N.P.G. Wax medallion by Peter Rouw (1809) – N.P.G. Print by John Hoppner (1805) – N.P.G. Numerous caricatures by Gillray, James Sayers and others – N.P.G. and British Museum. Drawing by Henry Edridge (c1800) – British Museum. Print by or after Thomas Gainsborough (1788) – Kenwood House Picture Gallery.

Statues and memorials

Above the main West Door of Westminster Abbey there is a statue of Pitt by Westmacott (1813). History is seen recording his words while Anarchy cowers in chains. Statue by J G Bubb – Guildhall, EC4. Bronze statue by Sir Francis Chantry (1831) – Hanover Square, W1.

Memorabilia

Pitt's will – Public Records Office, Chancery Lane, WC2.

Eleanor Rathbone

(12 May 1872 – 2 January 1946)

Eleanor Florence Rathbone, vigorous feminist, Member of Parliament and the moving spirit for family allowances, was born in London. There was a long tradition of civic service and philanthropy in her family. Her father, William Rathbone, was Liberal MP for the city of Liverpool.

Eleanor attended Kensington High School and then went up to Somerville College, Oxford. She was a diligent student of political philosophy, intending to divide her time, after graduating, between philosophical writing and work for social reform.

She applied her philosophical training to practical affairs when she began to do organised social work in Liverpool. Her impressively documented studies on the industrial conditions there were widely regarded as accurate and impartial, and many of the reforms which she proposed, regarding casual labour in the city's docks, were accepted and implemented, albeit years afterwards.

A committed feminist since her university days, she became increasingly aware that, while philanthropic projects offered temporary relief for the families she encountered during the course of her studies and social work in the docklands, it was only through political reforms that the particularly unfair condition of women (as dependent wives, mothers and widows) could be improved. She joined the suffrage movement and in 1897 became parliamentary secretary to the Liverpool Women's Suffrage Society; later she was elected to the executive committee of the National Union of Women's Suffrage Societies (NUWSS).

She became, in 1909, the first woman to be elected to the City Council of Liverpool. A committee which she called together in 1917 produced a pamphlet *Equal Pay and the Family: a Proposal for the National Endowment*, thereby initiating the long and arduous campaign for family allowances which was to be her major contribution to feminism.

In 1919 she succeeded Millicent Fawcett as president of the National Union of Societies for Equal Citizenship (formerly the NUWSS),

a position which she held until 1928. The main task which she set herself was to make family allowances a major plank in the NUSEC programme of reform. This she achieved through the conclusive arguments she marshalled in her presidential address in 1925 and through her book *The Disinherited Family*, about which Sir William Beveridge said at the time, "There are few whose opinions the book will leave unchanged."

She stood, unsuccessfully, as an Independent parliamentary candidate in 1924. In 1929 she stood again for Parliament – this time successfully – as the Independent candidate for the Combined English Universities. She was the only woman in Britain ever to stand successfully without the backing of a political party.

The plight of Indian women and children, revealed in Katherine Mayo's book *Mother India*, had strengthened her resolve to enter Parliament in order to help women of all nations and all classes. She went to India in 1931 to confer with national leaders, became involved in the campaign for women's suffrage in that country, and was particularly outspoken on the issue of child marriages. In these and other instances, as when she denounced the practices of female circumcision and forced marriages, she was accused of interfering in local (male) custom. She was a militant supporter of the League of Nations, and was tireless in her efforts on behalf of refugees. In the late 1930s and during the Second World War she strove to find ways of helping Jews in occupied territories and of pressuring the government to offer asylum to those who managed to escape or were released.

She continued to work on domestic reforms, while serving as chairman of the Family Endowment Society and of the Children's Nutrition Council. She was largely responsible for the Inheritance Family Provision Act of 1938, but family allowances still remained her major concern. It was said of her that "she belongs to the bulldog breed, and once she gets her teeth into a matter she worries it until she gets what she wants." The Labour movement gradually came to see family allowances as a way of alleviating poverty in large families, and the publiction of Eleanor's *Case for Family Allowances* in 1940 helped to instigate parliamentary action on the issue. At first the resulting Bill proposed, to Eleanor's horror, that the allowances be paid to fathers. The whole feminist argument, that payments should be made directly to mothers in order to end the "economic conditions of a glorified serfdom", would have been negated, and Eleanor threatened to vote against the Bill. She was joined in her protest by dozens of women's organisations, and eventually the government capitulated.

Throughout her political career Eleanor lived with Elizabeth Macadam. They had met, in the early 1900s, on the stage of St George's Hall, Liverpool, during the interval of a display of girls' club activities. Elizabeth, then a social worker, became warden of the Victoria Women's Settlement in Everton, of which Eleanor was a member of the committee. She later became Honorary Secretary of NUSEC and joint editor of its journal, the *Woman's Leader*.

Self-sacrifice, diligence and devotion to duty characterised Eleanor's public life, and with her predeliction for black clothes, her habit of peering over her half-spectacles, and her clipped speech, she was regarded as a rather austere, even severe, personality. When "off duty" she enjoyed relaxing at home with Elizabeth and their cat "Smuts". Every summer they would drive down to the coast in their battered old car which they named "Jane Austen".

Her battle for family allowances had taken nearly thirty years to win, but she felt that her faith in reformist politics and her "unquenchable belief in the ultimate goodness of human nature" had been vindicated.

Just a few months after moving into their new home in Highgate, Eleanor died from a heart attack as she sat at dinner with Elizabeth.

Works include

Memoirs of William Rathbone (1905) – edited by her; *The Disinherited Family: a Plea for Family Endowment* (1924); *Child Marriage: the Indian Minotaur* (1934); *War Can Be Averted* (1938); *The Case for Family Allowances* (1940); and various articles and reports on casual labour and women's work, including *How the Casual Labourer Lives* (1909) and *The Conditions of Widows under the Poor Law in Liverpool* (1913).

Also, she was one of the five contributors to *Our Freedom and its Results* (1931), edited by Ray Strachey.

Addresses

★ *14 Prince's Gardens, SW7* – birthplace.
★ *18 Prince's Gardens, SW7* – site. Her childhood home.
★ *Queen's Gate, SW7* – her mother's home. Eleanor stayed here during the First World War.
★ *50 Romney Street, SW1* – she and Elizabeth Macadam lived here from 1919 until the house was bombed in October 1940. (In 1931 Eleanor bought No. 52 and integrated it with No. 50 so that she had a study and office overlooking Smith Square.)
★ *5 Tufton Court, Tufton Street, SW1* – their home 1940–45.
★ *26 Hampstead Lane, N6* – their home from April 1945. (Eleanor died here.)

Portrait

Oil by Sir James Gunn (c1934) – National Portrait Gallery.

Memorabilia

Photograph of Eleanor Rathbone addressing a meeting; and several autograph letters – Fawcett Library.

Mary Renault

(4 September 1905 – 13 December 1983)

Mary Renault's erudition and her skilful and splendid imaginative reconstruction of the matriarchal societies and warrior kingdoms of the ancient Greek world have placed her among the most celebrated historical novelists of our time.

Born in Upton Manor, London, "Mary Renault" was the eldest daughter of Dr Frank Challans and Mary (Baxter) Challans. She was an imaginative and precocious child. At the age of eight she announced to her family that she had conceived the ambition of becoming a writer. Her first literary effort, a Western, which she composed in the family's grocery order book, was abandoned after one chapter.

Mary's fascination with Greece began during the years she attended Clifton High School, near Bristol, where her teachers encouraged her wide reading of ancient history and literature. As she explained in an interview (in 1979), "I was riveted by Plato. I ask myself and still do in my books: what was life really like then?"

While at St Hugh's College, Oxford, Mary wrote and published verse. She graduated with an Honours degree in English literature in 1928 and intended to make teaching and writing her career, but, as she later wrote, "my experience of life was largely derived from other people's books, which were good because their writers had got it at first hand." Having decided that what she needed, in order to be a successful novelist, was to find out for herself more about "human existence and how people react to illness and crises", Mary turned to nursing.

She began her training at Radcliffe Infirmary, Oxford, in 1933 and remained a nurse throughout the war, specialising in neurosurgical work at the Infirmary. Her first three novels were written in her free time and the occasional lulls in her nursing routine. *Purposes of Love*, which was published in 1939, sold well in Britain and was hailed by the *New York Times* as "an unusually excellent first novel", but her next two novels, *Kind Are Her Answers* (1940) and *The Friendly Young Ladies* (1944), were less well received by the critics, being considered to be much weaker than *Purposes of Love*. She continued to draw upon her nursing experience for *Return to Night* (1946), *North Face* (1948) and *The Charioteer* (1953), and these, also, were set in contemporary England.

Winning the Metro Goldwyn Mayer contest in 1946 for *Return to Night* (originally titled *The Sacred River*) brought her a prize of $150,000 and led to her rapidly gaining bestselling author status in the United States. (However, the novel, about a woman doctor in love with her patient, a much younger man, was never filmed.)

At the end of the war Mary gave up hospital nursing for a writing career and began travelling extensively in Italy, France, the Aegean Islands and Greece. "Of all these places," she wrote, "I have found Greece incomparably the most moving and memorable." When questioned later about her emigration to South Africa (in 1948) rather than to, say, Greece, she explained that because the Mediterranean was, in her view, "a man's world", she could not live there. Although none of her works has a South African setting, she thought that country an excellent field of study for a writer of historical fiction because "one can find preserved in it so many stages of human history, some so old, as to be, like the coelocanth, almost living fossils."

To ensure authenticity in her historical novels, Mary taught herself Greek, read widely in original sources and always kept abreast with new findings and theories in archaeology and social history. (She also specified that maps and bibliographies should be included with these novels.)

The Last of the Wine, her first historical novel, was published in 1956, but it is the second of her eight books in this genre which is possibly the best known. *The King Must Die* (1958), the first of two novels based on the Theseus myths, was a spectacular success, and she received lavish praise for her imaginative realisation of Theseus as a living being, the accomplished infusion of modern themes into mythology and ancient history, and her sound scholarship. Praise for its sequel, *The Bull from the Sea* (1962) was more muted.

Although her novels *The Mask of Apollo* (1966) and *The Praise Singer* (1978), in which the context is the Greek theatre in Plato's time, are generally well regarded, it is in those novels dealing with the warrior as hero that Mary Renault is most successful and her concerns of power, sexuality and the individual in society are most tellingly realised. Her renowned trilogy on Alexander the Great, *Fire from Heaven* (1970), *The Persian Boy* (1972) and *Funeral Games* (1981), constitutes a master-piece of the genre of historical fiction.

Mary Renault's novels have a wide homosexual readership. Of particular interest to lesbians and gay men are *The Friendly Young Ladies*, *The Persian Boy* and *The Charioteer* (the American publication of which was delayed by six years because of the frankness with which the theme of homosexuality was dealt.)

Neither her success as a novelist nor her position as a white writer living in South Africa was viewed with complacency by Mary Renault: she was an active opponent of apartheid and, as President of the PEN Club's South African chapter, was an outspoken critic of the country's censorship laws as well as the regime's banning of books on political grounds. (A typical statement of hers, about her political activities, was "I don't pass myself off as a heroine. You don't get locked up for writing protests.")

In her hillside home near Cape Town and overlooking the sea, Mary lived with her companion of nearly fifty years, Julie Mullard, whom she had met when they were both training at the Radcliffe Infirmary.

Among the honours she received were the Fellowship of the Royal Society of Literature in 1959, the Silver Pen Award in 1971 and, in the year before her death, Honorary Fellowship of St Hugh's College, Oxford.

Portrait

Photograph – National Portrait Gallery (Archives).

Address

★*Dacre Lodge, 49 Plashet Road, E13* – the Challans family's home in which Mary was born and in which her father, a physician, had his surgery.

Works include

Novels: *Purposes of Love* (1939) (in U.S. as *Promise of Love*, 1940); *Kind Are Her Answers* (1940); *The Friendly Young Ladies* (1940) (in U.S. as *The Middle Mist*, 1945); *Return to Night* (1947); *North Face* (1948); *The Charioteer* (1953); *The Last of the Wine* (1956); *The King Must Die* (1958); *The Bull from the Sea* (1962); *The Mask of Apollo* (1966); *Fire from Heaven* (1970); *The Persian Boy* (1972); *The Praise Singer* (1978); *Funeral Games* (1981).

Non-fiction: *The Lion in the Gateway: Heroic Battles of the Greeks and Persians at Marathon, Salamis and Thermopylae* (1964); *The Nature of Alexander* (1975).

Charles Ricketts
(2 October 1866 – 7 October 1931)
&
Charles Shannon
(26 April 1863 – 18 March 1937)

Ricketts was sixteen and Shannon nineteen when they met as students at the City and Guilds Technical Art School in Lambeth. For nearly fifty years they lived and worked together, devoting their lives to art. Their collection of paintings, sculpture, Persian miniatures and Oriental art was one of the finest in the world.

Charles de Sousy Ricketts was born in Geneva. His mother was French and his father, a naval officer, was English. For most of his childhood he lived abroad as his mother suffered from ill health and was unable to withstand the English climate. When she died in 1880 Ricketts returned to England. His father died two years later and he was given a quarterly allowance of £25 by his grandfather which enabled him to go to art school.

Charles Hazelwood Shannon was a clergyman's son and came from Quarrington in Lincolnshire. He was educated at St John's School, Leatherhead, where his skills as a footballer and his quiet blend of modesty and confidence won him many friends.

Soon after they left art school Ricketts and Shannon came to a remarkable agreement. Shannon would concentrate exclusively, for a period of five years, on perfecting his technique. His work would be seen and criticised only by Ricketts and he would not exhibit any of his paintings until he had become a master artist, whose considerable income would allow them both to live in comfort. In the meantime Ricketts would support him by doing illustrations for books and advertisements.

The outcome of their plan was in some ways unexpected. Financial pressures having been removed, Shannon began in his work to become self-indulgent and retrogressive, while Ricketts quickly acquired a reputation as a fine illustrator. Lord Leighton, the elderly President of the Royal Academy, was an early admirer of his work and paid him £5 for a drawing of "Oedipus and the Sphinx".

In 1889 Ricketts and Shannon set up the Vale Press (with £500 which Ricketts had inherited from his grandfather) named after the area in Chelsea in which they lived. With the help of the poets John Gray and Thomas Sturge Moore, they published the first issue of their sumptuously illustrated literary journal *The Dial* which contained the work of mostly unknown artists and writers.

After seeing a copy of *The Dial* Oscar Wilde visited the two artists and they became friends. Through Wilde Ricketts was able to decorate books more suited to his talents. Most of Wilde's major works were published at about this time and Ricketts (sometimes in collaboration with Shannon) designed all of them except *Salome* which was the work of Aubrey Beardsley.

Wilde became a frequent visitor to The Vale, describing it as "the one house in London where you will never be bored". He likened Ricketts to an orchid and Shannon to a marigold, and sometimes stayed for a supper of eggs and beer.

On Friday nights Ricketts and Shannon were at home to their friends. Visitors included Roger Fry, William Rothenstein, Charles Conder and Max Beerbohm who called them "The Sisters of the Vale" and lampooned them in a set of wickedly humorous drawings. On these occasions Shannon, tall and blond with the ruddy complexion of a countryman, would sit quietly at the back of the room entering little into the proceedings. It was the diminutive Ricketts with his grandee's beard and bright excited gaze who held the attention of their guests with the brilliance of his wit and conversation. To Rothenstein "the partnership seemed perfect; there was never a sign of difference or discord; each set the other off, in looks as in mind."

In 1899 a fire at the Ballantyne Press, where much of their printing was done, destroyed most of their engraved blocks which had taken five years to make. The Vale Press closed down and Ricketts threw the type matrices into the Thames, "as it is undesirable that these founts should drift into other hands than their designer's and become stale by unthinking use."

Shannon by this time was becoming successful both as a painter of portraits and as a lithographer. In a beautiful series of lithographs he revived what had become a forgotten art in England. Most are studies from the nude, and they have the gentle idyllic quality of many of his wood engravings.

Sir Edmund Davis, a South African millionaire, became their friend and patron and built studios for them near his home in Holland Park. Through his help their work became more widely known. They held joint exhibitions at Manchester City Art Gallery and in New York, but they kept apart from "common currents and popular aims". They were students of 19th-century masters, Shannon being a follower of Watts, while Ricketts was influenced to a great extent by Rossetti.

After 1904 Ricketts gave up printing and turned to painting and sculpture and to designing jewellery. In 1906 he began designing for the theatre and revolutionised the art of stage decoration, anticipating by some years the work of Leon Bakst for the Russian Ballet. His designs for the 1906 production of Wilde's *Salome* led to a meeting with George Bernard Shaw, who later commissioned him to design the sets and costumes for the first production of *The Dark Lady of the Sonnets* (1910) and *St Joan* (1924) – which was probably his finest achievement as a designer. Other notable designs were for *Henry VIII* (1925) and the 1926 D'Oyly Carte production of *The Mikado*.

Though Ricketts and Shannon never earned more than £1,000 a year between them, they were able, with their knack for finding unrecognised masterpieces, to build up a valuable art collection. Shannon was particularly interested in Japanese art and they purchased a number of Hokusai drawings for only £60. In 1908 Ricketts bought a Masaccio medallion in Bayswater for thirty-five shillings and presented it to the National Gallery. In the end their "treasure" was estimated to be worth £40,000, and in their joint will they left it to public collections, in particular the Fitzwilliam Museum in Cambridge and the British Museum.

Both men were elected to the Royal Academy, and in 1915 Ricketts was offered the directorship of the National Gallery. However, he turned it down when they refused to have flowers in all the rooms and to cover the walls with watered silk. In 1923 he was appointed art adviser to the National Gallery of Canada and became responsible for recommending and commenting on additions to their collection.

Shannon's home county belatedly paid tribute to him in 1928 with an exhibition of his work in Lincoln. In January 1929, while rehanging some of his pictures on the staircase of his studio, he fell from the ladder and hit his head on the marble floor. He never recovered and remained a physical and mental invalid for the rest of his life, unable to recognise or communicate with Ricketts. The beautiful partnership was effectively over. Ricketts was badly affected by the accident and although he continued to work on his stage designs he seemed to lose the will to live and died two years later. Shannon lived on for a further six years.

Their friend Thomas Sturge Moore wrote, "Between Ricketts and Shannon existed the most marvellous human relationship that has ever come within my observation, and in their prime each was the other's complement, but neither easily indulged the other; their union was more bracing than comfortable."

Addresses

★*Kennington Road, SE11* – they lived here between 1882–87.

★*1 The Vale, SW3* – site. Their home from 1887–94.

★*31 Beaufort Street, SW3* – site. They lived here between 1894–98.

★*Chalon House, 8 Paradise Road (formerly Spring Terrace), Richmond* – their home from 1898–1904.

★*Lansdowne House, Lansdowne Road, W11* – (Blue *plaque* erected 1979.) They lived here between 1904–23. These studios were built for them by their patron Sir Edmund Davis, who lived at 13 Lansdowne Road. (See also *Glyn Philpot*.)

★*Townshend House, Townshend Road, NW8* – *site* of their home 1923–31. (Ricketts died here.)

★*21 Kew Gardens Road, Kew* – site. (Shannon died here.)

Works include

Ricketts:

Books: *The Prado and its Masterpieces* (1903); *Recollections of Oscar Wilde* (1932); *Self Portrait: Letters and Journals* (1939).

Painting: "The Death of Montezuma" (c1905) – Victoria and Albert Museum.

Bronze: "Orpheus and Eurydice" (1906) – Tate Gallery.

Designs, illustrations and drawings: – in the Tate Gallery, Courtauld Institute Galleries, Theatre Museum, Victoria and Albert Museum, British Museum, and Richmond-upon-Thames Libraries.

Shannon:

Paintings: Portrait of W B Yeats – Courtauld Institute Galleries. "Les Marmitons" (1897) – Tate Gallery. Portrait of Mrs Patrick Campbell (1907) – Tate Gallery.

Lithographs: "Atlanta" (1896), for *The Dial* No. 4 – Courtauld Institute Galleries. Portrait of Thomas Sturge Moore (1893) – Courtauld Institute Galleries. Portrait of Sir Max Beerbohm (undated) – National Portrait Gallery.

Drawings: Chalk portrait of Thomas Sturge Moore (?1925) – N.P.G. Chalk portrait of Gordon Bottomley (1924) – N.P.G. Pencil and chalk portrait of F J. Furnivall (undated) – N.P.G.

Portraits

Ricketts: Canvas by Shannon "The Man in the Inverness Cape" (1898) – N.P.G. Chalk by Shannon (1899) – N.P.G. Pencil by Laura Anning-Bell (undated) – N.P.G. Two photographs by G C Beresford (1903) – N.P.G. Lithograph by Shannon (1894) – Victoria and Albert Museum. Drawing by Francis Dodd (1905) – British Museum.

Shannon: Canvas self-portrait "The Man in the Black Shirt" (1897) – N.P.G. Lithograph self-portrait (1918) – N.P.G. Four photographs by G C Beresford (1903) – N.P.G. Photograph by A L Coburn (1907) – N.P.G. Photograph by Elliott & Fry (undated) – N.P.G. Wood engraved medallion by Ricketts (1902) – Victoria and Albert Museum. Drawing by Sir William Rothenstein (1903) – British Museum.

Ricketts and Shannon: Lithograph by Sir William Rothenstein (1897) – N.P.G. Photograph by G C Beresford (1903) – N.P.G. Canvas by Jacques-Emile Blanche (1904) – Tate Gallery.

Fictional portrait

Oscar Wilde is believed to have based the character of Basil Hallward in *The Picture of Dorian Gray* (1891) on Shannon.

Memorabilia

Papers, diaries and journals – British Library. Their collection of Oriental art – British Museum. A number of their engraved wood blocks – British Museum. Ricketts's album *Designs for Jewellery* – British Museum. Ricketts's original page layouts for Wilde's *The Sphinx* were presented by Robert Ross to – British Museum. Costume and decor designs, photographs of the artists designing such, etc. – Theatre Museum.

Chalon House, 8 Paradise Road (formerly
8 Spring Terrace), Richmond

Lansdowne House, Lansdowne Road, W11

Arthur Rimbaud
(20 October 1854 – 10 November 1891)

&

Paul Verlaine
(30 March 1844 – 8 January 1896)

Rimbaud, a poet of precocious talent, said of himself: "I write of silences, of degrees of darkness; I express the ineffable. I fix my gaze on the vertiginous depths." He has long been acknowledged as one of the strongest influences on modern, and not only French, poetry. The legend of his life and his ideal of self-fulfilment through the spurning of conventional values, whether in the matter of morals, politics, religion, poetry, or in the mundane affairs of day to day living, gained him the admiration of the Surrealists; his revolutionary concept of the human condition in the modern world remains attractive to successive generations of intellectuals and rebellious young men and women.

Jean-Nicholas-Arthur Rimbaud grew up in Charleville in the Ardennes. His father, Frédéric Rimbaud, an army officer, abandoned the family when Arthur was six years old. Vitalie Rimbaud, a dour, fanatically religious woman, regarded her struggle to rear and educate her two sons and three daughters as a kind of martyrdom.

A highly intelligent child, Arthur Rimbaud was, until about the age of sixteen, a model pupil at the Collège de Charleville. Georges Izambard, a young teacher who arrived there in 1870, fostered his interest in literature and lent him "dangerous" books which the local library would not stock. With Izambard's help, Rimbaud published his first poem at the age of fifteen. That same year (1870) he wrote another twenty-one strikingly mature poems.

Excited by the outbreak of the Franco-Prussian war and stirred by revolutionary ideas and his growing fear of "decomposing in the dullness, in the nastiness, in the greyness" of his environment of repressive family and patriotic, bourgeois neighbours, Rimbaud fled to Paris. He was arrested and jailed for not having paid his train fare. Izambard came to his rescue, but returned him to *"la bouche d'ombre"* (as Rimbaud irreverently referred to his mother). Again Rimbaud left home. This time he walked via Belgium to the north of France to visit Izambard, to whom he had written, "One is an exile in one's own country."

Forced to go back to Charleville, he refused to return to the Collège (which had reopened as the war was drawing to a close). Instead he spent his time reading dozens of works on illuminism, mysticism and black magic, as well as the poetry of the "Parnassians". His refusal to wash or have his hair cut and his drinking and brawling in squalid cafés distressed his family. On another of his flights from home Rimbaud was picked up and raped by a party of soldiers. (His ambiguous response to this savage initiation into sex is recorded in his poem "Le coeur supplice".)

Writing to his friend Paul Démeny in May 1871, Rimbaud described his revolutionary theories about life and poetry. In this now celebrated "Lettre du voyant" he says that, to go beyond good and evil and express the inexpressible, the poet must practise "the long, immense and reasoned deranging of all his senses": that only by experiencing "all the forms of love", vice and self-induced states of delirium could he reach a transcendent state – "the unknown".

In the late summer of 1871 Rimbaud sent some of his poems to Verlaine, a poet he greatly admired. Verlaine's answer to the sixteen-year-old poet's appeal for help was a letter, stating, "Come, dear great soul, you are called, you are awaited," and some money for his train fare to Paris. Shortly before leaving for Paris, the elated Rimbaud wrote what is perhaps his finest poem, "Le bateau ivre" ("The Drunken Boat").

Paul Verlaine, a native of Metz, was then aged twenty-six. He had recently moved into the home of his parents-in-law, the de Fleurvilles, in Montmartre, because he had lost his job in the civil service as the result of the disclosure of his past association with revolutionaries of the Commune and his "intemperance". His wife, Mathilde, was seventeen years old and pregnant. She and her mother hoped that the birth of the child and the stability of the de Fleurville household would have the effect of transforming Verlaine into a model husband content with a peaceful bourgeois existence. At first they regarded Verlaine's invitation to Rimbaud to stay with them in their home as the generous act of the respectable man of letters they wished him to be.

From their initial meeting Verlaine was captivated by the younger poet. He thought Rimbaud, shock-headed, ill-clad and dirty though he was, "quite, quite beautiful", and sensed in him the seeds of genius. The literati of Paris, such as Albert Mérat, Théodore de Banville and Charles Cros, to whom Verlaine introduced his new friend and protégé, admired Rimbaud's work but found his arrogance, obscene language and hooligan ways less charming than Verlaine did.

Mathilde Verlaine and her parents were outraged by Rimbaud's increasingly offensive behaviour and the influence he exerted over Verlaine, and, shortly after the birth of the Verlaines' son in October 1871, they evicted their drunken guest. A violent family row ensued, in which Verlaine tried to strangle his wife. Before long Verlaine moved out of the home and joined Rimbaud in the studio which he had rented for him. There the two men became lovers.

Each was to have an important effect on the poetry of the other, but their relationship proved to be as calamitous for Verlaine as it was productive for Rimbaud. In his passion for Verlaine, Rimbaud found his sexual identity, and from the older, more experienced poet he learned how to subordinate his wild experiments in poetic form and language to the demands of art. To Rimbaud the violence and debauchery which characterised their affair was an essential means to self-understanding, but for Verlaine his own role of *compagnon d'enfer* contributed to the ruin of his marriage, his career and his talent. While the passion and vigour of Rimbaud served to inspire the finest of Verlaine's work, *Romances sans paroles* (and some of his own purity of style and clarity came to infuse the major works of Rimbaud), the result of their association has been, historically, for Verlaine to be considered, in the inevitable comparison of the two poets, the lesser associate of a writer of genius.

Until September 1872 Rimbaud and Verlaine tramped around France and Belgium. They frequently argued and separated; their reconciliations, usually initiated by Verlaine, were rapturous, but then there would be another violent quarrel. Finally they decided to go to London together, where things might be better for them and where they hoped they might escape from their families who had in the preceding months tried to intervene and "put matters right".

London, the "flat, black bug" as Verlaine described it, did not provide them with the distraction they wanted. They made contact with few people and thought Londoners and their pubs dreary. When Verlaine's money ran out Rimbaud gave French lessons to pay for their food and lodgings. However, they usually spent these earnings on drink, hashish and opium, which they obtained from sailors they met in the East End and the docklands.

Verlaine grew tired of their poverty and of being abused sadistically by Rimbaud who told him he despised his "weakness and vacillation", and so, in April 1873, they returned to France. Rimbaud went to his mother's farm and Verlaine returned to his parents-in-law's home where he sought a reconciliation with his wife.

At the farm at Roche, near Charleville, Rimbaud began to write *Une Saison en Enfer* ("A Season in Hell"), of which Delirium I is manifestly a poetic transposition of his life with Verlaine, with himself as the Infernal Bridegroom and Verlaine as the Foolish Virgin.

Rimbaud had decided to break with Verlaine, but nevertheless, within a month, he returned to London with him. Their second spell of living together here was hellish for both of them, and in July 1873 Verlaine fled from Rimbaud and London and went to Brussels. Rimbaud joined him there after Verlaine had threatened to shoot himself or return to his wife. In the event, it was Rimbaud that he shot, wounding him in the wrist. He was charged with attempted murder. Although the charge was reduced to one of "criminal assault" after Rimbaud had pleaded in his friend's favour, when the nature of their relationship became known to the court little leniency was shown and Verlaine was sentenced to two years imprisonment.

Rimbaud returned to Roche where he completed *Une Saison en Enfer*, the only one of his works which he himself published. In prison Verlaine became a devout Catholic convert. His wife gained, during this time, a legal separation from him on the grounds of immorality and cruelty.

At the height of his powers, at about the age of twenty, Rimbaud renounced literature and burnt most of his remaining manuscripts, probably as the deliberate, nihilistic act of the "*voyant*" (rebel "seer") he had striven to become. Between 1873 and 1879 he wandered around Europe, the Mediterranean and the Middle East, taking odd jobs and often sleeping rough. He visited London in 1874 with the homosexual writer Germain Nouveau and in the following year briefly met up again with Verlaine in Stuttgart. There Verlaine, "with a rosary in his paw" (according to Rimbaud), tried to convert him, but Rimbaud, denouncing him as a miserable failure, beat him up and, after depositing the manuscript of *Les Illuminations* with him, fled.

From 1880 until just before his death Rimbaud lived in self-imposed exile in Aden and at

Harar in Ethiopia. He was unsuccessful as a trader and arms dealer there, but received some recognition from the Société de Géographique for his work in exploring the area. When he developed an excruciatingly painful tumour (of syphilitic or cancerous origin) in his right knee the local doctors, afraid to operate on it, arranged for Rimbaud to be shipped back to France.

In Marseilles Rimbaud's leg was amputated. For a few months he stayed with his mother and sister, Isàbelle, on the farm at Roche, but he longed to return to Harar where his beloved Djarmi, his servant and "only consolation", was. Against his family's and medical advice he set out for Marseilles, where he fell ill. His sister, who had accompanied him to Marseilles, later reported that Rimbaud, as he lay dying in the hospital, renounced his lifelong revolt against the Church and his anti-Christian attitude. (This claim is generally regarded as an attempt, like that of Mathilde Verlaine's burning of most of her husband's and Rimbaud's letters to each other, to "clean up" the poet's reputation for posterity.)

In Paris Rimbaud's major works were being published and studied, but the poet died completely unaware of this. Verlaine had devoted a chapter to Rimbaud in his book *Les Poètes maudits* (1884) and had edited the first edition of *Les Illuminations*, published in 1886. He also wrote the introduction to the Vanier edition of the collection *Poèmes, Les Illuminations* and *Une Saison en Enfer*, published in 1891, through which Rimbaud's work became more widely known.

Verlaine had met (in 1879) Lucien Letinois, a young man who reminded him of Rimbaud. Together they visited London and, like Rimbaud before him, Letinois inspired much of Verlaine's verse. Letinois' death of typhoid at the age of twenty-three was perceived by Verlaine as a divine judgement on himself. Nevertheless, he continued to seek love in several more relationships with men and did not give up his heavy drinking or the use of drugs. During his last stay in England he delivered an acclaimed lecture at Oxford. The theme of the lecture was autobiographical: "The poet should live fully, live in all the senses."

Rimbaud

Verlaine

Addresses

★*35 Howland Street, W1 – site*. Rimbaud and Verlaine rented a room here (1872–73). A *plaque* commemorating their stay there was unveiled by Paul Valéry in 1922. (In the 1930s the house was demolished and a telephone exchange was built on the site.)

★*8 Royal College Street (formerly Great College Street), NW1* – they stayed here between May and July 1874. (*Tablet.*)

★*178 Stamford Street, SE1* – Rimbaud and Germain Nouveau shared a room here in 1874. (*Site.*)

★*Fountain Court, The Temple, EC4* – (top floor, overlooking the court). This was Arthur Symons's home, where Verlaine stayed during his last visit to London.

Works include
Rimbaud:

Poèmes, Les Illuminations, Une Saison en Enfer (1891). (*Arthur Rimbaud: A Season in Hell/The Illuminations* – a new translation by Enid Rhodes Peschel; 1973); *Complete Works* – translated by Paul Schmidt (1967); *Oeuvres complètes* (1972).

Verlaine:
Poèmes saturniens (1866); *Fêtes galantes* (1869); *La bonne chanson* (1870); *Romances sans paroles* (1874); *Sagesse* (1881); *Parallèlement* (1889); *Les Poètes maudits* (1884) – criticism; *Confessions* (1895) – autobiography; *Selected Poems* – edited by J Richardson (1974).

Fictional portrait

Verlaine appears as Choulette in *Le Lys rouge* (1894) by Anatole France.

Frederick Rolfe, 'Baron Corvo'

(22 July 1860 – 26 October 1913)

"He who desires must pursue his desire though the whole world obstructs him. He who pursues has his path with obstructions bestrewed," wrote Frederick Rolfe. Despite the many real and imagined obstacles which he encountered in his life he determinedly practised what he preached in his brilliant, epigrammatic and obviously autobiographical fiction.

Frederick William Serafino Austin Lewis Mary Rolfe was born into a Dissenting family that manufactured musical instruments. From boyhood he was drawn to the religious life, and in his teens he formed plans for a career in the Church. (The profoundity of his vocation was expressed in a typically eccentric manner by his having a cross tattooed on his chest when he was fourteen.)

After leaving North London Collegiate School, in Camden, at the age of fourteen, Rolfe became a pupil teacher; later he went up to Oxford, but did not graduate. During his early twenties he earned a living as an assistant master in several provincial schools, a task at which he excelled.

In 1886 Rolfe became a Catholic convert, and in the following year he began studying for the priesthood at St Mary's College, Oscott. After nine months he was dismissed from there for unexplained reasons, but probably for pursuing his interest in painting, photography and poetry at the expense of his devotions. He resumed his training a year later when, under the sponsorship of the Archbishop of Edinburgh, he entered the Scots College in Rome. Again his waywardness and independence incurred the wrath of his superiors, and again he was dismissed; this time the college servants had to forcibly remove him from the premises. His rejection by the Church caused him lifelong embitterment and frustration and it deepened his sense of persecution.

He spent the summer licking his "spiritual wounds" at the villa of the Duchess of Sforza-Cesarini in the Alban Hills, where he met a young peasant called Toto. This refuge and his relationship with Toto confirmed Rolfe's love for Italy which forms the background of nearly all of his work.

When Rolfe reappeared in England he was calling himself Baron Corvo. For over six years he wandered around the country, earning a pittance from his work as a tutor, painter, photographer's "learner" and journalist, and trying to get financial backing for the inventions he claimed to be working on. Debts and fierce rows with friends and landlords drove him continually on.

His Toto stories, which he began to contribute to *The Yellow Book* in 1895, caused quite a stir and seemed about to mark a change in his fortunes. His new career, however, was to be similarly lacking in financial reward as his earlier efforts had been.

At the start of his literary career in London he had the admiration, encouragement and support of Henry Harland, Sholto Douglas and many others, but when Rolfe (now using "Baron Corvo" as his pseudonym) encountered setbacks in making his way as a writer he roundly attacked his erstwhile benefactors, calling them jealous, persecuting agents of misfortune. His ingratitude and libellous denunciations swiftly led to his being shunned by the literary establishment.

Nevertheless, with characteristic independence of spirit, Rolfe persevered with his writing, and during the ten years of his London career he produced some remarkable books, the best known of which is *Hadrian the Seventh*, his fantasy of his becoming Pope and getting his own back on the Church which had rejected him by making sweeping innovations in Rome. Throughout his life Rolfe affected a manner of dress which suggested holy orders; at times he even referred to himself as a priest, and chose to mislead further by using, particularly as authorial title for his later works, the contraction of his first name "Frederick" to "Fr." which could be read as the clerical title "Father". (His fraudulent claim to the title of Baron Corvo was exposed in a Scottish newspaper in the 1890s and Rolfe was socially disgraced and ostracised; his precarious financial position worsened accordingly, and for a time he was forced to seek shelter in a workhouse in Wales.)

In the summer of 1908 an Oxford don, Prof. R M Dawkins, took Rolfe on holiday to Venice. When the holiday ended he refused to return to England: in Venice he had found an emotional refuge and, in the gondoliers and stevedores he had met, the beautiful, young and eager lovers he had always dreamed of. As his debts increased he wrote floods of letters home, demanding money from his friends and acquaintances and from his solicitors (to whom he had already yielded the rights of his literary works). Those who denied him assistance and those who gave it were all finally subjected to Rolfe's vituperation.

For months on end he was homeless and on the verge of starvation. Usually he tramped the streets and slept in an open boat; for a time he worked as a gondolier for an English family. "But I am not humbled, nor will be. Better by far to wear ruin as a diadem," he wrote to Charles Masson Fox, an occasional benefactor. (The begging letters to Fox were "sweetened" with descriptions of the charms of the youths whom Rolfe offered to procure for him when he revisited Venice.)

For a predictably brief period Rolfe gained the patronage of an Anglican clergyman, the Reverend Justus Serjeant, and he was finally able to indulge some of his eccentric fantasies, such as renting a palace, and gliding down the canals in an ornate sandolo in which he reclined on a leopard-skin while his young lovers, dressed in livery, rowed. On one occasion, piqued at not having been invited to a society funeral, he stood outside the church dressed as a cardinal and, to the horror of the mourners, hurled invective after the coffin. Thus he added to the legends of modern Venice.

At the end of his life Rolfe was suffering acutely from undernourishment and exposure, but, fearing that he was being robbed of his literary career, he applied himself steadfastly to his writing.

He died (according to some accounts) as he was making love with a Venetian youth.

Addresses

★*61 Cheapside, EC2* – site of his birthplace.
★*69 Broadhurst Gardens, NW6* – site. He had a small room here 1900–03. It was here that he worked on *Hadrian the Seventh*. (The house was bombed in the Second World War.)
★*15 Cheniston Gardens, W8* – he completed *Hadrian the Seventh* while living here in 1904.

Works include

Short stories: *Stories Toto Told Me* (1898); *In His Own Image* (1901).
History: *Chronicles of the House of Borgia* (1901); as *A History of The Borgias* (1931).
Novels: *Hadrian the Seventh* (1904); *Don*

Tarquino: a Kataleptic Phantasmatic Romance (1905); *The Weird of the Wanderer, Being the Papyrus Records of Some Incidents in One of the Previous Lives of Mr Nicholas Crabbe, Here Reproduced by Prospero and Caliban* – with C H C Pirie-Gordon (1912); *The Desire and Pursuit of the Whole: a Romance of Modern Venice* (1934); *Hubert's Arthur, Being Certain Curious Documents Found Among the Literary Remains of Mr N C* – with C H C Pirie-Gordon (1935); *Nicholas Crabbe, or, The One and the Many* – edited by Cecil Woolf (1958); *Don Renato: an Ideal Content* – edited by Cecil Woolf (1963).

Verse: *Tarcissus: The Boy Martyr of Rome in the Diocletian Persecution* (1880); *Collected Poems* – edited by Cecil Woolf (1974).

Translation: *Rubaiyat of 'Umar Khaiyam* (1903) – translated from a French version into "diaphotick verse".

Letters: Successive collections of his letters to various correspondents have been edited by Cecil Woolf (1959, 1960, 1962, 1963 and 1974) and by Miriam K Benkovitz (1977).

Fictional portraits

He appears as Enid in R H Benson's *Initiation* (1914).

169

Robert Ross

(25 May 1869 – 5 October 1918)

Robert Baldwin Ross was the third son of the Canadian Attorney-General. His grandfather, Robert Baldwin, had been the first Prime Minister of Upper Canada. Shortly before Ross was born his father died, leaving instructions that his children were to receive an English education, so Mrs Ross brought them to live here.

Ross was educated at private schools and at King's College, Cambridge, where he read history and rowed in the second college eight. However, his aesthetic mannerisms and long hair made him unpopular with many of his fellow undergraduates. After a ducking in the college fountain he contracted pneumonia and left university without taking a degree. Thereafter he supplemented his allowance from his mother by contributing book reviews and articles on art and drama to several newspapers.

It was in 1886 while he was living in Oxford that "Robbie" Ross had first met Oscar Wilde, already celebrated as a poet and wit. Ross became his lover for a time (he claimed to have been Wilde's first "boy"), and remained his closest friend, even after Wilde formed his disastrous liaison with Lord Alfred Douglas.

Ross was with Wilde at the Cadogan Hotel on the day of his arrest, pleading in vain with him to leave the country while there was still time. "It is too late," Wilde kept repeating, "the train has gone". After Wilde had been taken into custody Ross's mother gave him £500 for Wilde's defence, and promised, on condition that her son would go abroad, to give financial support to Lady Wilde who was entirely dependent on Oscar. So, accompanied by his friend Reginald Turner, Ross took the boat train to Calais. After the trial he returned to England and visited Wilde in Reading Gaol.

In 1900 Ross bought the Carfax Gallery in St James's which he ran with More Adey. They exhibited the works of many young artists who would later gain wider notice, such as William Strang, Max Beerbohm and Augustus John.

Within a few months of the purchase of the gallery Oscar Wilde, in exile in Paris, became ill and Ross and Turner took turns in looking after him and were with him when he died.

Wilde died intestate and bankrupt and Ross was appointed his literary executor. In order to satisfy the creditors it was first necessary to interest the public again in Wilde's books and plays. Ross accomplished this by publishing in 1905 the first (expurgated) edition of *De Profundis*. This book was an immediate success; five editions were issued in the first year alone, and soon Wilde's books were back in the shops and his plays were being performed again in the West End. On 1 December 1908 *The Works of Oscar Wilde*, edited by Ross, were published, and that evening at a dinner given in his honour at the Ritz to mark the event he announced that he had finally been able to pay off Wilde's creditors in full.

In 1913 Lord Alfred Douglas sued Arthur Ransome for libel over a statement he had made in his biography of Wilde. During the trial the unpublished parts of *De Profundis*, the long letter which Wilde had written to Douglas from prison, were read out to the court. Ross had sent a typescript of *De Profundis* to Douglas who, after reading the first few pages, destroyed the letter and later denied having received it. Ross had then given the original manuscript to the British Museum on condition that it would remain sealed for fifty years. However, he allowed it to be used in Ransome's defence and, as a result, Douglas lost the case.

Now Douglas, who had renounced his homosexuality on marrying and becoming a Catholic, sought revenge. He hounded Ross in much the same way as his father had hounded Wilde, publicly insulting him and gathering evidence about his homosexuality. Ross eventually sued him but was compelled to drop the case when he realised that he could be destroyed by Douglas's revelations in court about his sexual practices.

Soon afterwards Edmund Gosse raised a public subscription for Ross. A gift of £700 and three hundred and fifty signatures, including those of the Prime Minister and the Bishop of Birmingham, was presented to him.

During the First World War Ross worked to secure official recognition for war artists and, when eventually this was achieved, he served on the first British War Memorials Committee, selecting artists to be commissioned for war work. This led to the establishment of the Imperial War Museum where their pictures are now exhibited.

Although his chief interest was in painting, Ross also helped many of the soldier-poets who sent their manuscripts back to him for criticism, and he encouraged Siegfried Sassoon in the writing of his anti-war verse. Arnold Bennett described him as one of the most indirectly creative men he had ever known.

When Robert Ross died of a heart attack at the age of forty-nine, "It was," said Sassoon, "the only time that his heart had ever failed him." In his will he asked for his ashes to be placed in Wilde's tomb at the cemetery of Père Lachaise in Paris. This was done at a ceremony on 30 November 1950, the fiftieth anniversary of Wilde's death.

Oscar Wilde, in discussing his epitaph with Ross, had said, "When the last trumpet sounds and we are couched in our porphyry tombs, I shall turn and whisper to you 'Robbie, Robbie, let us pretend we do not hear it'."

Addresses

★*7 Bury Street, SW1* – he lived here in 1890.

★*54 Old Church Street (formerly Church Street), SW3* – he lived here in 1892.

★*11 Upper Phillimore Gardens, W8* – his home 1896–1900.

★*24 Hornton Street, W8* – he lived here with More Adey c1905.

★*86 Kensington Church Street (formerly 10 Sheffield Gardens), W8* – he stayed here, at the home of Reginald Turner, in 1905; and again in 1908 with More Adey. (See also *More Adey*.)

★*15 Vicarage Gardens, W8* – he lived here 1906–08 with More Adey. In November 1907 Ross gave a dinner party here to celebrate the 21st birthday of Vyvyan Holland, son of Oscar Wilde. The guests were: Sir William Richmond, R.A., Charles Shannon, Charles Ricketts, Henry James, Reginald Turner, William Rothenstein, Sir Coleridge Kennard, Ronald Firbank, More Adey and Cyril Holland, Wilde's other son.

★*5 Hertford Street, W1* – *site* of his home in 1909.

★*3 Chesterfield Hill (formerly John Street), W1* – he lived here 1911.

★*Mayfair Chambers, Broadbent Street (formerly Little Grosvenor Street), W1* – he lived here c1912–15. (Reginald Turner had rooms here too.)

★*40 Half Moon Street, W1* – he had a flat here c1916–18. "There he would stand in his loose grey alpaca jacket, wearing a black silk skull-cap and smoking his perpetual cigarette in its jade-green holder, emphasising his lively pronouncements with controlled gesture of the left hand, on the third finger of which was a fair sized scarab ring" – Siegfried Sassoon. The ring had been given to Ross by Charles Ricketts. (See also *Ronald Firbank* and *Wilfred Owen*.)

★*(24 Bury Street, SW1* – The Carfax Gallery, 1900–08).

Works include

Life of Charles Robert Maturin (1892) – with More Adey; *Aubrey Beardsley* (1908); edited *De Profundis* (1905) and *The Works of Oscar Wilde* (1908); *Masques and Phases* (1909); *Really and Truly* (1915).

Portrait

In "Prominent Men, 1895–1930" collection, by Sir William Rothenstein – National Portrait Gallery (Archives).

Memorabilia

The Importance of Being Earnest (1895) by Oscar Wilde is dedicted to Ross.

Vita Sackville-West

(9 March 1892 – 2 June 1962)

The Hon. Victoria Mary Sackville-West, poet, novelist, biographer and critic, was born and grew up at Knole, Kent. She was the only child of the third Baron Sackville and Lady Sackville and the granddaughter of an internationally famous Spanish dancer, Pepita (from whom she claimed she had inherited her impulsive and passionate nature).

Vita's childhood was a lonely and miserable one. Feeling herself to be a source of disappointment to her mother, a beautiful and popular society hostess, she decided that "if I couldn't be popular, I would be clever," and turned to reading and writing. By the time she was eighteen she had written five plays and eight novels, with plots based on the stories of her ancestors, the Sackvilles, and dozens of poems.

The rituals involved in "coming out into society" were distasteful to her. However, during her season as a debutante in 1910 she met Harold Nicolson, a young man in the Diplomatic Service, to whom she was married three years later. She spent several months in 1914 in Constantinople, where Nicolson had been posted, and she reluctantly assumed the role of "the correct and adoring wife of the brilliant young diplomat". Soon after they were recalled to England their first child, Benedict, was born; their second, Nigel, was born in 1917, the year in which Vita began her new career as a "serious" writer with the publication of her first volume of poetry.

When her husband informed her, early in their marriage, that he was homosexual, Vita felt, in a way, released, and she began acknowledging what she called her "dual nature". During her engagement to Harold she had had a passionate, but secret, love affair with Rosamund Grosvenor; however, the frankness with which she conducted her relationship with Violet Trefusis caused a crisis in her marriage. They created a scandal when, as Julian, a wounded soldier (Vita) and his demure fiancée, Lushka (Violet), they went dining and dancing together in London and in Paris. The women's three-year affair ended after their husbands sought them out in Paris

and persuaded them to return home. (The mutual trust and frankness and the refusal to interfere in, or be jealous about, each other's sexual relationships, which later developed with their growing friendship and love for each other, became the basis of Vita and Harold's long and extraordinarily successful marriage.)

A large part of Vita's renown stems from her association with the Bloomsbury Group, with which she became acquainted in the early 1920s, and, particularly, from her relationship with Virginia Woolf. The short novel *Seducers in Ecuador* was written for Virginia in 1924 and was Vita's literary wooing of the novelist and woman whom she admired and loved. Their sexual relationship was brief, but their friendship was deep and enduring. ("A treasure and a privilege" was how Vita described this relationship to her husband.) Virginia Woolf's novel *Orlando* (1928) has been described by Vita's son Nigel Nicolson as "her most elaborate love-letter, rendering Vita androgynous and immortal: it transformed her story into a myth, gave her back to Knole" (which only a male heir could inherit, a fact which Vita always resented).

In 1930, the year in which the Nicolsons purchased Sissinghurst Castle, the first of Vita's best-selling novels, *The Edwardians*, was published by Virginia and Leonard Woolf at their Hogarth Press. *All Passion Spent* (1932), probably her best work, was well received by the critics and public alike, as was *Family History* (1933). The formal gardens at Sissinghurst, which she spent much time developing, and her writing about gardening, in articles in the *Observer* and in books, later brought her a new and different renown.

Individualism and the independence of women were, as in many of her books, the main themes of Vita's lectures on literature which she gave during a lecture tour of the United States with her husband in 1933 and in broadcasts for the BBC in the 1930s and 1940s.

Vita's need for solitude and stability was intensified when she lost her closest friend, Virginia Woolf, who committed suicide by drowning in 1941. The war years saw a decline in her creative output as she sought solace from her grief in her gardening and in war work. She became the organiser of Kent's Women's Land Army, for which she wrote a history as recruiting propaganda, and was designated as an ambulance driver in the event of air raids in the vicinity.

Winning the Hawthornden Prize in 1927 for her long poem *The Land* (1926), in which was distilled her deep love of traditional English rural life and the knowledge of how the countryside was threatened by industrial and agricultural progress, had brought her significant literary attention. For another long poem, *The Garden* (1946) she received the Heinemann Award for Literature in 1947, and her spirits were further lifted when, in the following year, she was made a Companion of Honour for her services to literature.

Throughout Vita's long literary career, in which she brought a poetic consciousness to bear in novels, histories, biographies, travel books, works on gardens and stately homes, and literary criticism (chiefly essays for the Royal Society of Literature, of which she was a Fellow), reviewers drew attention to the beauty of her prose and to her skill in treating modern themes while staying within traditional forms.

Her last novel, *No Signposts in the Sea*, written during an ocean cruise to South Africa, was published in 1961. At the outset of a winter cruise which she and Harold made early the following year Vita was taken ill. An operation which she underwent on her return to England revealed advanced cancer. She died at Sissinghurst a few days after coming home from hospital.

Addresses

★*34 Hill Street, W1* – the Sackvilles' London home (during Vita's childhood and early womanhood).

★*182 Ebury Street, SW1* – Vita lived here in the 1920s.

★*4 King's Bench Walk, The Temple, EC4* – Vita and Harold Nicolson's pied-à-terre (1930–45).

★*10 Neville Street, SW7* – Vita and Harold Nicolson's London home during the 1950s.

Works include

Poetry: *Poems West and East* (1917); *The Land* (1926); *Collected Poems* (1933); *The Garden* (1946).

Novels and short stories: *Heritage* (1919); *The Heir* (1922); *Challenge* (1923); *Seducers in Ecuador* (1924); *The Edwardians* (1930); *All Passion Spent* (1931); *Family History* (1932); *Grand Canyon* (1942); *The Easter Party* (1953); *No Signposts in the Sea* (1961).

Biographies & histories: *Knole and the Sackvilles* (1923); *Aphra Behn: The Incomparable Astrea* (1927); *St Joan of Arc* (1936); *Pepita* (1937); *The Eagle and the Dove: A Study in Contrasts* (1943) – (about St Theresa of Avila and St Thérèse of Lisieux); *The Women's Land Army* (1944).

Travel: *Twelve Days: An Account of a Journey Across the Bakhtiari Mountains in South-Western Turkey* (1928).

Gardening: *Country Notes* (1939); *In Your Garden* (1951); *More for Your Garden (1955)*.

Portraits

Photographs by Cecil Beaton – National Portrait Gallery. Photographs (various, 1930s) by Howard Coster – N.P.G. Photographs by Walter Stoneman – N.P.G.

Fictional portraits

Challenge (1923) contains a fictional self-portrait – Julian Davenant. (Eve, the woman he loves, is a portrait of Violet Trefusis.) The titular hero/heroine of *Orlando* (1928) by Virginia Woolf is a portrait of Vita. (The original Hogarth Press edition contained a photograph of Vita, with the caption "Orlando in about 1840".) She appears as Georgiana in Roy Campbell's *The Georgiad* (1933) – (Campbell's wife, Mary, was one of Vita's lovers). Firbank portrayed Harold Nicolson and her as The Hon. Harold and Mrs Chilleywater in *The Flower Beneath the Foot* (1923).

Memorabilia

Several autograph letters – Fawcett Library.

'Saki'
(Hector Hugh Munro)

(18 December 1870 – 14 November 1916)

"I'm God! I'm going to destroy the world," cried the young Hector Munro, waving about him a burning hearth-brush as he chased his sister around the nursery. As a writer he set out to destroy the world of those who believe in restraint, decorum and respectability.

Hector Hugh Munro was born in Burma, where his father was Inspector General of Police. His mother died shortly after his birth and Hector and his older brother and sister were sent to England to be brought up by two aunts, "Tom" and Augusta.

The aunts loathed children almost as much as they loathed each other, and the children grew up under a regime of great severity. (Ethel Munro recollected that Aunt Tom, the less nasty of the aunts, might have been "a reincarnation of Catherine the Great".) Munro admitted to autobiographical elements in his work, and it is not difficult to read his best known short story "Sredni Vashtar" as his dream as a small boy of taking sweet and bloody revenge on his aunts.

Munro was a sensitive, often sickly child with a love of practical jokes, history, animals and the countryside. His early education was provided by governesses and attendance at a private school in Exmouth. Release from the tyranny of his aunts came when, at the age of fifteen, he went to Bedford Grammar School. ("You can't expect a boy to be vicious till he's been to a good school," says a character in "The Baker's Dozen".)

Between the ages of seventeen and twenty-three Munro travelled with his father, who had retired, and his brother and sister in France, Switzerland and Germany. He learned several European languages and became a cultured and reasonably sophisticated young man with a sense of artistic discrimination and a knowledge of cosmopolitan society.

In 1893 he secured a post in the police force in Burma, but after fifteen months, in which he suffered from bouts of malaria and home-sickness, he resigned and returned to England.

After recuperating in Devon, he moved to London in 1896 and decided to make writing his career. *The Rise of the Russian Empire* (1900), which he wrote in the British Museum library, was not well received, probably owing to the gruesome sense of humour and lack of respect for convention and religion which he displayed in it. He distinguished himself, however, as a political satirist and sketch-writer in the *Westminster Gazette* from 1900 to 1902. These political sketches were published anonymously with Carruthers Gould's original cartoons as *The Westminster Alice* in 1902. Less popular or successful were *The Not-So Stories*, his parody of Kipling's *Just So Stories*.

Munro was foreign correspondent for the *Morning Post* from 1902 to 1908 and worked in the Balkans, Warsaw, St Petersburg and Paris. On his return to London he continued to contribute political and other sketches to several papers, but concentrated on writing short stories.

Reginald (1904), a collection of short stories which had first appeared in the *Westminster Gazette*, was the first of Munro's books to be published under the pen name "Saki". (It is the name both of the cup-bearer in the Rubaiyyat of Omar Khayyam and of a type of small bushy-tailed South American monkey, though the reasons for Munro's choosing this pseudonym are not clear.)

Several of Saki's characters are patently gay and are almost certainly the mouthpieces for his own angry, sarcastic (and, unfortunately, sometimes misogynistic) observations on the hypocrisy and high regard for "proper behaviour" and arbitrary authority of the world of his aunts and the society in which he lived. Little is known of Hector Munro's life as a gay man, as his sister destroyed most of his papers and effects after his death, but it is clear that his proclivities were fairly well known in the literary society of the early 1900s, that he had relationships with several young men and lived with them (which Ethel Munro described as "chumming"), that the symbols in his diary refer to homosexual alliances, and that he – like several of the characters in his stories – frequented the notorious Jermyn Street baths.

The irrepressible wit and defiance of conventional standards of his political sketches and his first collection of Reginald stories continued through *Reginald in Russia* (1910), *The Chronicles of Clovis* (1911), and *Beasts and Super-Beasts* (1914).

The bleakness of *The Unbearable Bassington* (1912) and its air of foreboding give it a prophetic resonance, but his other novel *When William Came* (1913), about life in England after a successful German invasion, is disappointingly sentimental and the patriotic tone

of some of its passages is fulsome.

Although, as Hugh Walpole related, "he was to be met with at country houses and London parties, apparently rather cynical, rather idle, and taking life so gently that he might hardly be said to be taking it at all," Munro possessed a strong, and curiously conventional, sense of personal responsibility and duty.

At the outbreak of the First World War he enlisted in the 22nd Royal Fusiliers and refused to take a commission or a comfortable job as a linguist. Towards the end of 1915 he went to the Front in France and was promoted to lance-sergeant. Of the war he is reported to have said, "Awful, my dear. The *noise!* and the *people!*"

Still ill from a bout of malaria Munro took part in the attack on Beaumont Hamel in November 1916. In the early hours of the 14th a fellow soldier heard Munro shout from a shallow crater where he was resting: "Put that bloody cigarette out!" A few seconds later he was shot through the head.

Address

★*97 Mortimer Street, W1* – he had rooms here from 1909 until his death.

Works include

Short stories and sketches: *The Westminster Alice* (1902); *Reginald* (1904); *Reginald in Russia, and Other Sketches* (1910); *The Chronicles of Clovis* (1911); *Beasts and Super-Beasts* (1914); *The Toys of Peace, and Other Stories* (1919); *The Square Egg, and Other Sketches* – with three plays (1924); *The Short Stories of Saki* (1930).

Novels: *The Unbearable Bassington* (1912); *When William Came: a Story of London under the Hohenzollerns* (1913); *The Novels and Plays of Saki* (1933).

Studies: *The Rise of the Russian Empire* (1900).

The Complete Saki (1981).

Ethel Sands

(6 July 1873 – 19 March 1962)

Ethel Sands, a central figure in English cultural society for over half a century, was born in Newport, Rhode Island. Her parents brought her to England, and settled here, when she was just a few months old. Her father, Mahlon Sands, was a wealthy businessman with a fortune which came from his family's drug importing company. Her mother, Mary Hartpence Sands, was a celebrated beauty and socialite who entertained the Prince of Wales at her London home, and was painted by Sargent.

Her mother's beauty was a cause of suffering for Ethel. "Are you really Mrs Sands's daughter?" people would enquire on meeting the tall, gaunt woman whose long face, square protruding teeth and receding chin gave her a rather equine appearance.

Despairing of ever being able to find a suitable husband for Ethel, her parents allowed her to withdraw from the social scene and to study art in Paris. There she met and fell in love with another American art student, Anna Hope Hudson (1869–1957), known to her friends as "Nan" (and to her detractors as "Man"). She was outspoken, confident and warm-hearted, while the young Ethel was painfully shy and self-conscious. They loved each other from the moment they met and lived together for over sixty years.

When she left art school Ethel returned to London with Nan and took a house in Knightsbridge. Both of her parents had died by this time, and she and Nan were left in charge of her two younger brothers.

In 1908, at the Royal Albert Hall, Ethel and Nan's paintings were exhibited for the first time. Then in Paris, in 1911, Ethel had her first one-woman show. The following year a joint exhibition of Ethel's interiors and still lifes and Nan's landscapes was held at the Carfax Gallery. They were founder members of the Fitzroy Street group of artists which, with Walter Sickert as their guiding light, became known as the London Group.

Ethel bought a country house in Newington, Oxfordshire, and she and Nan began giving house parties. Their guests included Henry James, Howard Sturgis, Lady Ottoline Morrell and Robert Ross. Ross was a particularly close friend and stayed with Ethel after his court case against Lord Alfred Douglas.

Lytton Strachey was a guest in 1913, with Gertrude Stein and Alice B Toklas, at Ethel's studio in Chelsea. He described her as "dressed in white satin and pearls . . . thickly powdered and completely haggard" with "appreciative shiny teeth". What Ethel thought of Strachey has unfortunately not been recorded.

During the First World War Newington was turned into an army hospital. Ethel became forewoman of an overall factory and then went to France, where she and Nan worked as hospital nurses. After the war she returned to London, where she resumed her round of cinema and theatregoing, and began again to give her elegant parties. Nan spent several weeks of each year painting landscapes in Normandy, where they had bought a château.

After the outbreak of the Second World War Ethel and Nan went back to France and again worked as nursing auxiliaries. When the Germans invaded France they returned to England. While they were doing hospital work in Surrey a parachute mine gutted their London house. Most of their paintings were destroyed. Others were lost when the Château d'Auppergard was looted by the French and then occupied by the Germans.

They came back to London after the war and bought a house near the ruins of their old home. Then they went back to Normandy to clear the mess of war from their French home. One day in 1951, while they were out walking together, Nan was knocked down by a car. She was taken to hospital and had to undergo two orthopaedic operations. They missed each other more than they had ever done, and exchanged letters every day when they were apart. Separation was almost unbearable for them, with, as Nan said, "no one to giggle with".

Nan never fully recovered from the accident and was never again free from pain. Ethel looked after her at home for as long as she could, but in 1957 Nan's condition grew worse and she was taken to a nursing home in Kilburn, where, in her few lucid moments, she cried out for Ethel. She died a week after her eighty-eighth birthday and was buried in Normandy, in the churchyard facing the Château d'Auppergard.

Shortly after Nan's death their friend L P Hartley wrote to Ethel, "Nan's and your beautiful life together makes a memorial to love which still, when it is over, warms the heart and helps one to believe in eternal values."

Ethel survived Nan by just four and half years, comforted in her loneliness by the memories of many friendships and of her long, happy life with Nan. She died peacefully at her home in Chelsea Square. Her funeral service was held at Chelsea Old Church and her ashes were buried next to her brother Morton in Putney Vale Cemetery.

3 Durham Place, SW3

Addresses

★*(Clive Lodge), Queen's Gate, SW7* – she lived here with her family 1876–77.

★*St George Street (formerly George Street), W1* – she lived here with her mother 1877–88.

★*40 Portland Place, W1* – her home 1888–97.

★*42 Lowndes Street, SW1* – her first London home with Nan (1906–13).

★*15 The Vale, SW3* – their home 1913–37.

★*3 Durham Place, SW3* – their home 1937–38.

★*51 Chelsea Square, SW3* – they lived here 1938–41. (Bombed in 1941.)

★*18 Chelsea Square, SW3* – they lived here 1944–62. Ethel died here.

Works include

Colour print "The Chintz Couch" (c1910) – Tate Gallery.

Portrait

(Probable) portrait in the canvas "Tipperary" (1914) by W R Sickert – Tate Gallery.

Memorabilia

L P Hartley's novel *The Boat* (1950) is dedicated to Ethel Sands.

Siegfried Sassoon

(8 September 1886 – 1 September 1967)

Siegfried Louvain Sassoon was born in Kent into a wealthy Jewish banking family. His parents separated when he was five and he saw little of his father, who died when Sassoon was nine.

His mother was a talented amateur artist and the sister of the sculptor Hamo Thorneycroft. It was she who recognised her son's literary talent when, at the age of eleven, he presented her with a collection of his poems.

Sassoon went to Marlborough College and to Clare College, Cambridge. He was more interested in sport and poetry than in his studies, and left university without taking a degree. Thereafter he divided his time between the country, where he fox-hunted and played cricket, and London, where he spent his days writing poetry and his evenings at the theatre.

Between 1906 and 1912 Sassoon published nine privately printed collections of poems. All the time he "muddled along, making corrections . . . I had no one to whom I could show any poems in MS and [my own publications] were a sort of private hobby." However, in 1913 he met Edward Marsh who gave him all the encouragement and advice he needed and introduced him to his circle of literary friends which included Rupert Brooke.

At the outbreak of the First World War Sassoon joined the Royal Welch Fusiliers and was posted to France. He soon saw action in the front line, where his reckless bravery earned him the nickname "Mad Jack". In 1916 he was awarded the Military Cross for rescuing, under heavy fire, a lance-corporal who was lying wounded close to the German lines. A year later he captured, single-handedly, some German trenches and remained in the enemy position, reading a volume of poetry, seemingly oblivious of the danger.

Sassoon was attracted to a nineteen-year-old soldier named Gibson who was killed during the battle of the Somme. "Part of me died with all the Gibsons I used to know," he wrote in 1921. "Their memory makes Gabriel taste like a cheap liqueur." (The artist Gabriel Aitkin was Sassoon's lover for several years after the war.)

His closest relationship was with a young subaltern, David Thomas, who was also killed in action. Sassoon paid tribute to him in *The Memoirs of a Fox-hunting Man* and commemorated him in his poems "The Last Meeting", "A Letter Home" and "A Subaltern". In his Diaries he recalled the summer before the war when he and Thomas "lived together four weeks in Pembroke College in rooms where the previous occupant's name, 'Paradise', was written above the door". When he heard of Thomas's death, Sassoon went into the woods to grieve alone, and hung a garland on a tree where he had chalked his friend's name.

In April 1917, after being invalided back to England with a bullet wound in his shoulder, Sassoon began to take a different view of the war. He threw his Military Cross ribbon into the River Mersey and made public the "Soldier's Declaration" which he sent to his commanding officer, attacking "the political errors and insincerities for which the fighting men are being sacrificed. On behalf of those who are suffering now I make this protest against the deception which is being practised on them."

He expected to be court-martialled, but the War Office, in an effort to hush up the matter, announced that his "act of wilful defiance" was the result of shell-shock, and he was sent to Craiglockhart War Hospital on the outskirts of Edinburgh. There he met Wilfred Owen whose poetry he influenced and encouraged.

On leaving Craiglockhart, early in 1918, Sassoon decided that his protest could be more effectively made from the Front, so he rejoined his battalion in France. Soon afterwards he was wounded again, this time by one of his own NCOs who mistook him for a German, as he returned from a dawn patrol.

By the end of the war Sassoon had established his reputation as a poet. He continued to write poetry but his work never again achieved the pungency or the passion of the "war poems". In 1928 his best known prose work, *The Memoirs of a Fox-hunting Man*, appeared. It was the first of his fictionalised memoirs, relating the life of "George Sherston", a lonely cricket-loving boy who joins the army and is sent to fight in the trenches, where he is brutally thrust into adulthood.

In 1957 Sassoon was awarded the Queen's Medal for Poetry, and in the same year he joined the Roman Catholic Church. In his later years he wrote mainly devotional poetry. He had married in 1933 and had one son.

Addresses

★*1 Raymond Buildings, WC1* – he lived here in 1914.
★*54 Tufton Street, SW1* – *site* of his home during the 1920s.

Works include

Poetry: *The Old Huntsman* (1917); *Counter-Attack* (1918); *War Poems* (1919); *Satirical Poems* (1926); *The Road to Ruin* (1933); *Collected Poems (1908–1956)* (1961).

Prose: *Memoirs of a Fox-hunting Man* (1928); *Memoirs of an Infantry Officer* (1930); *Sherston's Progress* (1936); *The Old Century* (1938); *The Weald of Youth* (1942); *Siegfried's Journey* (1945).

Diaries: *Diaries, 1915–1918* (1983) edited by Rupert Hart-Davis; *Diaries, 1920–1922* (1981) edited by Rupert Hart-Davis.

Portraits

Photographs by Cecil Beaton, Howard Coster, Bassano (1920), Walter Stoneman (1936), and by John Gunston (1916) – National Portrait Gallery.

Fictional portraits

He appears as George Sherston in several of his own books; as Siegfried Victor in *The Apes of God* (1930) by Wyndham Lewis; as David Casselis in *But It Still Goes On* (1930) by Robert Graves; and as Patient B in *Conflict and Dream* (1923) by William Halse Rivers. (Rivers was the army doctor who treated Sassoon for shell-shock.)

Memorabilia

Manuscript of *Memoirs of an Infantry Officer* – Imperial War Museum.

Edith Simcox

(21 August 1844 – 15 September 1901)

A shy, diffident, cultivated woman from a well-to-do middle class family, Edith Jemima Simcox was a radical social reformer who struggled, as she said, "to set the world to rights". She became a leading figure in the trade union movement and a tireless campaigner for women's rights.

Edith had always wanted to be a writer and was delighted when in 1869 she was offered a job as a reviewer for the *Academy* magazine. She soon realised, however, that her talent with words could be put to better use. She began writing articles for magazines such as *Nineteenth Century* and *Frasers* about the inequality and appalling hardships suffered by the working classes. She was a supporter of women's suffrage and of the trade unions. She lectured in Working Men's Clubs on social and economic issues, campaigned against low pay and high rents, and organised a Lodgers' League in Stepney.

With her friend Mary Hamilton, Edith started, in 1875, a small cooperative shirt-making business, "Hamilton & Co", which began trading at 68 Dean Street, W1, and after three years moved to larger premises in Mortimer Street, W1. She was a keen supporter of the cooperative movement, though characteristically did not include her name in the firm's title. Also in 1875 Edith, representing the Society of Shirt and Collar Makers, and Mrs Paterson, of the Society of Bookbinders, were the first women admitted as delegates to the eighth TUC Congress. Edith told the story of Hamilton & Co in an article, "Eight Years of Cooperative Shirt Making", which appeared in June 1884 in *Nineteenth Century*.

As a trade unionist Edith visited tailors and stocking makers, and spoke on their behalf at trade union and cooperative congresses. In 1876 she began to write her "Autobiography of a Shirt Maker", which she described not as the story of a shirt maker, but of a lover.

The love that transformed and filled her life was for the novelist George Eliot. It is not known what led to their first meeting in December 1872. Perhaps Edith, as an admirer of George Eliot's books, had written asking for a meeting. For the next eight years until George Eliot's death Edith was her most adoring and attentive friend. Unfortunately the great writer did not respond beyond allowing Edith's total devotion, and all Edith's passion went into the "Autobiography", which sadly has never been published.

When George Eliot died Edith wrote of the sorrow which came from "thoughts of our being parted before the perfect union I always longed for had been quite reached". Through the following years she became a regular visitor to Highgate Cemetery where George Eliot is buried. It was her greatest wish that she would be buried near her friend, and she wrote as her epitaph, "Here lies the body of E.J.S. whose heart's desire lives wherever the name and memory of George Eliot is beloved."

She was, however, buried far away from Highgate, at Apsley Guise, which is nine miles south of Bedford, near Guise House, the family home. She was cremated and her ashes were buried in her mother's grave. She has no epitaph and no words are inscribed to tell where she is buried.

10 Lansdowne Road, W11

Addresses

★*1 Douro Place, W8 – site* of her childhood home.

★*Chenies Street, WC1* – she had a house here c1875–c1885

★*10 Lansdowne Road, W11* – her home 1899–1901.

Works include

"Autobiography of a Shirt Maker" (Manuscript – Bodleian Library, Oxford); *Natural Law: an Essay in Ethics* (1877); *Episodes in the Lives of Men, Women and Lovers* (1882); *Primitive Civilisations* (2 volumes, 1894).

Memorabilia

Material relating to her trade union activities – National Museum of Labour History.

Winnaretta Singer
Princesse Edmond de Polignac

(8 January 1865 – 26 November 1943)

Winnaretta Eugenie Singer was born in Yonkers, New York, the twentieth child of Isaac Merritt Singer, the wealthy founder of the sewing machine company. She was the second child of his second marriage, to a young Frenchwoman, Isabella Boyer Summerville. Between his two marriages Singer had fathered sixteen other children, all of whom he acknowledged.

When Winnaretta was two years old the family moved to Europe. They lived for a while in Paris and London before settling in Paignton, Devon, where Singer built a mansion which he called "The Wigwam". He died in 1875 and was buried in a newly created vault in Torquay Cemetery. Isabella took the children back to Paris in 1878. Soon afterwards she married a Belgian aristocrat and became a leading figure in Paris society.

Winnaretta showed an early interest in art and studied painting at the studio of Félix Barrias. Later she became interested in the new school of Impressionist painters. The particular influence of Manet was evident in a series of paintings she produced in the 1890s. Her first love, however, was music, and she was a gifted pianist.

Her ambition was to be a leader of society and a patron of the arts, with a salon which would be a centre for the social and cultural life of Paris. As an unmarried woman she had no social standing, so she began, at the age of twenty-two, to look around for a suitable husband: one who in return for a share of her huge fortune would give her a title and the place in society that she desired.

The man she chose to marry was an impoverished prince, Louis de Scey-Montbéliard. Despite the fact that she had made clear to her husband the conditions of the marriage, and assumed that he knew that she was a lesbian, he made persistent attempts to get into her bed. After a brief period they separated and were divorced.

Being a divorced woman put Winnaretta at a great disadvantage socially. She was not keen to remarry, but was persuaded by her friend Comte Robert de Montesquiou to marry his friend Prince Edmond de Polignac, whom he considered to be the perfect partner for her. The fifty-nine year old prince was charming, cultured and a talented composer. Two important points in his favour were that he came from a distinguished family and that he was a homosexual.

They were married in 1893 and, unexpectedly, became devoted to one another. Together they built up a considerable collection of Impressionist paintings and held annual exhibitions at the large house Winnaretta had bought for herself. Edmond died in 1901 and was buried in the Singer vault in Torquay.

There was no need for Winnaretta to remarry; as a widow she was still accepted in society. Her salon was always full of the rich and titled, who came to hear the latest music by Fauré, Ravel and Debussy, and to observe leading figures in the arts such as Diaghilev, Cocteau and Proust. Many of the musical works first performed in Winnaretta's salon were commissioned by her, and she was the chief backer of Diaghilev's Ballet Russe.

To many of her guests meeting her for the first time Winnaretta appeared cold and aloof. The determined set of her jaw and her ice-blue eyes gave the impression of an aggressive character. "I have seldom seen a woman sit so firmly," noted Harold Nicolson in his diary. "There was determination in every line of her bum"; but to her friends she was warm, generous and amusing. Maurice Baring called her "the wittiest woman in Europe".

She had love affairs with several celebrated women, including Ethel Smyth, Romaine Brooks, Violet Trefusis and the Romanian pianist Clara Haskil. Her deepest relationship was with the Baroness Olga de Meyer (reputed to have been the illegitimate daughter of Edward VII), whom she met in 1909. They were parted at the beginning of the First World War when Olga, a German citizen, was forced to flee with her husband to America.

In 1926 Winnaretta set up the Fondation Singer-Polignac to foster and endow artistic and scientific projects. "I owe to my father a considerable fortune," she wrote, "but I am sixty-one years old; I am now seriously preoccupied with the arrangements that I have to make for the future of the fortune." Archaeological expeditions to Greece were subsidised; the Musée Gauguin was built in Tahiti; the Institut Océanographique was presented with a ship, which they named the "Winnaretta Singer"; work on the properties of hallucenogenic mushrooms was financed; and a mobile laboratory was presented to the Institut Pasteur for its work in Dakar.

32 Grosvenor Gardens, SW1

Apart from the projects made possible by her bequest she also financed the building of Salvation Army hostels in Paris, modernised houses for the poor, and gave money to the Society for the Preservation and Rehabilitation of Young Girls.

She died in London, where she lived during the war, and is buried in the family vault in Torquay.

Addresses

★*32 Grosvenor Gardens, SW1* – she lived here with her family 1870–71.

★*Argyll Mansions, 303–323 Kings Road, SW3* – she lived in the flat above No. 321 from 1908 until c1916.

★*55 Park Lane, W1* – she lived here from 1939 until her death here in 1943.

Works commissioned by her include

Stravinsky's "Renard" (1915–16); Satie's "Socrate" (1918); Falla's "El Retablo de Maese Pedro" (1919; 1st perf. 1923); Françaix's "Le Diable Boiteux" (1937); Poulenc's Organ Concerto (1938).

Works dedicated to her include

Fauré's "Cinq Mélodies de Venise" (1891) – text by Verlaine; Ravel's "Pavane pour une Infante Defunte" (1899).

Fictional portrait

She is portrayed as Vinaigrette in Robert de Montesquiou's collection *Les Quarante Bergères* (1925).

Dame Ethel Smyth

(23 April 1858 – 8 May 1944)

"Because I have conducted my own operas and love sheepdogs; because I generally dress in tweeds, and sometimes at winter afternoon concerts have conducted in them; because I was a militant suffragette and seized a chance of beating time to 'The March of Women' from the window of my cell in Holloway Prison with a toothbrush; because I have written books, spoken speeches, broadcast, and don't always make sure that my hat is on straight; for these and other equally pertinent reasons, in a certain sense, I am well known."

Ethel Smyth was born in Sidcup and grew up in Frimley, near Aldershot. Her father was a general and he ruled over his wife and eight children in much the same way as he did his regiment. His sons were expected to follow him into the army, while his daughters were brought up by governesses to be demure, devout and submissive, so that they might become "good wives". In Ethel's case, however, the general's plans did not turn out at all as expected.

When she was twelve Ethel heard a new governess, who had studied music at the Leipzig Conservatory, playing some Beethoven piano sonatas. It was the first time she had heard classical music and immediately she knew that she wanted to become a composer. She made up her mind that as soon as she was old enough she too would go to Leipzig.

It took a long time for Ethel to overcome her father's opposition to her demands to go to Germany and study music, but eventually, after many fierce arguments and battles of will, he gave his consent.

As soon as she arrived at the Conservatory Ethel encountered male prejudice, and when she was introduced to Brahms he was "very kind and fatherly in his awkward way" but refused to take her music seriously because she was a woman. Tchaikovsky, on the other hand, listened to her music and thought that "she gave promise in the future of a serious and talented career". He encouraged her to change her musical direction away from the influence of Brahms and to find her own way. Ethel made her debut in England in 1890,

when her "Serenade in D" was performed at the Crystal Palace. But it was the performance of her "Mass in D" at the Albert Hall that established her reputation as the greatest English woman composer.

In 1910 she went to a meeting of the Women's Social and Political Union, which was being addressed by its leader, Emmeline Pankhurst. So strong an impact did the speech and the speaker have on Ethel that she decided then and there to join the movement for a period of two years, after which she would return to her work. She contributed to the cause by composing "The March of Women", which became the suffragettes' anthem; and she used her skills as a fast bowler to give Emmeline Pankhurst lessons in stone-throwing. In March 1912 Ethel was arrested while smashing the windows of the home of the Colonial Secretary, and spent three weeks in Holloway Prison.

During the 1920s her works were regularly performed, both in England and abroad. Ethel often appeared as conductor on these occasions, dressed in the regalia of a Doctor of Music, her mortar-board perched on top of a bright red wig. In 1922 she was created a Dame Commander of the Order of the British Empire. In 1930 she conducted the police band in "The March of Women" at the unveiling in the Victoria Tower Gardens of the statue of Emmeline Pankhurst, who had died two years earlier.

As she grew older Ethel became increasingly deaf. The specialists she consulted were unable to help her, and she was forced to abandon her musical career.

She published several volumes of memoirs in which she wrote of her relationships with women. Throughout her long, energetic life she fell passionately in love with a vast array of women, including Pauline Trevelyan (who inspired her to write the "Mass in D"), the Empress Eugénie, Winnaretta Singer, Lady Mary Ponsonby, and Edith Somerville. In her seventies she met Virginia Woolf, the last great love of her life. She pursued her with an ardour and exuberance which caused the frail, introspective novelist to reflect, "I daresay the old fires of Sapphism are blazing for the last time. In her heyday she must have been formidable."

Ethel died at "Coign", her house in Woking. Her brother, who had lived up to their father's expectations by becoming a general, scattered her ashes in the woodland next to Woking Golf Course.

Address

★*40 Moore Street, SW3* – she had rooms in this house, which belonged to her friend Lt-Col. The Hon. Denis Tollemache, and stayed here many times on her visits to London.

Works include

Operas: "The Wreckers" (1904); "The Boatswain's Mate" (1914).

Orchestral works: "Overture – Antony and Cleopatra" (1890); "Concerto for Violin, Horn and Orchestra" (1927).

Choral works: "Mass in D" (1891); "The Prison" (1930).

Song: "The March of Women" (1911) (words by Cicely Hamilton).

Memoirs: *Impressions That Remained* (2 volumes) (1919); *Streaks of Life* (1921); *Female Pipings in Eden* (1933); *As Time Went On* (1936) – dedicated to Virginia Woolf; *What Happened Next* (1940).

Portraits

Black chalk by John Singer Sargent (1901) – National Portrait Gallery. Canvas by Neville Lytton (1936) – Royal College of Music. Drawing by Powys Evans (undated) – Royal College of Music. Chalk by Antonio Mancini (1900) – Royal College of Music. Photographs – National Portrait Gallery and Museum of London.

Fictional portrait

She is caricatured as Edith Staines in E F Benson's *Dodo* (1893).

Memorabilia

Collection of unpublished letters – British Library. Several autograph letters and a manuscript sheet of music – Fawcett Library. Vernon Lee dedicated her play *Ariadne in Mantua* (1903) to her.

Simeon Solomon

(9 October 1840 – 14 August 1905)

He was, according to Burne-Jones, "the greatest artist of us all", yet today much of his work has been lost or is unaccounted for.

Simeon Solomon was born in Bishopsgate. His family were Italian-Jewish immigrants who had made a fortune by importing and manufacturing leghorn hats. His father, Michael Solomon, was the first Jew ever to be admitted to the Freedom of the City of London. Simeon's brother Abraham (1823–62) and his sister Rebecca (1832–86) were also successful artists.

As a boy he worked in his brother's studio in Gower Street and when he was fourteen he entered the Royal Academy Schools. In 1858 he exhibited for the first time at the Royal Academy (and was to do so annually until 1872) a painting entitled "And the Lord said 'Take now my son, thine only son Isaac and offer him there for a burnt offering upon one of the mountains I will tell thee of'".

His skill as a draughtsman and the sincerity and beauty of colour in his work were quickly recognised and he was taken up by Rossetti and other Pre-Raphaelites. For a time he was Millais's assistant. Influenced by Rossetti and later by Burne-Jones he developed a romantic style which, mixed with high camp and mysticism, appealed to aesthetes such as Pater, Swinburne and Wilde.

Scenes from the Bible and Jewish ritual provided the subject matter for most of his drawings and paintings. A feature of his work, perhaps especially in those pictures with mythological and allegorical themes, is his overt portrayal of homosexual and lesbian subjects.

Many critics, including Thackeray, regarded him as an important and influential figure in the Aesthetic movement. He was also a fine illustrator and in the 1860s he designed stained glass windows for William Morris & Co.

Walter Pater, who described Solomon as a "young Greek god", invited him to stay with him at Brasenose College, Oxford, and to paint his portrait.

Solomon often visited Rossetti's home at 16 Cheyne Walk, Chelsea, where his friend Swinburne was living in 1863. He and Swinburne used to slide naked down the stairs and race through the house, until a valuable vase belonging to Rossetti was smashed.

Through Swinburne, Solomon met Oscar Browning, the historian and educator, and stayed with him at Eton, where Browning was a master. In 1869 they went on holiday together to Italy, where Solomon fell in love with a Roman youth who was probably the inspiration for his prose poem *Vision of Love Revealed in Sleep*, which was published with his own illustrations in 1871.

On 11 February 1873 he and a man called George Roberts were arrested and charged with "committing an offence" in a public urinal in Stratford Place Mews, near Oxford Street. Solomon was sentenced to eighteen months imprisonment in the Clerkenwell House of Correction, but the sentence was suspended and he was placed under police supervision. Most of his friends deserted him. Swinburne, displaying appalling hypocrisy, denounced him as "a thing unmentionable alike by man and woman, as equally abhorrent to either – nay, to the very beasts".

As a result of the scandal Solomon received no more commissions and found it very difficult to sell his work, apart from the occasional pastel which he sold for a guinea apiece. He began to drink heavily, and in order to buy food, took to selling Swinburne's indiscreet letters. He turned down offers of help from his family, rather than lose his independence, even if it meant ending up in the gutter.

He became a vagrant, existing on the few pennies he made as a pavement artist in Brompton Road and by selling matches and shoelaces in Mile End Road. His companions now were pickpockets and petty thieves. His involvement in an attempt to steal gold leaf from Burne-Jones's studio led to his arrest. He was spared a prison sentence, on the grounds that he had once been a gentleman and an artist.

A chronic alcoholic, he spent his last years in St Giles Workhouse. Robert Ross visited him there and remarked on his cheerfulness and lack of recrimination. In May 1905 he collapsed in Great Turnstile and spent some time in King's College Hospital. He returned to the workhouse, where on 14 August 1905 he died suddenly in the dining hall. An inquest was held at which the cause of death was given as heart disease and chronic alcoholism.

He is buried in the Jewish Cemetery in Willesden.

Addresses

★*3 Sandys Row (formerly Sandys Street), E1* – birthplace.

★*18 Gower Street, WC1* – site. He worked here in his brother's studio.

★*18 John Street, WC1* – his mother's home. He lived here c1864.

★*26 Howland Street, W1* – he lived here mid-1860s. (*Site.*)

★*106 Gower Street, WC1* – he lived here with his sister Rebecca (late 1860s).

★*12 Fitzroy Street, W1* – site. He lived here with Rebecca 1869–73.

★*13 Newton Street, WC2* – site. He lived here c1886.

★*113 Gray's Inn Road, WC1* – he lived here c1888. (*Site.*)

★*81 Long Acre, WC2* – site of the house in which he lived 1889.

★*359 Edgware Road, W2* – he lived here c1896.

★*St Giles in the Fields Workhouse* (*site* at junction of Endell Street, WC2, and High Holborn, WC1). He was first admitted "as a pauper" on 15 July 1885, and stayed here at intervals over the next twenty years. (He died here.)

Works include

Drawing "David and Jonathan" (c1856) – Tate Gallery. Canvas "The Moon and Sleep" (1894) – Tate Gallery. Watercolour "Sappho and Erinna in the Garden of Mytilene" (1864) – Tate Gallery. Pen and ink drawing "Dante's first meeting with Beatrice" (1859–63) – Tate Gallery. Study for "Sappho . . ." (1862) – Tate Gallery. Pencil "The Bride and Bridegroom and Sad Love" (1865) – Victoria and Albert Museum. Watercolour drawing "In the Temple of Venus" (undated) – V & A Museum. Drawing "Study for 'Sacramentum Amoris'" (c1868) – British Museum. Drawing "Until the Day Break and the Shadows Flee Away" (1869) – British Museum. Facsimile of drawing – Portrait of Dante Gabriel Rossetti (c1864) – National Portrait Gallery. Facsimile of drawing – Portrait of Algernon Charles Swinburne (c1864–65) – N.P.G.

Prose poem: *A Vision of Love Revealed in Sleep* (1871).

Portraits

Pencil self-portrait (1859) – Tate Gallery. Albumen print (photograph) by David Wilkie Wynfield (c1870) – Royal Academy of Arts.

Nancy Spain

(September 1917 – 21 March 1964)

Nancy Brooker Spain, journalist, novelist and television personality, was born in Newcastle-upon-Tyne. Her mother was Irish. Her father was a soldier who also wrote for *Punch* and other magazines. She was educated at Roedean, where she excelled at sports and was selected to play cricket, squash and lacrosse at county level.

She returned to Newcastle after leaving school and at the age of seventeen became a freelance sports reporter for her local newspaper. At the same time she got a job with the BBC playing "dialect" parts in radio plays. Then she set up a business selling sports equipment with her friend Winifred Sargent, who "drank burgundy and fizzy lemonade for lunch and who I was mad about". Sadly Winifred died and the business was wound up.

In 1939 Nancy joined the WRNS as a lorry driver. Eventually she rose to the rank of Second Officer and was put in charge of recruitment for the London area. She described her often hilarious wartime experiences in her first book *Thank You Nelson*.

When she was invalided out of the WRNS in 1945 because of a weak chest Nancy decided to stay in London and to try to make a living as a freelance journalist. Soon she was busy writing articles for such diverse publications as *Good Housekeeping*, *Empire News* and the *New Statesman*. In her spare time she wrote detective novels. In four years she wrote six novels and a biography of her great-aunt, Mrs Beeton. With success in her career came confidence and independence. She cropped her hair with nail scissors and took to wearing dungarees or slacks and sweaters. As an aghast columnist reported in the *Daily Sketch*, "Sharp-witted Nancy . . . even wears slacks to the theatre."

It was when Nancy became editor of a magazine called *Books for Today* in 1951 that she met Joan Werner Laurie ("Jonnie"), who ran the Werner Laurie publishing house which had been founded by her father. Jonnie, who was two years younger than Nancy, was a widow with two young sons. "She saved my life," Nancy wrote. "She is certainly the only person who has ever let me be myself . . . the only person with whom I can cheerfully live in close disharmony. It is impossible for me to take a step without Jonnie."

Nancy was invited in 1952 to write for the *Daily Express*, first as a book critic and then as a special feature writer. She made her first television appearance in *Something to Shout About* in 1954 and soon became a household name through such programmes as *Jukebox Jury*, *Twenty Questions* and *My Word*. She enjoyed being a celebrity and carefully cultivated her public image. She sometimes shocked people, but never scandalised them. Her alleged love for Gilbert Harding (with whom she appeared on the television panel game *Who Said That*), which led to press speculation about their possible marriage, was merely a joke played on an unsuspecting public, which gave them both valuable publicity and kept them in the public eye.

In 1954 Nancy and Jonnie, together with Michael Griffiths, founded *She* magazine as an alternative to the staid, old-fashioned women's magazines of the time. Jonnie was the first editor and Nancy, while still working for the *Daily Express* (until 1961, when she joined the *News of the World*), spent every available moment writing articles for the new magazine.

On Grand National day 1964 Nancy and Jonnie set off from Luton Airport in a light aircraft to fly to Aintree, where Nancy was to report on the race for the *News of the World*. They had been given permission to land in the racecourse area, and the pilot flew low and circled twice to fix his position. Watched by thousands of horrified racegoers, the blue and white Piper Apache suddenly plunged into a cabbage field near the Canal Turn. Nancy and Jonnie and the three other people on board were killed.

Addresses

★*4 Randolph Gardens, NW6* – she lived here late 1940s.

★*2 Chesney Court, Shirland Road, W9* – she lived here c1950.

★*6 Baker Street, W1* – *site* of her home with Joan Werner Laurie c1950–51.

★*35 Carlyle Square, SW3* – they lived here 1951–53.

★*7 Clareville Grove, SW7* – their home 1953–55.

★*20 William's Mews, SW1* – *site* of their last home.

Works include

Novels: *Death Before Wicket* (1946); *Poison for Teacher* (1949); *Death Goes on Skis* (1949); *R in the Month* (1950); *Out Damned Tot* (1952); *The Kat Strike* (1955).

Biography: *Mrs Beeton and Her Husband* (1948).

Autobiography: *Thank You Nelson* (1945); *Why I'm Not a Millionaire* (1956).

Gertrude Stein

(3 February 1874 – 27 July 1946)

There are probably few of Gertrude Stein's readers who.would rate her as highly as she did herself: "Think of the Bible and Homer, think of Shakespeare and think of me."

She was born in Allegheny, Pennsylvania. Her childhood, she recalled, was one which any middle class Jewish girl of her generation might have had, but with more overseas travel than most.

At university she studied philosophy and experimental psychology, and went on to do fairly advanced work on brain anatomy. An unhappy love affair in which she and two other women were involved probably had much to do with her abandoning her studies and joining her brother Leo in London in 1902. (They had a small independent income from their late father's business interests.)

Most of Gertrude's time in London was spent making social contacts, reading in the British Museum and writing in the Bloomsbury flat which she and Leo shared. She did not like London and the exceptionally bad weather that winter added to her depression.

After a brief visit to New York Gertrude went to Paris where Leo had taken a *pavillon* and studio at 27 rue de Fleurus. Their search for paintings by Cézanne for their collection led them to the works of, among others, Renoir, Dérain, Matisse, Gauguin, Rousseau, Braque and Picasso. They recognised the significance of these artists and, through the fairly informal literary and artistic salon which they had established, brought them to the attention of a wider public. Gertrude was particularly vigorous in her championing of abstract painting.

The painters she became most friendly with were Matisse, Braque and Picasso. It was whilst Picasso, who became a lifelong friend, was painting her portrait (circa 1905–06) that Gertrude began work on *Three Lives*.

The paintings and philosophies of the Cubist and abstract painters, together with the teachings of William James, her psychology professor at Radcliffe College, were the most significant influences on her writing.

Alice B Toklas, a young Californian woman who had recently arrived in Paris, began visiting the salon in September 1907. It was soon evident that her interest was more in Gertrude than in the paintings in the Steins' collection. She recalled (in her memoir *What Is Remembered*, 1963), "Gertrude Stein . . . held my complete attention, as she did all the many years I knew her until her death, and all the empty ones since then." Before long she was doing the proof-reading of *Three Lives* for Gertrude and within a year had become an indispensable member of the Stein menage. Leo soon departed, leaving 27 rue de Fleurus to Gertrude and Alice. Thus began their long life together.

Alice devoted her life to Gertrude, serving her as typist, proof-reader, publisher, manager, critic, confidante and nurse. Although they always presented themselves to the outside world as "the writer" and her "secretary" or "companion", Gertrude and Alice nevertheless soon became legendary as a lesbian couple. Both, however, were reticent upon the nature of their relationship and their sexuality. It was probably for this reason that Gertrude's novel *Q.E.D.* (completed in 1903), which like several of her other early works has lesbian relationships as its subject, was "forgotten" and only published posthumously in 1950 as *The Way Things Are*.

With Alice's excellent practical support, loyalty and total agreement on her "genius", Gertrude thought, wrote, talked, criticised, self-publicised, lectured, held court. On the basis of such works as *Three Lives*, *Tender Buttons* and the "portraits" of her friends, Gertrude's reputation as a literary innovator grew during the 1920s and 1930s – she was on her way to becoming one of the most publicised but least read authors of this century. She lectured at Cambridge and Oxford in 1926 and on tour in America in the 1930s.

Although she was a prolific writer of fiction, verse, drama and criticism, it was only with the publication in 1933 of *The Autobiography of Alice B Toklas* that Gertrude reached a wide readership and began to earn some money from her writing.

That same year her opera *Four Saints in Three Acts*, with music by Virgil Thomson, was performed to acclaim in Hartford, Connecticut, and New York. During their 1934–35 visit to America Gertrude and Alice found themselves fêted celebrities. The peculiarity and eccentricity of the couple, like that strangeness which Gertrude aimed at in her writing as a means of revitalising language and literature, captured the imagination of the public.

From 1937, 5 rue Christine became their Paris home; summers and autumns were spent in a country house at Billigny which they began renting in 1928. Unlike their fellow expatriates, they did not return to America during the war, but remained in occupied France, a course either particularly courageous or naive, given their vulnerability as well-known elderly Jewish aliens.

During the First World War they had entered the war effort by enlisting as an ambulance unit with a van which Gertrude imported and learned to drive, but now they withdrew to the countryside where Gertrude devoted herself to her writing. Works such as *Ida, a Novel*, *Wars I Have Seen* and *Paris France* date from this period.

Gertrude and Alice returned to Paris in December 1944 after the liberation of the city. There they were hailed as heroines by the American servicemen, and the novel *Brewsie & Willie* is Gertrude's tribute to them.

On 27 July 1946 Gertrude underwent surgery for an abdominal tumour. On briefly regaining consciousness she asked Alice, "What is the answer?" When she received no reply she demanded, "In that case, what is the question?" She died shortly afterwards.

After Gertrude's death Alice zealously nurtured her friend's literary reputation, and, through her lectures, talks and writings (memoirs, letters, journalism and her famous cook-books), won appreciation on her own account.

Gertrude and Alice are buried in Père Lachaise Cemetery, Paris, beneath a headstone designed by Gertrude's protégé, Sir Francis Rose.

Address

★*20 Bloomsbury Square, WC1* – Gertrude stayed here with her brother Leo during the winter of 1902–03.

Works include

Three Lives (1909); *Tender Buttons* (1914); *How to Write* (1931); *Before the Flowers of Friendship Faded Friendship Faded* (1931); *The Autobiography of Alice B Toklas* (1933); *Portraits and Prayers* (1934); *Picasso* (1938); *Paris France* (1940); *What Are Masterpieces* (1940); *Ida, a Novel* (1941); *Wars I Have Seen* (1945); *Brewsie & Willie* (1946); *Blood on the Dining-Room Floor* (1948); *Things As They Are* (1950).

Portrait

Plaster sculpture by Jacques Lipchitz (undated) – Tate Gallery. (The widely reproduced painting of Gertrude Stein by Picasso and the photographs by Cecil Beaton of her and Alice B Toklas were greatly loved by both of them; less well liked was Pavel Tchelitchew's painting of them, "Big Chief Sitting Bull and the Knitting Maniac".) *Portrait on p. 192.*

Fictional portrait

Gertrude appears as Mrs Percival in Ford Madox Ford's *The Rash Act* (1933).

192

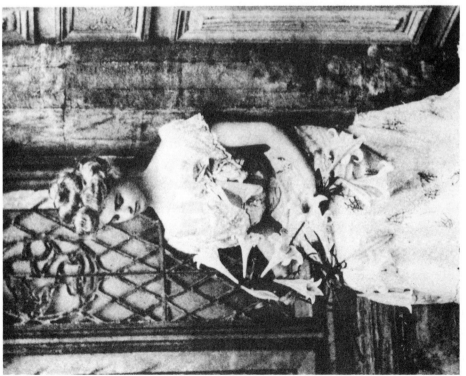

Count Eric Stenbock

(14 March 1860 – 26 April 1895)

Count Stanislaus Eric Stenbock lived in a haze of opium smoke and incense with a pet toad called Fatima and a snake which he coiled around his neck like a scarf.

He came originally from Estonia and owned a castle in an isolated region of Russia, but he preferred to spend most of his life in England. While an undergraduate at Balliol College, Oxford, he began to write love poems addressed to young men, and stories about witches, demons and werewolves based on the folk tales of his native land.

Stenbock was short and slightly built with fair, curly hair and china blue eyes. He had a habit of dipping his fingers into a gold vial of scent, which he carried with him, and then running them through his curls. It is sad to relate that by the time he was thirty most of his hair had fallen out and his fine chiselled features had become blurred and distorted by his over-indulgence in drugs and alcohol.

In his house Stenbock kept a shrine containing a statue of Buddha and a bust of Shelley, before which red votive lamps constantly burned. Once, when Oscar Wilde committed the sacrilege of lighting his cigarette from Shelley's altar lamp, Stenbock fell to the floor in a dead faint. Wilde, quite unconcerned, stepped over the prostrate body of his host, picked up his hat, and took his leave.

In 1891 Stenbock fell madly in love with the young theatrical composer Norman O'Neill (1875–1934), whom he met on the upper deck of a Piccadilly omnibus. When, two years later, O'Neill became a student at the Hoch Conservatorium in Frankfurt, Stenbock took a great interest in his progress, and sent him a series of humorous sketches by Aubrey Beardsley depicting him as "the English flower in the German conservatory".

Stenbock's circle of friends included More Adey and Robert Ross, and he was one of the few who kept in touch with Simeon Solomon after the artist's public downfall. Although he could not bring himself to visit Solomon in the squalor of the workhouse, he often sent him gifts and money via Ross and in 1886 gave a lavish reception in his honour at his Chelsea home.

By 1895 Stenbock's addiction to opium and alcohol had reduced him to a state where he was no longer able to look after himself. He became very ill and was taken to his mother's home in Sussex. There, in a drunken rage, he attacked someone with a poker and in so doing lost his balance, hit his head against the stone fireplace, and was killed. He died on the day that Wilde's trial opened at the Old Bailey.

In his will Stenbock left his young friend O'Neill £1,500 which enabled him to continue his studies for a further valuable year at the Conservatorium. O'Neill went on to become a successful composer of light music and songs, and wrote the incidental music to Maeterlinck's *The Bluebird* and Barrie's *Mary Rose*.

Addresses

★*11 Sloane Terrace, SW1* – Sloane Terrace Mansions stands on the *site* of his home 1886–90.

★*21 Gloucester Walk, W8* – his home 1890–95.

Works include

Poetry: *Love, Sleep and Dreams* (c1881); *Myrtle, Rue and Cypress* (1883) – with a dedication to Simeon Solomon; *The Shadow of Death* (1893).

Stories: *Studies of Death* (1894).

Translation: *Shorter Stories of Balzac* (1890) – with William Wilson (More Adey).

Sir Ronald Storrs

(19 November 1881 – 1 November 1955)

Ronald Henry Amherst Storrs, the distinguished and unusual Governor of Jerusalem, whom T E Lawrence described as "the most brilliant Englishman in the Near East", was born at Bury St Edmunds, Suffolk, the eldest son of the Rev. John Storrs, who later became Dean of Rochester, and his wife, the Hon. Lucy Cust.

He was educated at Charterhouse and at Pembroke College, Cambridge, and in 1904 entered the Egyptian civil service. He was posted to the Ministry of Finance and spent five years in this and other departments. But administration bored him: he preferred to spend his time getting to know the local people and collecting objets d'art.

In 1909 Storrs was appointed to the more interesting position of Oriental Secretary at the British Agency in Cairo, under Sir Eldon Gorst. There he was able to indulge his love of art, music and cooking, and to enjoy the company of all sorts and conditions of men. It was said of him that "he was ready, indeed anxious, to mix with all and sundry, with Turks, Jews, heretics and infidels, provided always that their company was worth while."

Gorst's term of office in Egypt was not without its problems, but Storrs, with his "almost feminine perceptions", understood him and remained loyal. With Gorst's successor, Lord Kitchener, he found himself naturally more in rapport. They were both ardent collectors of china and porcelain, and Storrs helped Kitchener to add to his collection while developing his own.

When Kitchener returned to England in 1914, Storrs remained in Cairo and became involved with the negotiations with the Sherif, afterwards King Hussein, an episode in his career which was written about by his friend T E Lawrence in *Seven Pillars of Wisdom*.

Storrs was appointed Governor of Jerusalem in 1917, at the beginning of the British mandate. It was a difficult time, and he and his staff had to be constantly on the alert. Characteristically, he left the administration to others while he began promoting musical societies and art exhibitions, and reviving the arts of glass blowing, pottery and weaving. Above all he set up the Pro-Jerusalem Society, to protect the city's monuments and to supervise the construction of new buildings with the local stone. He was awarded a knighthood in 1924. The previous year he had married Louisa Clowes, a widow with children.

In 1926 Storrs went as Governor and Commander-in-Chief to Cyprus where one of his first acts was the cancellation of the island's share of Turkey's war debt. He was popular for a time, but when agitation for union with Greece began he became a target for attack. In 1931 the wooden Government House was burned down and with it went Storr's entire collection of art objects and rare books which he had spent his life so patiently and skilfully bringing together. Within a fortnight order was restored by ships and troops from Malta and Egypt.

At the end of his term in Cyprus, in 1932, Storrs was appointed Governor of Northern Rhodesia, where he organised the transfer of the capital from Livingstone to Lusaka. Two years later he was taken seriously ill and forced to retire from the service.

In 1937 Storrs became a member of the London County Council, representing East Islington. In his later years he lectured and broadcast on Dante, Shakespeare and T E Lawrence.

Addresses

★*84 Elm Park Gardens, SW10* – his home c1938–40.
★*15 Alexander Square, SW3* – his home c1952–55.

Works include

Memoirs: *Orientations* (1937).

Portraits

Two photographs of him in uniform by Walter Stoneman (1919; 1931) – National Portrait Gallery.

Memorabilia

Sir Edward Marsh's translation of *The Odes of Horace* (1941) was dedicated to "The Three Ronalds" – Storrs, Knox and Fuller.

Lytton Strachey

(1 March 1880 – 21 January 1932)

Lytton Strachey's major achievement was to produce a new style of biography. In writing his concise, ironic, gossipy and witty studies of eminent social figures he treated his subjects as human beings and not as phenomena, and adhered to his dictum that "discretion is not the better part of biography". Discretion and that patriotic fervour which creates idealised national heroes were, for him, the hallmarks of the bourgeois Victorianism that he hated so intensely and in the struggle against which he was the spiritual leader.

Giles Lytton Strachey was born in London into an upper class family distinguished in the military, the civil service and in literature. At an early age he was encouraged by his mother, the noted essayist Lady Jane Strachey, to write verse, which was read aloud at family gatherings. An enthusiasm for the French language and literature was also inspired through his mother's teachings.

When he went up to Trinity College, Cambridge, in 1899 Strachey immediately impressed his tutors with his maturity, the depth of his intellect and the range of his reading. His undergraduate days were spent in reading 18th-century literature, both French and English (Horace Walpole was his greatest idol), and in having long, leisurely, intimate talks with such friends as Thoby Stephen (Virginia Woolf's brother), Leonard Woolf, Clive Bell and John Maynard Keynes. He also wrote verse and one of his poems, "Ely", won the Chancellor's English Medal. In a *Granta* interview around this time he was described as "robed in an embroidered silk dressing gown, reclining on a sofa, smoking scented cigarettes, sipping crème de menthe". In his aesthetics, his literary tastes and his idiosyncratic views on the study of history, Strachey had a dominating influence on the Cambridge intellectuals of his generation.

He left Trinity College in 1905, having failed to gain a Fellowship. However, he returned to Cambridge often over the next few years, in order to participate in the intellectual life of the university (particularly at King's College) and to be with Keynes who had become his lover.

Strachey was attracted to a succession of handsome young men who showed intellectual or artistic promise. One of these was his cousin Duncan Grant, and he was deeply distressed when Grant later made it clear that he preferred Keynes by going to live with him.

He began his writing career, after his return to London from Cambridge, as a literary critic and essayist for several journals and as the drama critic of the *Spectator* (which was then edited by his cousin St Loe Strachey). Although he hated doing this work he recognised that journalism gave him the opportunity for learning his craft and polishing his writing style, as his ambition was to write something more substantial than reviews. After his first book, *Landmarks in French Literature*, which he had been commissioned to write, appeared in 1912 and was well received, his friends and family arranged a subscription for him which would make him financially independent of journalism and enable him to concentrate on writing more books. (Easily distracted by the promise of good company and intellectual discussion, Strachey often had to retreat to the country in order to get some writing done.)

He was the focus of that literary and artistic network (whose "inner circle" comprised his Cambridge friends as well as Roger Fry, Virginia Woolf and her sister, Vanessa Bell) which came to be known as the Bloomsbury Group, or as Gertrude Stein called it, "The Young Men's Christian Association – without Christ of course". The contradictions in his personality and behaviour seemed to typify the ethos of "Bloomsbury": he was always well-mannered and sympathetic, yet often amusingly censorious and invariably the prime initiator of the malicious, albeit very witty, gossip which his friends found so delightful; a believer in frankness and loyalty, he was outrageously candid about his own and others' sexual activities, and viewed his emotional life with great irony. The impression he gave of a general debility and lack of energy – it was said that "he drooped if he stood upright, and sagged if he sat down" – belied the vitality, passion and sense of intellectual authority with which his presence infused the Bloomsbury gatherings.

In describing him Clive Bell wrote of "that air of flexible endlessness which was his prevailing characteristic". With his long russet-brown beard, "calamitous equine teeth", bulbous nose, owlish stare and a voice which would alter from a strong bass to a squeaky falsetto within a single sentence, Strachey seemed to be a caricature made flesh.

When, during the First World War, he was asked by a recruiting officer what he, as a conscientious objector, would do if a German soldier were to try to rape his sister, Strachey replied, "I should attempt to interpose my body." To Keynes he wrote of his intention to "knit a muffler in navy blue for the neck of one of our sailor-lads. I don't know which but I have my visions."

With *Eminent Victorians* (1918) Strachey found his literary niche. His next two major works were also biographical: a humanising portrait of Queen Victoria and Prince Albert, and a Freudian analysis of Elizabeth I. All three books were best-sellers, and his earnings from them enabled him to buy a large country house, Ham Spray, near Hungerford, Berkshire. There he lived with the talented artist Dora Carrington (1893–1932), her husband Ralph Partridge (with whom he was in love), and Partridge's lover, Frances Marshall. Despite the fact that Carrington was fiercely jealous of her independence, for years she made herself virtually a servant of Strachey, whom she loved dearly and regarded with great reverence. An occasional member of the household was the major love of Strachey's later years, Roger Senhouse (1899–1970), a translator of Colette and a partner in the publishing business Secker and Warburg.

Two months after Strachey died of cancer Carrington shot herself with a borrowed gun. In her diary she had set out her reasons for wishing to die: without Strachey to share the jokes and gossip and the appreciation of books and art, life was pointless for her and could only become a tiresome burden.

Addresses

★*(Stowey House,) Clapham Common South Side (between Elms Road and The Crescent), SW4* – (*site?*). Birthplace.
★*69 Lancaster Gate, W2* – the Strachey family's home c1884–c1905. (Now part of the Charles Dickens Hotel.) (See also *Duncan Grant*.)
★*51 Gordon Square, WC1* – he lived here in 1909. (Blue *plaque*.) (See also *André Gide*.)
★*6 Belsize Park Gardens, NW3* – he lived here c1915.

Works include

Landmarks in French Literature (1912); *Eminent Victorians* (1918); *Queen Victoria* (1921) –

awarded the James Tait Black Memorial Prize; *Books and Characters, French and English* (1922); *Pope* (1925); *Elizabeth and Essex: a Tragic History* (1928); *Portraits in Miniature, and Other Essays* (1931); *Characters and Commentaries* (1933) – edited by James Strachey.

Diary: *Lytton Strachey by Himself: a Self-Portrait* (1971) – edited by Michael Holroyd.

Portraits

Pastel by Simon Bussy (1904) – National Portrait Gallery. Chalk by Nina Hamnett (undated) – N.P.G. Photographs (various, in the Strachey Collection) – N.P.G. (Archives). Canvas by Duncan Grant (c1909) – Tate Gallery. Canvas by Henry Lamb (1914) – Tate Gallery. Bronze head by Stephen Tomlin (c1928–30) – Tate Gallery. Pencil study by Henry Lamb – Victoria and Albert Museum. Caricature by N Bentley (1950) – V & A Museum.

Fictional portraits

He appears as Risley in E M Forster's novel *Maurice* (published posthumously in 1971). *The Apes of God* (1930) by Wyndham Lewis contains a satirical portrait of him as Matthew Plunkett. Wyndham Lewis portrayed him as Cedric Furber in *Self-Condemned* (1954). Leonard Woolf modelled one of the "epicures" in his novel *The Wise Virgins* (1914) on him. The character of Neville in Virginia Woolf's *The Waves* (1931) is based in part on Lytton Strachey.

Memorabilia

His personal copy, bearing his own signature, of *Monday and Tuesday* (1921) by Virginia Woolf – Fawcett Library.

Mary Anne Talbot

(2 February 1778 – 4 February 1808)

Mary Anne Talbot was known in her day as the "British Amazon".

Her mother died in giving birth to her and her father is believed to have been William Talbot, 1st Earl Talbot, who died when she was four years old. She went to school in Chester, but was removed from there after a few years and sent to live with a so-called guardian, a Mr Sacker, in Shropshire.

Mr Sacker "gave" or sold her to a disreputable naval officer, Captain Bowen, who raped her and forced her to accompany him on his voyage to St Domingo as his footboy, "John Taylor".

Later she was compelled by Captain Bowen, under threat of being sold as a female slave, to join the army as a drummer-boy. In this guise she went to Flanders (1792) and took part in the capture of Valenciennes (28 July 1793). Captain Bowen was killed in battle, and, freed from her "protector", Mary Anne deserted from the army.

Begging food and shelter as she went, still dressed as a man, she made her way through Luxembourg to the Rhine where John Taylor signed on as a cabin-boy on a French lugger, the *Le Sage*. The lugger was later captured by Lord Howe (subsequently British Admiral of the Fleet) and Mary Anne served as a British sailor in several campaigns.

She worked as a cabin-boy and powder-monkey on the *Brunswick* and during the battle of 1 June 1794 she sustained grapeshot wounds to the ankle and lower leg. These injuries kept her ashore for four months.

Shortly after her return to sea she, along with her shipmates, was captured and gaoled in France. She secured her release in November 1796, after eighteen months' imprisonment, by revealing to her captors that she was a woman.

By temporarily dropping the disguise of John Taylor she was able to extricate herself from other difficult situations, such as when she was kidnapped by a press-gang which, she believed, had been set on her by a ship's officer jealous of her relationship with the captain's niece, who had hopes of marrying John Taylor.

Having been able to secure for herself a small pension in consideration of the wounds she had received during active service, she returned to London.

As a result of her being press-ganged in Wapping, the fact that John Taylor was really a woman soon became public knowledge.

The ever resourceful Mary Anne then went on the stage, performing in several Covent Garden theatres and appearing in *Babes in the Wood* at a theatre in Tottenham Court Road. She enjoyed a brief period of fame as the "well-known patriot and male impersonator".

There followed bouts of imprisonment for debt and the petty offence of swearing. Mary Anne served a term in Newgate Prison for not paying the rent on a house which she shared with her lover. This woman's income from needlework helped provide Mary Anne with food and other necessities during this time.

Upon her release she rejoined her lover in their home and they tried to earn their living by taking in laundry and doing needlework.

In 1804 Mary Anne became a domestic servant in the home of the publisher Robert S Kirby, who wrote of her exploits in the second volume of his *Wonderful Museum* (1804) and *The Life and Surprising Adventures of Mary Anne Talbot* (1809; reprinted in *Women Adventurers*, 1893).

She worked for Kirby for three years but her rapidly failing health (probably due to her wounds and the severe hardships which she had endured) caused her to leave his employ at the end of 1807. She went to live with a friend in Shropshire, where she died two months later.

"John Taylor" had provided her with the means of getting a job, attaining a degree of independence and freedom from the threat of sexual assault, and a pension and medical care (for her wounds), but it was the many women who knew her as Mary Anne who gave her support and love, as she gratefully acknowleges in her "autobiography".

Addresses

★*62 Lincolns Inn Fields, WC2 – site* of her birthplace.

★*Marylebone Street (formerly Little St Marylebone Street), W1 – site*. She had lodgings (end 1803–beginning 1804) in the home of a Mr Joseph Bradley.

★*11 London House Yard, Paternoster Row, EC4 – site* of Robert S Kirby's home and bookshop, where she lived whilst in his employ (1804–07).

Portraits

Engraving by G Scott after James Green, in Robert S Kirby's *Wonderful Museum* (1804) – British Library. Engraving by unknown artist, in Robert S Kirby's *The Life and Surprising Adventures of Mary Anne Talbot* (1809) – British Library.

Related artefact

Painting of the Battle of 1 June 1794, by P J de Loutherbourg – National Maritime Museum, Greenwich.

Ernest Thesiger

(15 January 1879 – 14 January 1961)

"A lank, weedy, cadaverous, plaintive-eyed ninny with a nose as sharp as a pen" was how the *Pall Mall Gazette* described Ernest Thesiger in 1915. He was appearing in a farce *A Little Bit of Fluff*, playing the sort of role for which he later became well known: a dignified but dim-witted upper class English gentleman.

He was the grandson of a Lord Chancellor and the cousin of a Viceroy of India, and he went to school at Marlborough. Instead of entering the Civil Service as expected, he persuaded his parents to let him study art at the Slade School. There he fell in love with a fellow student, Willie Ranken. They became inseparable lifelong companions and walked about town together with bouquets in their buttonholes.

While still a student Thesiger got involved in amateur dramatics and appeared at charity matinees. He enjoyed performing in front of an audience and decided to concentrate on acting as a career. His friend Robert Ross helped to get him his first job, as an understudy at the St James's Theatre.

Soon after the outbreak of the First World War Thesiger was wounded while serving on the Western Front with the Queen Victoria Rifles. He returned to the stage and quickly established a reputation for himself, with his polished and restrained style of acting. He became one of Shaw's favourite actors and "created" several Shavian characters, including the Dauphin in *St Joan* (which was perhaps his greatest role) and Charles II in *Good King Charles's Golden Days*. Shaw also considered him to be the perfect Professor Higgins in *Pygmalion*.

Among Thesiger's other notable roles were those of Piers Gaveston in *Edward II* and the Eunuch in Bennett's *Judith* in which he was described by Rebecca West as being "exquisite as a lady's lampshade with his swinging skirts and fringes, evil as the slash of a poisoned scimitar in an Eastern alley". He once complained to Somerset Maugham about his never having written a part for him. "But I am always writing parts for you, Ernest," Maugham replied. "The trouble is that some-body called Gladys Cooper will insist on playing them." Thesiger appeared in drag with Douglas Byng in a 1925 Cochran Revue. They played two middle-aged women disrobing in a bedroom, in a sketch by Noel Coward.

In 1917 Thesiger married Willie Ranken's sister Janette. Willie was so upset that he shaved off his hair. The marriage seems to have been founded upon a mutual adoration of Willie and was never consummated. Janette was in love with Margaret Jourdain who dedicated her *Poems* (1911) to her.

All his life Thesiger combined a refusal to conform with an outward display of moral and social rectitude. He delighted in showing his green-painted toenails to guests at conventional dinner parties and often caused further consternation by unbuttoning his shirt and pulling out the strings of pearls he always wore next to his skin. "I have the perfect skin for healing pearls," he would explain.

As a founder member of the Men's Dress Reform Society Thesiger designed many of his own clothes. He was very proud of his legs and enjoyed showing them off in pale moleskin shorts or in a blue velvet pair with matching silk blouse and muffler.

One of his closest friendships was with Ivy Compton-Burnett. Every week they went shopping together and spent the evening doing their needlework, like the Scroves in *The Present and the Past*. "He was like a butterfly," another visitor to Ivy's home remarked. "Or more like a mosquito."

In later life he modelled himself on Queen Mary and grew more and more to resemble her, with his pursed lips, regal bearing and haughtiness of manner.

Thesiger was, as he put it, "engaged in a film studio" for the first time in 1932 and gave several memorable screen performances, including a wonderfully camp portrayal of the sinister Professor Praetorius in James Whale's 1935 film *The Bride of Frankenstein*.

In 1959 he celebrated fifty years on the stage and the following year was appointed CBE. He died in his sleep the day before his eighty-second birthday, just a few weeks after his last West End stage appearance.

Addresses

★*6 Montpelier Terrace, SW7* – the home of Thesiger and his wife, c1917–c1939, where Thesiger worked his own gros point carpets, appliquéed the curtains, painted the Chinese wallpaper, marbled the bathroom and frescoed a sky on his wife's bedroom ceiling.

★*8 St George's Court, Gloucester Road, SW7* – Thesiger's home from c1939 until his death here in 1961.

Works include

Books: *Practically True* (1927) – autobiography. Thesiger said he charged people £50 for a mention and £75 to be left out. *Adventures in Embroidery* (1941).

Painting: "Ruins of Old Chelsea Church" – Victoria and Albert Museum.

For the reconsecration of Chelsea Old Church in 1958, Thesiger embroidered two kneelers. One of them commemorates Henry Patenson, Sir Thomas More's jester, "a Man of Special Wit", who is pictured in the costume of the time with cap and bells. (For Queen Mary's dolls' house at Windsor Castle, Thesiger made the Aubusson carpet and the dining-room firescreens, and Willie Ranken did the still life over the sideboard.)

6 Montpelier Terrace, SW7

Portraits

Canvas by Sir Gerald Kelly (1920) – National Portrait Gallery. Photographs by Karl Pollak and by an unknown photographer – N.P.G. Chalk by Sir W R Flint (c1945) of Thesiger as Voltaire – British Museum. Bronze bust by Eric Schilsky (1925) – Theatre Museum.

Portrait on p. 192.

Fictional portrait

Ivy Compton-Burnett based Mortimer Lamb in *Manservant and Maidservant* (in U.S. *Bullivant and the Lambs*) (1947) on him.

Memorabilia

Photographs, programmes, playbills, etc. – Theatre Museum.

Renée Vivien

(11 June 1877 – 18 November 1909)

In her short life Renée Vivien wrote over twenty volumes of poetry and prose. Her celebration of lesbian passion and mysticism, and her condemnation of male injustice to women, contributed to her lack of literary recognition. However, there has lately been a renewal of interest in her work and life, and her reputation as a lesbian feminist writer is beginning to grow.

Pauline Mary Tarn, later known as Renée Vivien, was born in London of an American mother and a Scottish father. The family's considerable wealth derived from their large clothing and household furnishings business, William Tarn & Co.

When she was about seventeen Renée was sent to study at an academy in Paris for a couple of years to complete her education and prepare her for a respectable marriage. In Paris she met Violet Shilleto, who was to become one of the central figures in her life. The friendship between the young women, who shared an interest in death and religion, was close but Renée's passion for Violet was never consummated.

On her return to London Renée dutifully prepared for her entry into society, and was presented at Court in 1897. Her parents were probably disturbed by her preoccupation with Violet and with poetry and by her urge to travel, but they nevertheless agreed to her returning to Paris in 1898 and gave her an allowance.

Free from family constraints, the aspiring poet began to indulge her taste for the exotic and the nostalgic, by living in rooms filled with Oriental artefacts, white lilies and the smoke of incense; dressing as an 18th-century courtier to receive friends at home; and writing poetry influenced by Baudelaire.

In the winter of 1899 Renée met Natalie Barney through Violet Shilleto. Natalie found the fragile beauty of Renée, with her halo of blonde hair, heart-shaped face and sad laughter, irresistible, and christened her "My Angel". Renée, however, perceived their love as being poetic and spiritual, that of "souls vibrating in harmony", and wrote many of her poems about Natalie.

Despite their shared lesbian consciousness, Renée and Natalie were emotionally incompatible. Renée blamed herself when Natalie, for whom being "wanted through Sappho" was not enough, was unable or unwilling to remain monogamous and worship her alone.

During the winter of 1900–01 Renée and Natalie visited London, where they explored the Greek antiquities sections of the museums, read translations of the poetry of Sappho and met Olive Custance, whose poems they admired and with whom they began making plans to establish a colony of women writers on the island of Mytilene (Lesbos). On their return to Paris they visited Pierre Loüys to pay homage to the man who had celebrated the "cult of Sappho" in his *Chansons de Bilitis*.

Renée's first collection of poems, *Studies and Preludes*, was published in 1901 under the name of Renée Vivien, which she had begun using around 1899.

Early in 1901 Violet Shilleto invited Renée to visit the South of France with her. Preferring to spend the rest of the season with Natalie in their new home at Neuilly, Renée made plans to join Violet later. However, shortly afterwards she received a telegram informing her that her friend was dying. She rushed to Nice to be with Violet, who died a few days later.

Renée mourned endlessly for Violet, trying to expiate the guilt she felt for neglecting her and, somehow, causing or allowing her to die. She wrote scores of poems in which she compared her friend to the flower whose name she bore. (This led to Renée being called, later, "the violet muse".) In her grief she took to taking chloral and drinking gin in large amounts.

The news that Natalie had had an affair with Olive Custance during her absence in Nice compounded Renée's ambivalent feelings toward Natalie and confirmed the link she saw between sensuality, betrayal and death. She spent the summer with Natalie at Bar Harbor, Maine, where Natalie's earlier amour, Eva Palmer, was much more sympathetic towards Renée's grief than Natalie was.

While Renée went to London to visit her family Natalie stayed on in America, and they arranged to meet back in Paris. This separation provided Renée with the opportunity of breaking free from Natalie. She tried unsuccessfully to console herself with a liaison with Olive Custance (who, the following year, married Lord Alfred Douglas). Before Natalie's return to Paris Renée had become involved in another intense relationship: with the Baroness Hélène de Zuylen de Nyevelt.

Renée refused to see Natalie, in spite of her many attempts to woo her back, which included getting the opera singer Emma Calvé to serenade her.

According to her friend and neighbour, Colette, Renée was dominated by her new lover, whom she called "The Master" and who, she confided to Colette, would kill her with her love-making. (The Baroness, an immensely wealthy Dutch woman, had the unflattering soubriquets *la Brioche* and "the Valkyrie" and she scandalised polite society by wearing white tie, tails and a moustache to the opera.)

With Eva acting as intermediary Natalie finally managed to re-establish contact with Renée in 1904. She convinced Renée that their love for each other was as strong as before. They revived their dream of establishing a lesbian colony on Mytilene, where they went to resume their relationship. However, the Lesbos idyll was interrupted by the news of the Baroness's intention of coming to the island to reclaim Renée. In haste Renée returned to the Baroness and later she wrote to Natalie breaking off their relations. That year Renée revised her novel *Une femme m'apparuit*, which she had written in 1901 in an attempt to come to terms with the failure of her relationship with Natalie.

Although her health was seriously undermined by anorexia and her addiction to drugs and alcohol, Renée travelled widely, between 1905 and 1909, in the Middle East and the Orient, continued to write prolifically and had a few love affairs. Romaine Brooks was for a time a sympathetic friend, but she grew to abhor Renée's obsession with death.

Shortly before her death Renée converted to Catholicism, as Violet had done. She died at the age of thirty-two, weighing only 30 kilograms, and was buried at Passy. The last few lines of the epitaph which she wrote for herself read (in translation):

My ravished soul, from mortal breath
Appeased, forgets all former strife,
Having, from its great love of Death,
Pardoned the crime of crimes – called Life.

Addresses

★*94 Lancaster Gate, W2 – site* of her birthplace and childhood home. (Barrie House stands on the site.)

★*10 Green Street, W1 –* during her visit to London in 1901 she stayed here at the home of her recently widowed mother.

10 Green Street, W1

Works include

Poésies Complètes (in 12 volumes, 1901–10; in 2 volumes, 1934); *Vagabondages* – a posthumous collection of her prose poems.

(The lesbian feminist Naiad Press in the United States has in recent years published translations from the French of several of her works, including: *At the Sweet Hour of Hand in Hand, The Muse of the Violets* and *A Woman Appeared to Me*).

Fictional portrait

Lucie Delarue- Mardrus portrayed Renée and the Baroness de Zuylen de Nyevelt as Aimée de Lagres and Countess Taillard in *L'Ange et les pervers* (1930). *Portrait on p. 193.*

Horace Walpole

(24 September 1717 – 2 March 1797)

Known today as one of the greatest letter writers in the English language, Horace Walpole was famous in his time as the author of *The Castle of Otranto*, the first Gothic romance, and as a wit, connoisseur and arbiter of fashion.

He was the youngest son of the Prime Minister, Sir Robert Walpole, and his wife, Catherine Shorter. His first ten years were spent at his father's house in Chelsea and he was then sent to Eton where he began his friendship with the future poet Thomas Gray. At King's College, Cambridge, he proved an indifferent classics scholar and left without taking a degree. Fortunately, his father gave him some sinecures, including the offices of Controller of the Pipe and Usher of the Exchequer, which brought in £1,200 a year.

After a two year Grand Tour of Europe with Gray, Walpole went to live at his father's house in St James's because he disliked living at Houghton Hall, the vast family mansion in Norfolk. When his father died in 1745 he left the London house and £5,000 to him, which enabled him to lead a leisurely literary life. He wrote occasional poems and began writing the first of his long sparkling letters.

In 1747 Walpole rented a small house at Twickenham from the proprietor of a sweet-shop: "It is a little play-thing house that I got out of Mrs Chevenix's shop, and is the prettiest bauble you ever saw. It is set in enamelled meadows, with filigree hedges." The following year he bought it, renamed it "Strawberry Hill" and set about transforming it into "a little Gothic castle". He added a refectory, library, cloister, battlements and a round tower. The rooms were filled with paintings, books, china and a collection of knick-knacks, or what he called "serendipity".

Strawberry Hill became so famous that the King, the nobility and visiting foreign dignitaries demanded to see it. The clamour for admission became so great that Walpole was obliged to issue tickets. He welcomed his guests wearing a lace cravat carved in wood by Grinling Gibbons and an enormous pair of 'oves embroidered up to the elbows, which once belonged to James I. He was very thin, with lively dark eyes and a quiet voice, and had a way of entering a room with "affected delicacy", holding his hat and darting about on tiptoe "like a peewit". He dressed in lavender suits and waistcoats embroidered in silver, and was fond of ruffles and frills. "It is charming," he wrote, "to totter into vogue."

For most of his life Walpole was hopelessly in love with his cousin Henry Seymour Conway, a soldier. Walpole enthused over "the beauty of his person and the harmony of his voice" and when Conway married, he offered him half his fortune and helped to advance his career. Conway, however, was a cold, insensitive man, and a heterosexual who found difficulty in dealing with Walpole's feeling for him. When Walpole sent him one of his favourite Latin poems he replied: "The avowing a passion for a youth . . . is so notoriously impious and contrary to nature, as well as morality and religion, that it is impossible not to be offended at it."

When Conway achieved power (he eventually became a field-marshal and Secretary of State) he turned his back on Walpole, who lamented, "Such failure of friendship or to call it by its truer name, such insensibility, could not but shock a heart at once so tender and so proud as mine."

In 1757 Walpole set up a printing press at Strawberry Hill (the first private press to be established in England), and began printing and selling, at a shilling a copy, the poems of Thomas Gray, whose genius he had been among the first to recognise.

Walpole's Gothic novel *The Castle of Otranto* was published in 1764 and was a huge popular success. It was inspired by Strawberry Hill, "a very proper habitation of, as it was the scene that inspired, the author of *The Castle of Otranto*". Its influence extended to, among others, William Beckford, "Monk" Lewis, Mary Shelley and Bram Stoker. Walpole's greatest achievement, however, was his three thousand letters. Full of wit, anecdote and epigram, they reflect his many interests and give a brilliant insight into the manners and artistic taste of the 18th century.

On the death of his nephew in 1791, Walpole became the fourth and last Earl of Orford. Towards the end of his life he enjoyed the close friendship of the young Berry sisters, Mary and Agnes. He gave them a house, Little Strawberry Hill, near his own, and the three of them became inseparable. He died of palsy and was buried in the little church at Houghton near his family home. He left Strawberry Hill and its contents to Anne Damer, the daughter of Henry Seymour Conway.

Strawberry Hill, Waldegrave Road, Twickenham

Addresses

★*22 Arlington Street, SW1 – site*. Birthplace.
★*Royal Hospital Road, SW3* – he spent much of his childhood in a house which was later turned into the Infirmary of the Royal Hospital, Ward 7 being the old drawing room.
★*10 Downing Street, SW1* – he lived here 1741–42.
★*5 Portland Place, W1 – site*. He lived here in 1743.
★*5 Arlington Street, SW1* – he lived here 1743–79. (Society of Arts *plaque* erected 1881.)
★*Strawberry Hill, Waldegrave Road, Twickenham* – his home from 1747 to 1796. (Now St Mary's R C Training College. Admission only by prior application to the Principal.)
★*11 Berkeley Square, W1 – site* of his home between 1779–97. (He died here.)

Works include

Novel: *The Castle of Otranto* (1764).
Verse drama: *The Mysterious Mother* (1768).

History: *Historic Doubts on the Life and Reign of King Richard III* (1768).
Art criticism: *Anecdotes of Painting in England* – 5 volumes (1762–71).

Portraits

Canvas by John Giles Eccardt (1754) – National Portrait Gallery. Pencil drawing by George Dance (1793) – N.P.G. Pencil drawing by Sir Thomas Lawrence (c1795) – N.P.G. Prints by W Greatbach (1842) – N.P.G. (Archives). Prints by D P Pariset – N.P.G. (Archives) and British Museum. *Portrait on p. 193.*

Memorabilia

A letter dated 28 March 1769 from Walpole to Thomas Chatterton – British Museum. Walpole Gardens, W4, is named after him. (He used the "Pack Horse" staging post which was situated here, on his journeys to and from London.)

Sylvia Townsend Warner

(6 December 1893 – 1 May 1978)

Sylvia Townsend Warner, poet, novelist, short-story writer and biographer, was born at Harrow School, where her father was a housemaster and head of the Modern side. An only child, she was educated by her parents and a French governess. At an early age she began reading voraciously and had the run of her father's extensive library.

As a young woman her first interest was music, and she would have studied composition with Arnold Schoenberg in Vienna if the outbreak of the First World War had not prevented this. She went to work in a munitions factory instead, and her account of the experience earned her the first money she made from writing. Through her friendship with the music master at Harrow she was drawn into the field of musicology. In 1917, the year after her father died, she moved to London (from Devon), having been invited onto the editorial board of the Church Music Project. She was one of the four music scholars who undertook the editing of *Tudor Church Music*, published in ten volumes between 1922 and 1929.

Sylvia delighted in character and idiosyncracy, and she was thrilled and flattered by the overtures of friendship made by the novelist and eccentric T F Powys, whom she met in Dorset in 1923. Powys was a great influence on her poetry and fiction, and for many years she worked on a biography of him (which was never published).

Another friend whom she met around this time was David Garnett. Garnett, then a partner with Francis Birrell of the renowned literary bookshop "Birrell and Garnett" in Bloomsbury (later in Soho), was enthusiastic about her poetry and recommended it for publication to Chatto and Windus. Her first book of poems, *The Espalier*, appeared in 1925. It was followed a year later by a novel, *Lolly Willowes* (about the "conversion" of an inhibited maiden aunt with the discovery that he is "a witch by vocation"), which was the "Book of the Month" in the United

made her first visit to New York, as guest critic of the *Herald Tribune*, in 1927. Her second novel, *Mr Fortune's Maggot*, published that year, consolidated the success of her first and won her considerable respect in both Britain and the United States. (She was to become a Fellow of the Royal Society of Literature, in 1967, and an Honorary Member of the American Academy of Arts and Letters, in 1972.)

Not long after her return to England she met Valentine Ackland (1906–69). Valentine was a neighbour and acquaintance of Powys and his wife Violet, and she too wrote poetry. Their first meeting was not a success because Valentine, extremely shy and sensitive, felt almost overwhelmed by Sylvia's witty talk and enthusiasm, but both women recognised the strong attraction between them. When Sylvia decided to settle permanently in the country (around 1930), Valentine responded with alacrity to her invitation to come and live with her in the cottage which she had bought. They lived first in Dorset, then in Norfolk, and finally they settled again in Dorset in a house a few yards from the River Frome and a short walk from the village of Maiden Newton.

On the flyleaf of a book which she gave Valentine for Christmas, Sylvia wrote: "'Never heed,' said the girl, 'I'll stand by you'." Valentine referred to this in the covering letter to an autobiographical essay she wrote for Sylvia in 1949 during a crisis in their relationship: ". . . I am a coward, my love, and I have heeded far too often, but that has made no difference to the truth of this that you wrote down for me: let it be true to our lives' end."

In 1933 Sylvia and Valentine published a joint collection of poems, *Whether a Dove or Seagull*. Two years later they joined the Communist Party, having concluded that communism was the only defence against fascism. Together they twice visited Spain during the Civil War. They attended a conference for "concerned writers" in New York in 1939, and during the next decade Sylvia was a regular contributor to several Party-oriented publications, chiefly to the *Left Review*. (She remained a left-wing socialist and in her later years called herself an anarchist.)

Sylvia had begun contributing work to the *New Yorker* in 1936, and over the years it published nine of her poems and 144 of her short stories. (Explaining her abandonment of the novel form after *The Flint Anchor*, which appeared in 1954, she once said: "I melted into the background as best I could, to continue sniping. You can pick your enemies off, you know, by aiming a short story well.")

When Sylvia was not engaged in writing – apart from her fiction and poetry she wrote on average three letters a day to friends – she enjoyed tending her herb garden and cooking, especially curries. Valentine preferred bird-watching, angling and attending auctions in the neighbouring villages in the pursuit of interesting items for the antique shop which she opened in a sideroom of Frome Vauchurch, their home. After their black chow dog William died they kept a succession of cats. Siamese cats were animals with which they both had an affinity; Valentine's poodles, however, were rather less popular with Sylvia.

Sylvia was an unequivocal atheist, and Valentine's decision (taken in 1955) to become a practising Catholic again irked her, but she came to recognise the spiritual comfort which Valentine obtained from her struggle to regain her faith, particularly during her friend's final illness.

Their last trip abroad, to Italy in 1963, was a happy one, despite Valentine's poor health. Shortly after their return home Sylvia was commissioned to write the biography of T H White (who, with A E Housman, had been among her staunchest supporters). The next few years were tranquil ones for both women, and creative too: Valentine began' writing again, both nature poems and deeply religious "private" poems. In 1968 Valentine was operated on for cancer, but the illness was too far advanced. Sylvia nursed her at home and even accompanied her to the Quaker meetings which she now attended.

After Valentine's death in November 1969 Sylvia wrote to a friend, "Don't think I am unhappy and alone . . . I am not. I am in a new country and she is the compass I travel by." She lived on in Frome Vauchurch alone, writing stories and poetry. She died peacefully at home and was buried in the churchyard in Chaldon Herring (East Chaldon) where Valentine had been buried eight years earlier.

Sylvia had once exclaimed "I propose to be a posthumous poet." A new volume of her later poems was published after her death, as were her *Collected Poems*, and her earlier volumes, which had been out of print for nearly forty years, were re-issued.

Addresses

★*Harrow School, High Street, Harrow* – birthplace and childhood home.

★*127 Queensway (formerly Queens Road), W2* – she had a flat here in 1917.

★*121 Inverness Terrace, W2* – site of her home c1924.

★*113 Inverness Terrace, W2* – site of her home 1928.

Works include

Poetry: *The Espalier* (1925); *Time Importuned* (1928); *Opus 7* (1931); *Whether a Dove or Seagull* (1933) – with Valentine Ackland; *Boxwood* (with engravings by Reynolds Stone) (1957; new edition 1960); *Twelve Poems* (1980); *Collected Poems*, edited with an introduction by Claire Harman (1982).

Novels: *Lolly Willowes* (1926); *Mr Fortune's Maggot* (1927); *The True Heart* (1929); *Summer Will Show* (1936); *After the Death of Don Juan* (1938); *The Corner That Held Them* (1948); *The Flint Anchor* (1954).

Short stories (Collections): *A Moral Ending* (1931); *The Salutation* (1932); *More Joy in Heaven* (1935); *A Garland of Snow* (1943); *The Museum of Cheats* (1947); *Winter in the Air* (1955); *The Cat's Cradle Book* (1960); *A Stranger with a Bag* (1966); *The Innocent and the Guilty* (1971); *Kingdoms of Elfin* (1977); *Scenes of Childhood* (1981).

Biographies: *Jane Austen* (1951) – a British Council "Writers and their Work" pamphlet. *T H White* (1967).

Translation: *By Way of Sainte-Beuve* (1958) – a translation of Proust's *Contre Sainte-Beuve*.

(Valentine Ackland's autobiographical essay was published in 1985 as *For Sylvia: An Honest Account*).

Portraits

Several photographs by Howard Coster – National Portrait Gallery.

Denton Welch

(29 March 1915 – 30 December 1948)

Maurice Denton Welch, the youngest of four brothers, was born in Shanghai. His father had substantial business interests in the Far East and Welch's early childhood was spent in China.

He was educated in England, and, after his mother's death, when he was eleven, he spent his school holidays at his grandfather's house in Sussex. At fourteen he joined his brother Paul at Repton, but he hated the restrictive atmosphere of the school and, after two years, ran away.

In 1933 he enrolled as a student at the Goldsmith School of Art and went to live in lodgings in Greenwich, at the home of Miss Evelyn ("Evie") Sinclair, who was later to become his housekeeper and one of his closest friends.

On 7 June 1935 Welch was knocked off his bicycle by a car and suffered terrible injuries to his spine, bladder and kidneys, from which, thirteen years later, he was to die. His response to the accident, and to the knowledge that he would never fully recover, was to turn back to memories of childhood and adolescence. Hitherto he had been preoccupied with painting, but now, by recording in minute detail the events of his past, he realised his genius as a writer. His three novels, the collections of short stories, and his journals, were all in effect written while he was dying.

After his release from hospital and until his death, Welch lived in Kent, in and around Tonbridge. He refused to be beaten by his illness and seemed for a few years to be making a remarkable recovery. He went for long walks or bicycle rides in the surrounding countryside, and learned to drive a car. In his journal he described the events and discovery of his day to day life: forays to antique shops; the calm of an old village church; the careful restoration of his dolls' house; naked youths bathing in the river; and semi-clad farm boys working in the fields. "How I longed," he wrote, "to be strong and lusty, not ill!"

Although his finest works, his last novel and his journals, were not published until after his death, Welch did enjoy critical acclaim and encouragement from many distinguished writers and critics. Edith Sitwell, one of the few writers whom he actually met, hailed him as "that rare being, a born writer".

Welch felt a special kinship with the poet Gerard Manley Hopkins, and, enraged by a particularly pompous and evasive article about him in the *Times Literary Supplement*, wrote, "It is an insult to hide his secret – to pretend that he was 'normal', in other words, ordinary." Welch was determined to be honest about himself and never tried to conceal his homosexuality.

He first met Eric Oliver (1914–), with whom he lived for the last few years of his life, in November 1943. He had been lying in bed one day, when a friend arrived to visit him, accompanied by Oliver, who was working on a farm and living in a hostel in Maidstone. Welch's first impression of his "new hearty land-boy friend" was of "someone in green battle-dress trousers, Wellingtons, and a jersey and white shirt, open, also white tops of pants showing above the trousers, large leather belt, face red-brown, with a very good throat". Oliver became a regular visitor, and soon moved into Welch's cottage.

In the last entry which Welch made in his journal, he described a visit which he and Oliver made to Sissinghurst, the home of Vita Sackville-West and Harold Nicolson. Vita wore cord riding breeches, which "disappeared into tall laced canvas leather boots" and a large straw hat. She offered them crumpled cigarettes and cucumber sandwiches, and a choice of cider, tea or water. Fortunately for him, Welch chose tea, for "tiny flies had got into the keg of cider, and Vita fetched an old silver funnel through which to strain it."

Four months later, Denton Welch died. After the funeral service at Wateringbury parish church near Tonbridge, his coffin, draped in the red aldermanic gown which he used to wear when writing in bed, was taken to Charing, and there, dressed in a priest's cassock of which he was fond, he was cremated.

Addresses

★*33 The Little Boltons (formerly The Grove),
SW10* – he stayed here in 1931 after he ran
away from school. It was the home of his
cousin May Beeman.

★*Robert Adam Street (formerly Adam Street),
W1* – he stayed here in 1933 at his brother Bill's
flat.

★*34 Croom's Hill, SE10* – he lived here
1933–35.

Works include

Autobiographical novels: *Maiden Voyage*
(1943); *In Youth is Pleasure* (1945); *A Voice
Through a Cloud* (1950).

Short stories: *Brave and Cruel, and Other
Stories* (1949).

Fragments – poems and short stories: *A Last
Sheaf* (1951); *I Left My Grandfather's House*
(1958); *Dumb Instrument* (1976).

Journals: *The Denton Welch Journals* edited
by Jocelyn Brooke (1952); *The Journals of
Denton Welch* edited by Michael De-la-Noy
(1984).

Portrait

Oil self-portrait (undated) – National Portrait
Gallery.

Fictional portraits

Self-portraits in his novels and stories.

Memorabilia

After Welch's death his 18th-century dolls'
house, which he had spent many months
restoring, was presented by Eric Oliver to the
Bethnal Green Museum of Childhood.

James Whale

(22 July 1889 – 30 May 1957)

James Whale, the director of *The Bride of Frankenstein* and several other classic horror films, was born into a working-class family in Dudley, Worcestershire. After leaving school, where his favourite subjects had been literature and drawing, he trained in graphic art. From 1910 until the outbreak of the First World War he worked as a newspaper cartoonist on the *Bystander*.

Whale spent much of the war interned in a prisoner-of-war camp in Germany, and it was there that he began acting. On his return to England he joined the Birmingham Repertory Company as an actor and occasional designer, and made his first professional appearance on the stage in 1918 as Mr Slaney in *Abraham Lincoln*.

The offer of a job as stage manager at the Savoy Theatre brought him to London early in 1923. Two years later he made his debut on the West End stage as Gas Jones in *A Comedy of Good and Evil*. Over the next three years he played a number of supporting roles in comedies by Chekhov and Farquhar, but it was in J R Ackerley's *The Prisoners of War* (which he also designed) in 1925, and in *The Man With Red Hair* (in which he played Herrick, the insane son of Mr Crispin, played by Charles Laughton) in 1928, that he gave his most notable performances.

In 1928 Whale turned from acting to directing for the stage. He had a tremendous success with his first production, R C Sherriff's pacifist drama *Journey's End*. He went to New York in the following year to direct the American stage production of this play, and then moved on to Chicago to produce *One Hundred Years Old*.

While in America he became involved in the film industry, in a small way, as dialogue director on Howard Hughes's *Hell's Angels*. Not unnaturally, as the director of successful stage productions of *Journey's End*, he was given the job of directing the film version of it as a "British talkie" in Hollywood in 1930. The cast was recruited locally from among the "ex-pat colony", except for Whale's friend, Colin Clive, who was brought over especially from the West End cast to play the lead, Captain Stanhope.

Under contract at Universal and under the patronage of studio production head Carl Laemmle Jnr, Whale started work on his next project, filming Robert Sherwood's First World War melodrama *Waterloo Bridge*. The heads of Universal were impressed with the results, and when the original director of *Frankenstein*, in preparation at the studio, dropped out, Whale was assigned to the film. He promptly hired two of his friends, Colin Clive and Boris Karloff, to play the scientist and the monster. The film was an enormous success and made Whale a studio hero.

His next films, his finest and his most personal, were, with a few exceptions, in the same genre of Gothic horror fantasy: *The Old Dark House*, a quirky, schlock-horror film with the characteristic in-joke of the bearded 102-year-old man in the attic being played by a woman; *The Invisible Man*, which made a star of Claude Rains (as *Frankenstein* had made one of Boris Karloff); and *The Bride of Frankenstein*, with which Elsa Lanchester as "the Bride", with her bandages and towering, lightning-streaked shock of hair, will always be identified, and in which Ernest Thesiger gave a wonderfully camp performance as Dr Praetorius.

In addition to his masterly command of narrative, Whale displayed in his Gothic fantasy films a genius for finding beauty and humour in horror, and through his intelligent use of wilful scenic distortion, expressionistic lighting and witty musical scores, realised both the spirituality and pathos of the creatures and the fear and loathing which they evoked.

Whale's quirky sense of humour and camp sensibility were appreciated by Elsa Lanchester; she remembered him as a dazzling tango dancer when he used to visit her cabaret-nightclub, the "Cave of Harmony", in Soho, and she admired his talent as a director. Her husband, Charles Laughton, shared this opinion about Whale's talent, but thought him vulgar and a snob, and nicknamed him "The Would-Be Gentleman", from the title of a play in which Whale had acted. Laughton, repressed and self-loathing, probably resented Whale's "don't give a damn" attitude and his refusal to conceal his homosexuality; others in Hollywood also thought him "dangerously indiscreet".

His snobbery and hauteur were, for the most part, elements in a pose he adopted: essentially Whale was a quiet, introspective man; but he certainly loved money – "I'm pouring the gold through my hair and enjoying every minute of it," he told Laughton – and he lived in showy style. Referring to the high salaries he commanded and to his lifestyle, he observed in an interview in 1936: "Who's worth it? But why not take it? . . . I can have modernistic designs one day and an antiquated home overnight! All the world's made of plaster of Paris!" The home which he shared with his lover David Lewis (who became a gifted producer at MGM and Warners) was filled with works of art and musical instruments, and, as in his films, his choice of decor was rather Italianate and a bit gothic.

After *The Bride of Frankenstein*, Whale abandoned horror for more theatrical films. His memorable *Showboat*, with Irene Dunne, Paul Robeson and Helen Morgan, is probably the best film version of this musical. However, his later films seem less personal. It is believed that he may have lost interest in the cinema after the unexpected sudden death of his close friend Colin Clive in 1937.

Showboat was a great commercial success for Universal, but, surprisingly, Whale, one of the studio's top directors, was demoted and given small-scale, sometimes B-feature, films to direct. One of the theories advanced to explain this demotion and Whale's precipitate retirement from film-making is that he had been involved in a sex scandal.

Whale retired in 1941, supposedly to concentrate on his painting. He made an unsuccessful attempt to return to the medium of the film in 1949; later he did a little theatre work in California and in England.

In 1957 he was found dead "under mysterious circumstances" – floating in the swimming pool behind his Brentwood, California, home.

Suspicion (1938); *The Man in the Iron Mask* (1939); *Green Hell* (1940); *They Dare Not Love* (1941); and an episode (*Hello Out There*) in an unreleased film in 1949.

Memorabilia

Playbills, programmes, etc. – Theatre Museum. Film stills, photographs, etc. – British Film Institute.

Address

★*402a Kings Road, SW10* – his home c1925–30.

Films directed

Journey's End (1930); *Waterloo Bridge* (1931); *Frankenstein* (1931); *The Impatient Maiden* (1932); *The Old Dark House* (1932); *The Kiss Before the Mirror* (1933); *The Invisible Man* (1933); *By Candlelight* (1934); *One More River* (1934); *The Bride of Frankenstein* (1935); *Remember Last Night* (1935); *Showboat* (1936); *The Road Back* aka *Return of the Hero* (1937); *The Great Garrick* (1937); *The Port of Seven Seas* (1938); *Sinners in Paradise* (1938); *Wives under*

Oscar Wilde

(16 October 1854 – 30 November 1900)

Oscar Fingal O'Flahertie Wills Wilde was born in Dublin. His father, Sir William Wilde, was an eminent eye surgeon, and his mother, under the name "Speranza", wrote Irish nationalist verse.

At the Portora Royal School Wilde obtained a scholarship to Trinity College, Dublin, where he won the Berkeley gold medal for Greek. In 1874 he went up to Magdalen College, Oxford. There he discovered "the dangerous and delightful distinction of being different from others". Accepted student pursuits such as rowing and football bored him, and he felt disinclined to pander to the academic expectations of the dons, most of whom he despised. Nevertheless, he gained a double first in Classics and won the Newdigate Prize with his poem "Ravenna". His greatest problem at university was, he said, learning to live up to the blue china he had installed in his rooms.

While at Oxford Wilde became a follower of Walter Pater's doctrine of Art for Art's Sake. Pater maintained that everyone has the right to enjoy a work of art regardless of moral prejudices and that the pursuit of beauty in all its forms is the finest of life's endeavours.

When Wilde came to London in 1879 he set about establishing himself as the leader of the "Aesthetic Movement". He wore velvet coats edged with braid, knee breeches, loose wide-collared shirts and flowing ties, and carried a jewel-topped cane and lavender-coloured gloves.

In 1881 Wilde's collected poems were published. The following year, being short of money, he accepted an invitation to go on a lecture tour of America. There he met Walt Whitman. They got tipsy on elderberry wine, and Whitman called him "a great big splendid boy". Wilde told Whitman, "There is no one in the great wide world of America whom I love and honour so much."

The tour was a great success and Wilde returned to London richer by several thousand pounds. In 1884 he married Constance Lloyd, the daughter of an Irish barrister. They had two sons, Cyril, born in 1885, and Vyvyan, in 1886. Meanwhile, Wilde was to be seen around town with young men whom he met through Alfred Taylor, a transvestite at whose house in Westminster he became a regular visitor.

One day in 1891 the poet Lionel Johnson came to tea at Wilde's house in Tite Street, and brought along with him the handsome young poet son of the Marquis of Queensberry, Lord Alfred Douglas (1870–1945), known to his friends as "Bosie". Wilde and Bosie were instantly attracted to one another. Bosie was fascinated by the brilliance of Wilde's conversation and wit, and Wilde was entranced both by Bosie's looks and by his title.

Between 1891 and 1895 all of Wilde's great social comedies were produced. Nothing like them had been seen since Sheridan and they were greeted with rapturous applause. These were the years of his greatest triumph.

On 18 February 1895, four days after the first night of *The Importance of Being Earnest*, the Marquis of Queensberry left a visiting card at Wilde's club, the Albemarle, on which he had written "To Oscar Wilde posing as a somdomite" (his spelling). Urged on by Bosie, whose hatred for his father was greater than his regard for his friend, Wilde foolishly sued Queensberry for criminal libel. Queensberry defended himself in court by presenting incriminating evidence against Wilde and was acquitted.

Having lost the case, Wilde went with Bosie and Robert Ross to the Cadogan Hotel where Bosie had rooms. At between seven and eight o'clock that evening the police arrived with a warrant for his arrest. As the curtain rose in the West End on *The Importance of Being Earnest* and *An Ideal Husband* Wilde was taken in custody to Bow Street Police Station. He was charged with homosexual offences under an act unique to Victorian Britain. At his first trial the jury failed to agree; at the second he was found guilty and sentenced to two years' hard labour. Alfred Taylor, who refused to turn Queen's Evidence against Wilde, received the same sentence.

Wilde served the first six months of his sentence at Wandsworth and was then sent to Reading Gaol. He was forced to shred tarred rope with his bare hands and to turn the handle of a metal drum against an inbuilt resistance 10,000 times a day. He was placed in solitary confinement and his meals consisted mostly of gruel, suet, water and greasy cocoa. Robert Ross, More Adey, Charles Ricketts and several other friends went to see him, but he neither saw nor heard from Bosie.

While he was in prison Wilde was declared

bankrupt and his house and all his possessions were sold to pay his creditors. His wife obtained a separation and a legal guardian was appointed for his children, whom he never saw again.

In the early morning of 19 May 1897 Wilde was released. More Adey and Stewart Headlam, a socialist clergyman who had stood bail for Wilde between his trials, were waiting for him outside the prison. He spent the morning at Headlam's house and then went to Victoria Station and caught the boat train to Dieppe.

Under the name of Sebastian (the well-known martyr) Melmoth (from his kinsman Charles Maturin's novel *Melmoth the Wanderer*) Wilde spent his last three years moving restlessly about Europe, experiencing what Ricketts described as "the bitterness of those who cannot forgive the victim the wrong they have done".

In a letter to Ross written towards the end of his life, Wilde wrote: "To have altered my life would have been to have admitted that Uranian love is ignoble. I hold it to be noble – more noble than other forms."

Addresses

★*13 Salisbury Street, WC2 – site.* Shell Mex House, The Strand, now stands on the site of Wilde's home between 1879–80.

★*44 (formerly Keats House, 26) Tite Street, SW3* – he lived here between 1880–81.

★*9 Carlos Place, W1* – he lived here in 1883.

★*34 (formerly 16) Tite Street, SW3* – his home between 1884–95. *Blue plaque* erected 1954.

★*10–11 St James's Place, SW1* – he had rooms here between 1893–94.

★*2 Courtfield Gardens, SW5* – he stayed here at the home of Ernest and Ada Leverson while on bail in 1895.

★*Bedford Way (formerly 31 Upper Bedford Place), WC1* – site of the home of Rev. Stewart Headlam, where Wilde spent his last hours in England.

Works include

Plays: *Lady Windemere's Fan* (1892); *A Woman of No Importance* (1893); *Salome* (1893); *The Importance of Being Earnest* (1895); *An Ideal Husband* (1895).

Stories: *The Canterville Ghost* (1887); *The Happy Prince* (1888); *The Picture of Dorian Gray* (1891); *Lord Arthur Saville's Crime* (1891).

Poems: *The Sphinx* (1894); *The Ballad of Reading Gaol* (1898).

Essays: *The Soul of Man under Socialism* (1890); *De Profundis* (1897).

Portraits

Pencil drawing by A S Boyd (1883) – National Portrait Gallery. Two photographs by Napoleon Sarony (1882) – N.P.G. Photograph by W & D Downey (undated) – N.P.G. (Archives). Caricature by Carlo Pellegrini (1884) – N.P.G. Caricatures by Sir Max Beerbohm (1916) and by Aubrey Beardsley (1894) – Tate Gallery. Drawing "Greenery Yallery" by Osbert Lancaster (1939) – Tate Gallery. Drawings by Frederick Pegram and by S P Hall (1888–89) – Victoria and Albert Museum. Many photographs and cartoons – Theatre Museum.   *Portrait on p. 216; photo of 34 Tite St on p. 217.*

Fictional portraits

He appears as Esmé Amarinth in the novel *The Green Carnation* (1894) by Robert Hichens. Reginald Bunthorne in Gilbert and Sullivan's opera *Patience* (1881) was widely believed to have been based on Wilde, but it was originally meant to be a caricature of Swinburne. The character of Toad of Toad Hall in *The Wind in the Willows* (1908) by Kenneth Grahame was modelled on Wilde. Claude Davenant in *Mirage* (1887) by George Fleming (pseud. Julia Constance Fletcher) is believed to be a portrait of Wilde. Cardinal Pirelli in *The Princess Zoubaroff* (1920), the play by Ronald Firbank, is thought to be a composite of Wilde and the author himself. Wilde appears again in the same play as Lord Orkish. Gabriel Nash in Henry James's *The Tragic Muse* (1890) is believed to be a part portrait of Wilde.

Memorial

Stone bas-relief of Wilde's head, with representations of Dorian Gray and Salome, on the facade of St James's House, 23–24 King Street, SW1, which stands on the site of the St James's Theatre, where *Lady Windemere's Fan* and *The Importance of Being Earnest* were first performed.

Memorabilia

Holograph manuscript of *The Importance of Being Earnest* – British Museum. Playbills, programmes, photographs, cartoons, etc. – Theatre Museum.

Oscar Wilde

34 Tite St, SW3 (Oscar Wilde)   217

Select Bibliography

My Father and Myself by J.R. Ackerley (Bodley Head) 1968
The Simple Life: C.R. Ashbee in the Cotswolds by Fiona MacCarthy (Lund Humphries) 1981
W.H. Auden: The Life of a Poet by Charles Osborne (Eyre Methuen) 1979
Sir Francis Bacon by Jean Overton Fuller (East-West Publications) 1981
The Better Fight: The Story of Dame Lilian Barker by Elizabeth Gore (Geoffrey Bles) 1965
The Amazon of Letters by George Wickes (W.H. Allen) 1977 [a biography of Natalie Barney]
Between Me and Life by Meryle Secrest (Macdonald & Janes) 1976 [Romaine Brooks]
Samuel Butler: The Incarnate Bachelor by Philip Henderson (Cohen & West) 1953
Edward Carpenter: Prophet of Human Fellowship by Chushichi Tsuzuki (Cambridge University Press) 1980
Emily Carr: The Untold Story by Edythe Hembroff-Schleicher (Hancock House Publications, Saanichton, British Columbia) 1978
Cavafy: A Critical Biography by Robert Liddell (Duckworth) 1974
Life of Frances Power Cobbe: As told by herself Introduction by Blanche Atkinson (Swan, Sonnenschein) 1904
Edy: Recollections of Edith Craig edited by Eleanor Adlard (Frederick Muller) 1949
Theatre In My Blood by John Percival (The Herbert Press) 1983 [John Cranko]
Charlotte Cushman: Her letters and memories of her life edited by Emma Stebbins (Houghton, Osgood) 1878
Anne Seymour Damer: A Woman of Art and Fashion by Percy Noble (Kegan Paul, Trench, Trübner) 1908
Menlove: The Life of John Menlove Edwards by Jim Perrin (Victor Gollancz) 1985
Erasmus of Rotterdam by George Faludy (Eyre & Spottiswode) 1970
The Prancing Novelist by Brigid Brophy (Macmillan) 1973 [Ronald Firbank]
With Friends Possessed: A Life of Edward FitzGerald by Robert Bernard Martin (Faber & Faber) 1985
E.M. Forster: A Life by P.N. Furbank (Secker & Warburg) Vol. 1 1977, Vol. 2 1978
In the Dorian Mode: A Life of John Gray 1866–1934 by Brocard Sewell (Tabb House) 1983
Thomas Gray: His Life and Works by A.L. Lytton Sells (Allen & Unwin) 1980
Our Three Selves: A Life of Radclyffe Hall by Michael Baker (Hamish Hamilton) 1985
Jane Ellen Harrison: A Portrait from Letters by J.G. Stewart (The Merlin Press) 1959
Harriet Hosmer: Letters and Memories edited by Cornelia Carr (Moffat, Yard & Co., N.Y.) 1912
A.E. Housman: The Scholar Poet by Richard Perceval Graves (Routledge & Kegan Paul) 1979
Naomi Jacob: The Seven Ages of Me by James Norbury (William Kimber) 1965
Love and Work Enough by Clara Thomson (University of Toronto Press) 1967 [Anna Jameson]
Geraldine Jewsbury: Her Life and Errors by Susanne Howe (George Allen & Unwin) 1935
The Life of Sophia Jex-Blake by Margaret Todd (Macmillan) 1918
Edward Lear: The Life of a Wanderer by Vivien Noakes (Collins) 1968
"Vernon Lee": Violet Paget 1856–1935 by Peter Gunn (Oxford University Press) 1964
Christopher Marlowe: A Biography by A.L. Rowse (Macmillan) 1964
Edward Marsh: A Biography by Christopher Hassall (Longmans) 1959
Constance Louisa Maynard by C.D. Frith (Allen & Unwin) 1949
Charlotte Mew and Her Friends by Penelope Fitzgerald (Collins) 1984
Harold Monro and the Poetry Bookshop by Jay Grant (Routledge) 1967
Prick Up Your Ears: The Biography of Joe Orton by John Lahr (Allen Lane) 1978
Wilfred Owen: A Biography by Jon Stallworthy (Chatto/Oxford) 1974
Pitt The Younger by Robin Reilly (Cassell) 1978
Eleanor Rathbone: A Biography by Mary D. Stocks (Victor Gollancz) 1949
The World of Charles Ricketts by Joseph Darracott (Eyre, Methuen) 1980
Arthur Rimbaud by Enid Starkey (Faber & Faber) 1938
The Quest for Corvo by A.J.A. Symons (Cassell) 1934

Robert Ross: Friend of Friends by Marjory Ross (Jonathan Cape) 1952
Vita: The Life of Vita Sackville-West by Victoria Glendinning (Weidenfeld & Nicolson) 1983
Saki: A Life of Hector Hugh Munro by A.J. Langguth (Hamish Hamilton) 1981
Miss Ethel Sands and Her Circle by Wendy Baron (Peter Owen) 1977
Edith Simcox and George Eliot by K.A. McKenzie (Oxford University Press) 1961
The Food of Love: Princesse Edmond de Polignac and Her Circle by Michael de Cossart (Hamish Hamilton) 1978
Impetuous Heart: The Story of Ethel Smyth by Louise Collis (William Kimber) 1984
Charmed Circle: Gertrude Stein and Company by James R. Mellow (Phaidon Press) 1974
The Strawberry Hill Set: Horace Walpole and His Set by Brian Fothergill (Faber & Faber) 1983
Letters of Sylvia Townsend Warner edited by William Maxwell (Chatto & Windus) 1982
Denton Welch: The Making of a Writer by Michael De-la-Noy (Viking) 1984
The Bloomsbury Group edited by S.P. Rosenbaum (University of Toronto Press) 1975
Coming Out by Jeffrey Weeks (Quartet Books) 1977
Eighteenth Century Women: An Anthology by Bridget Hill (George Allen & Unwin) 1984
Homosexuals in History by A.L. Rowse (Weidenfeld & Nicolson) 1977
Independent Women by Martha Vicinus (Virago) 1985
Omega and After: Bloomsbury and the Decorative Arts by Isabelle Anscombe (Thames & Hudson) 1981
Surpassing The Love of Men by Lillian Faderman (Junction Books) 1980
Women of Ideas by Dale Spender (Routledge & Kegan Paul) 1982

Index